The Final Few Years of British Steam

Part One

Summer 1958 – Summer 1966

An enthusiast's recollection of exploits and adventures while following the decline of steam on British Railways.

Les Wheeler

Dedicated to my late uncle, Roy Derry, who encouraged me to photograph such an engaging and worthwhile subject and without whose generosity in supplying me with so many rolls of film, the vast majority of pictures featured would never have been taken.

Cover Illustrations.

Front cover: The last of the 'A3's to be withdrawn: No.60052 Prince Palatine moves off Edinburgh St Margarets Motive Power Depot, her home shed, on 16th July 1965.

Back cover, top: ex-GWR 'Grange' No. 6859 Yiewsley Grange in the south yard of Tyseley Motive Power Depot, October 1965. Allocated to Severn Tunnel Junction, the 4-6-0, would be withdrawn shortly after this photograph was taken.

Back cover, bottom: 'Castle' class No. 7023 Penrice Castle rests in the yard of Bristol Barrow Road MPD c1963. Stored serviceable after hauling the last express passenger train from Worcester to London Paddington on 7th September 1963, the 4-6-0 as a result of diesel availability and failures impacting heavily on the delivery of the Winter Timetable, was put back into traffic to help out and would continue its main line duties until the following June.

First published in February 2017

Published by Grange Publications and Les Wheeler.
Hawthorn Terrace
Shilbottle
NE66 2XA
Telephone 01665 575 287

ISBN 9 780995 554801

Printed in Great Britain by The Amadeus Press Ltd.

Proceeds from the sale of this book will go towards the upkeep of the last steam engine to carry out a normal duty for British Railways on 4th August 1968, Stanier 'Black 5' No. 45212.

I think I'm goin' back to the things I learned so well in my youth

Let everyone debate the true reality
I'd rather see the world the way it used to be…

So catch me if you can I'm goin' back

Song: Goin' Back

Songwriters: Gerry Goffin and Carole King

Singer: Dusty Springfield (recorded 15th June 1966)

Introduction

With their number in excess of sixteen thousand for much of the decade, as a young boy growing up in the 1950's, the many steam engines going about their daily business enticed me, and indeed many others, to watch them whenever possible. Six decades later, I still find myself looking to see what opportunities are in the offing to see steam working on the mainline or on the many heritage railways we are so fortunate to have; for me, their appeal has remained timeless, my affinity for them not abating one little bit over the years since they finished employment on BR.

It all began, though, way before I was able to make use of a notebook and pencil to record each engines number. My mother often reminded me how she had great difficulty trying to whisk me away from the side of Golden Hillock Road Bridge, next to Small Heath and Sparkbrook station, to continue our homeward journey after visiting my grandmother. A few trainspotters would invariably be found here, and it was from this spot that I first saw the 'Kings' of the old GWR working the express passenger trains on the main line between Wolverhampton, Birmingham and London. As I sat in my pushchair, the railings in front of me didn't help to enhance the view, but when grabbed hold of they came in very useful to delay what was always a reluctant and tearful departure!

While watching a 'warts and all' steam video a number of years ago, the thought that, perhaps, some of my photographs, together with various recollections of journeys in search of steam, might interest a wider audience seemed distinctly possible. The producers of the video were quick to point out that the pictures were not edited, and reflected the quality of their cameras and the budget available at the time. Well, suffice to say that my images, also taken using very basic cameras, together with various musings and memories, hopefully reflect the last few years of an era fast coming to an end; a period of transition before the Modernisation Programme permeated and changed for good so many aspects of our railways infrastructure, operation and above all its motive power.

The diesels and electrics beginning to appear in the late 1950's were no match for steam's charisma and character. For many, the new forms of motive power were dull and uninteresting by comparison. However, having become used to what seemed to me like the same sounds emanating from an ever growing number of different diesel locos (apologies to all enthusiasts of such technology!), I came across one that, I must confess, left me in no doubt that it stood out from the crowd and, as diesels go, was something special. It happened in the summer of 1965 while I was standing next to an English-Electric 'Deltic' in Newcastle station waiting to witness its departure. So at odds with the outline of Gresley's 'A4's, which it had helped push aside on the east coast mainline, its authoritative and imposing shape concealed two throbbing 18 cylinder Napier engines that suddenly burst into life with a roar that shook both the platform and me, and left a lasting impression of its presence and power that remains to this day.

From the summer of 1964, rather late in the day sadly, I made my first efforts to record on film some of the steam engines I would normally have only noted in my logbooks. Taking such pictures was really incidental at first, but as time passed by I became more determined to record on film a form of motive power whose decline was in freefall and would only too soon become a memory. Partly for comparison purposes, or because of being noted on paper but, unfortunately, not on emulsion, a few photographs of engines working in preservation are also included. There are a number taken by other photographers too, and these help to provide a wider pictorial flavour for the few years prior to the beginning of my own efforts and to supplement where appropriate my own photographs taken between 1964 and 1968. Also featured are a few pictures discovered amongst family and holiday snaps - a mixture of negatives with no prints and vice versa - so my apologies to anyone who realises they should have been credited with taking them and, indeed, for any inaccuracies in the accompanying captions. The primary focus throughout may be on the steam locomotive but, because of the nature of the motive power changes taking place at the time, a few pictures of diesels are included as well.

As the end of steam drew ever closer, pictures of grubby engines were frequently taken with basic cameras in far from perfect circumstances - often in poor light, pouring rain, thick mist or any combination of these; it wasn't always possible to forgo an opportunity for a photograph in the hope that both the sun and another suitable subject would appear later. Yet there are, out of a few hundred snapshots taken, a number that I believe deserve to find their way on to the pages that follow and, in some small way, help to take the process of recording a bygone era a little further. A number of pictures were even taken in sunshine!

By my tenth birthday steam had started to disappear at an alarming rate; over eleven hundred were withdrawn during 1960, and as early as the beginning of 1962 footplate men were complaining openly about the condition of their engines. Locomotives that remained in service during the last two years or so of steam operation were dreadfully dirty and frequently in poor mechanical condition. Very often without number plates (chalked numerals were often scrawled in their place), stripped of their names, leaking water and steam from places where neither should have escaped and covered by layer upon layer of grease and grime, they continued to give as good a service as could be expected. Neglected as they were, looking scruffy and unkempt, they still managed to hold my interest and proved to be as engaging as ever right up until their final fires were dropped; better to see and be hauled by shabby steam locos than pristine diesels!

Following the fortunes of steam on BR once 1961 had passed would prove to be an ever-greater challenge. It would signal, for me, the beginning of a six and a half year period of constantly bidding goodbye to more and more locomotives, culminating in the ultimate farewell to the few that completed their duties at the beginning of August 1968. Unsurprisingly, I offer no apologies for my sometimes rather nostalgic reflections on the role these engines played until the conclusion of their replacement by diesel and electric traction.

Looking at my old notebooks - my jottings first started around 1957 - I find it difficult to believe the journeys I had made before I'd reached my teens. In August 1960, at 10 years of age, I went off, unaccompanied, on my first visit to Derby for its Works Open Day. This was over twice as far as Tamworth, previously my furthest destination from home, and no doubt my excitement was evident to everyone I came in contact with that day. In 1961, at the age of eleven, I made my first visit to London, eager to watch and record locomotives that I had only seen pictures of in my Combined Volume and Locospotters' and Trains Annuals. Sadly, my notes have been lost along the way and I have no written record of the many engines seen during this very special trip. In 1962, Manchester and Doncaster were added to my foray list, and in the summer of 1964, while on holiday in South Devon, I managed to persuade my parents to let me opt out of the normal seaside activities and go instead to Exeter and Exmouth Junction where I could see some of the Southern steam engines still working. From 1965 to 1967 my travels became even more adventurous and far reaching. But by 1968 it wasn't necessary to journey to different distant places - steam by this time could only be found working in one area, the north west of England.

Extracts from my surviving logbooks, together with a fair spread of pictures and a few anecdotes, make up the pages that follow. Also included are relevant snippets of railway news mainly, but not entirely, linked to the effects of the introduction of diesel and electric motive power on steam operation. I was lucky to travel as far and wide and visit as many sheds as I did and, because of this, my reflections I believe are reasonably varied and not too parochial in nature. Having said that, I must mention one shed in particular, Saltley. It was a depot I would unofficially visit many, many times. Why so many, I'm not sure; it certainly didn't have lots of glamorous engines allocated to it, although a few 'Jubilees' and 'Royal Scots' put in brief appearances and rubbed shoulders with the more commonplace, some would say uninteresting, engines that made up the majority of its stock of steam power. Perhaps it was because of the ease with which I managed to bunk the shed without my presence being called into question... well, for the most part!

Formerly of the Midland Railway and then the LMS, Saltley was first and foremost concerned with the supply of engines for freight workings. By 1954, its pool of over 190 engines meant it was the LMR's most important shed in terms of the size of its allocation. The many trucks and wagons carrying all sorts of manufactured and other goods, after being systematically sorted out in the large marshalling yards such as Bromford, Lawley Street, Washwood Heath and Water Orton, needed suitable motive power to despatch these trains to a wide variety of destinations. The shed was required to provide engines for passenger work too, but this was mainly for suburban duties, although there were a few express turns to places such as Sheffield and Bristol. Top-link in Saltley terms, then, was not so much to do with passenger services as was the case with many sheds; it was the domain of the Road Link, and more specifically Link 1 the long-distance freights with the Carlisle and Glasgow being the cream of the crop. Known as lodging turns, they were the longest through freights in the country using a single crew, and every effort was made to have the best engines with the best coal available for these duties.

Throughout the period covered here, visits to Birmingham's depots of Saltley, Tyseley and to a lesser extent Aston are reported on frequently and remain a thread running through this and part two (covering the last two years of steam operating on BR) until their respective closures. But plenty of other visits elsewhere are reported on, too, and create, hopefully, a wider picture of the motive power transformation that was taking place during the final few years of British steam.

For some, what follows will be a reminder of the time when, with duffel bag filled with jam sandwiches, lemonade, biscuits and of course notebook and Combined Volume, they could sprint to catch a locos number and not be out of breath. Times, too, when on arrival back home rather than responding to the wash and brush up directive, the first thing to do was underline (with a ruler, of course) all the day's cops. This is not a book in any way attempting to display steam photography at its best, nor is it a book steeped in research with lots of statistics and data, although there is a reasonable amount of information accompanying the various pictures as well as added details to enhance my description of some of the places visited. It is really the story of a young trainspotter developing into a steam enthusiast with a desire to record, albeit in perhaps a basic, raw and no frills way, a few images together with a personal portrayal of what was a fast fading scene. I hope that it will stimulate recollections and memories of days now long past - days for many readers when responsibilities were few and hobbies and interests of topmost importance.

1954 - 1959 (Early Recollections)

Residing close to the heart of a big city in the 1950's meant one was never very far from a busy railway line. Certainly living in Birmingham's inner city areas of Bordesley Green, Winson Green and Small Heath meant that I grew up with the familiar sights and sounds of the railways. The house in Bordesley Green, the first suburb I lived in, was only a few minutes from Adderley Park on the Birmingham to Coventry line, and I can remember occasionally walking down to the station with my mother to meet my father off the train after his days work at the Coventry Radiator and Presswork Company.

Adderley Park station, Birmingham. It was here at the top of the steps seen on the left of the picture that I would wait impatiently with my mother for my father's train to arrive from Coventry. D J Norton (courtesy of Mark Norton).

Shortly after my fourth birthday in February 1954, we moved to Winson Green with the former GW line from Snow Hill to Wolverhampton less than a two-minute walk away. Our "new" house was a back-to-back, one of thousands built during the 19th century to accommodate the rapidly expanding workforce of industrial towns. One room deep and quite cramped, it was three storeys high and I had the 'penthouse suite' but, unfortunately, without a view of the railway! All I could see was the rooftops of other similar houses, our courtyard and the outbuilding where Mum and other women regularly did their washing using the communal tub or 'copper' as it was called.

In time this facility became redundant as more and more families began to use the new labour-saving twin tub washing machine. Once the 'copper' had gone the outbuilding was turned into a storage area for refuse bins. It was also a place to hide, and not only for children. On one occasion my mother had the fright of her life when, just as she was disposing of some rubbish, a patient from the nearby Psychiatric Hospital jumped out from behind the bins and ran off. Change is always with us and like the old methods of washing laundry being improved upon, so too was the type of house we were living in. Slowly but surely homes like ours were being demolished to make way for more modern developments. Fortunately, in 2004, as a reminder of what it was like to live in such accommodation, the National Trust saved the city's last few remaining examples of back-to-back type housing.

It was while living in Winson Green that my attraction to the railway, or more specifically the steam engines in charge of its daily traffic, really developed. Like a number of other lads living nearby, I began to do what they were doing - making a note of their numbers, some of which I recorded in the back of my old schoolbooks, unfortunately now long disposed of. I used to start off early for school, which was reached by crossing over the main line by the station, so that I could watch the trains for a while before, most reluctantly, making my way to the playground, ready to line up for registration. At weekends and after school in the summer, I could often be found on or near Winson Green station collecting the numbers of the engines passing by. My parents gradually got used to me spending hour upon hour watching and recording the locomotives working near where we lived; they accepted that it was a popular hobby and thought that at least it would keep me out of trouble and, of course remain, initially at least, relatively close to home.

When you are only seven going on eight, there seems to be a good deal more than twenty-four hours in a day. Playing football (in the road, rather than in the park, only a few minutes walk a way!), and all the other things - including trainspotting - that young boys would get up to in their spare time, didn't appear to have any impact on how slowly the days seemed to pass. But the pace of life was changing, and so too were our railways - the Modernisation Plan, of which I was blissfully unaware, would see to that.

Many a happy hour was spent on this Birmingham station. Heading south, Oxley-based Churchward 2-8-0 No. 3865 trundles through Soho & Winson Green with a mixed freight during the summer of 1958. This engine was one of twenty of the class to be converted to oil firing during 1946-1949 and was renumbered 4851 until reconverted to coal firing. D. Montgomery. (M.L. Boakes collection).

Diesels, although relatively few in number when I began spotting, were becoming more firmly established and, by the time I was eight or nine, the influx was truly underway. My Combined Volume of summer 1957 reminds me of the fact that, as well as deliveries of 0-6-0 shunters continuing, the first diesels capable of taking over passenger as well as freight duties would be entering service this year, too. Two years later, the same reference book, published November 1959, would reflect the speed at which such changes were taking place. Not only did diesel locomotives feature more significantly, so too did diesel multiple units (dmu's) of which there was a rapidly growing number. Steam's supremacy was being threatened on all fronts - its main express passenger duties, local and suburban duties and, of course, it's day-to-day movement of goods both in terms of shunting and general freight responsibilities.

I didn't have any idea of what was about to happen, or the effect the transformation planned for our railway would have on a young boy simply watching and collecting the numbers of passing steam engines. My notebooks of 1958 and 1959 list locos seen at Snow Hill, New Street and, at a newly discovered location known to local spotters as the 'Button Factory'. Here, at the back of the building, one could see both the ex-GWR route into Snow Hill and, albeit with a degree of neck stretching while on tiptoes, the old LNW line into New Street. Moor Street, the other former GWR station, could also be observed across the way from this vantage point. My records reveal that, on occasions, I would not note a solitary diesel locomotive (See appendix 2), but such steam-dominated jottings were about to change.

From time to time I would visit my aunt and uncle who lived in Bordesley Park Road next to the former Midland Railway line. The section between Landor Street Junction and King's Norton was known locally as the Camp Hill line and passed next to Birmingham City's Football ground. It then climbed up over the old GWR line at Bordesley. A picture giving an idea of the view I had looking down and along the line towards St Andrew's is shown below. I would spend hours sitting on the Anderson air-raid shelter watching the trains go by until encouraged (pardon the pun) to make tracks home! Many years later I found out that, under the cover of darkness and with bucket in hand, my uncle would descend the embankment, make his way to the side of the signal box and help himself to some coal from the adjoining bunker. This fuel was still very much in short supply after the war, and I suppose 'borrowing' a little from British Railways to help keep the house warm was too great a temptation to resist.

An unidentified Stanier '8F', having waited for the 'right away' begins to move its mixed freight train on to the old Midland line and under the Coventry Road / Arthur Street bridge. Out of view, a few yards back along the embankment, is Bordesley Junction signal box, which controlled movements to and from the former GWR line (see next picture). Summer 1965.

Bordesley Junction signal box. The two lines to the right of the picture connect the old Midland Railway to the ex-GWR main line from Paddington to Birmingham Snow Hill and also provided access to Bordesley Junction sidings (see page 22). D. J. Norton, Courtesy of Mark Norton.

The view overlooking what was a quite busy freight line was a good place for spotting, with trains frequently having to be assisted by a '3F' from Saltley shed when battling their way up the incline, which by St Andrew's was as steep as 1 in 62. However, being able to hear and not see the engines on the Snow Hill to Paddington route close by was always frustrating, so one day I decided to try and find somewhere by the spur joining the two lines that would provide a vantage point allowing me to view both at the same time. Eventually, close to the railway bridge over Bordesley Park road, I found a place where I could easily see the locos on both routes and, as can be seen in the picture below, I was almost within touching distance of the engines on the up line!

In charge of a mixed freight, an unidentified 'Hall' heads for The Camp Hill line (in the background), and passes a light-engine Brush Type '4' about to join the ex-GWR main line. From this bridge over Bordesley Park Road I could watch and record engines working on both routes.
Summer 1965.

In the spring of 1959 we moved house again, and once more I found I was near the old Great Western route, with Small Heath and Sparkbrook station less than five minutes away. Like Winson Green the area was a working class one, with the BSA Works situated close to the station. Along Armoury Road, adjacent to the factory, with their back gardens running down to the railway, were rows of terraced houses in which lived the families of key workers employed there. One of my early pictures taken on the station, on what was evidently a good day for washing, has the rear of some of the houses as a backdrop. As mentioned earlier, it was here next to the railway bridge that I first glimpsed steam engines from my pushchair.

Our new home in Sparkbrook was about a mile away from the ex-GWR shed at Tyseley, and my earliest recorded visit there was a few months later during the summer holidays. Hearing older fellow spotters talking about their bunking exploits had tempted me to think about doing the same for sometime, and early in August I plucked up the courage to have a go myself.

I can recall as though it were yesterday, walking along the towpath of the Grand Union Canal from where it passed under Anderton Road to where it was crossed by the GWR mainline and accessing the shed for the first time from here via the north yard. With the prospect of being frog-marched to the shedmaster's office if apprehended, and dreading what might follow a good ticking off, I recall how I carefully made my way from one part of the shed to another, taking down the numbers of the engines as quickly as possible before retracing my steps back up the yard to the canal. I didn't delineate between engines noted while spotting at Small Heath before and after visiting the depot, so cannot accurately say what locos were on shed, but the results of the day's spotting (most likely 8th August 1959) can be seen in appendix 1. The event had been daunting yet so enjoyable too; the combination of experiencing first-hand the atmosphere of a working steam shed and being so close to the engines it housed, was something that would have a lasting impression and continuing appeal.

'Hall' class 4-6-0 No. 4965 Rood Ashton Hall crosses over the Grand Union Canal shortly after leaving Tyseley for Snow Hill with the Shakespeare Express on 3rd August 2008. It was here that I used to gain access to the line leading into the north yard of the shed (at the back of the trees on the right).

Unable to resist the lure and attraction of Tyseley, I made further visits to the depot and, as my confidence grew, I began bunking the city's other depots, too. Fortunately, not long after moving to Sparkbrook, I had my first bicycle, which gave me greater freedom, and I could travel independently and reasonably quickly to Saltley, Aston and Monument Lane sheds; I would not have to trouble Mum and Dad anymore with requests for money for bus fare. I had no shortage of interests at this time, and as well as playing football or cricket, fishing was another hobby that I enjoyed as much as trainspotting, and I could often be found, rod in hand, at the side of the pool in Small Heath Park, together with a friend, Chris Allard, who lived nearby. As will be revealed later, I eventually discovered Utopia - somewhere I could fish and trainspot at the same time!

Recorded during one of a number of visits to Saltley MPD in the autumn of 1959, 'Crab' 2-6-0 No. 42816 was transferred shortly afterwards from 21A to Gorton where it would remain until its withdrawal at the beginning of October 1964. The engine is seen on Saltley shed in the south yard on 29th April 1959. H. C. Casserley. Courtesy of R.Casserley.

Built in November 1950, Collett 4-6-0 No. 7821 Ditcheat Manor is seen at the head of an ordinary passenger train next to the up platform of Paignton station. Together with four other classmates (No's. 7806/8/18/24), the engine had been transferred from Tyseley to Newton Abbot at the end of June 1959 to assist with the increased traffic during the summer months. I believe my father took this and the following three pictures while we were on holiday two months later in August.

Above. Paignton on a bright summer's day in August 1959: in charge of the up Torbay Express is Newton Abbot-based 'Castle' No. 5032 Usk Castle. Recently fitted with double chimney, the 4-6-0 would become an Old Oak Common engine in March 1960 and complete a further two and a half years service before being condemned in September 1962. Left. Seen on the same day is sister engine No. 7001 Sir James Milne (formerly Denbigh Castle), renamed in February 1948 after the last general manager of the GWR.

As early evening approaches, one of Laira's five 'Grange' class engines is seen standing alongside the up platform of Paignton station in charge of an express passenger turn. 'Granges' were often used on through expresses to the Midlands and the North, normally running to Exeter or Bristol. A total of eighty of these engines were built between 1936 and 1939 and all had been withdrawn by January 1966.

As a nine year old, regularly watching and noting the numbers of steam engines as an end in itself, meant I was not really aware of the developments and plans that had occurred during 1959. At the beginning of the year, the British Transport Commission released information concerning what was to be the biggest batch of orders for BR main line diesels since the pronouncement of the Modernisation Plan. These included further EE Type '4's and Type '1's, BR Type '4's and a new EE design classified as Type '3', the first thirty of which would be for the Eastern Region. Perhaps the most significant of the orders, was the 137 locomotives that would be built at Crewe and Derby and would become known to trainspotters as the 'Peaks.' Total cost for all these new engines was estimated to be in the region of £16 million (approximately £335 million today - 2015).

It wasn't only BR motive power that was beginning to feel the effects of 'The Plan.' Changes were also in the offing with regard to some of our larger stations; the North Eastern Region, for example, divulged further details of the £4 1/2 million scheme to rebuild and enlarge Leeds City station to accommodate traffic from Central station and, of course, facilitate its closure. The forecast was for a completion date of 1963-4, but this would prove to be rather over optimistic and wouldn't happen until sometime later in the spring of 1967.

By September, the first of the 193 'Peaks' ultimately built, No D1, had officially entered revenue earning service after quite lengthy trials and had been named Scafell Pike at a ceremony held on Carlisle Citadel station. And, although the last few of the '9F's were still to be built, lets not forget that electric traction was about to further threaten steams pre-eminent position; quickly following the introduction on the SR of the Doncaster built E5000 class, the first of many of the

3,300hp locomotives (No. E3001) had been allocated to Longsight (Manchester) by the end of the year.

On a lighter note, it was reported in the April issue of Trains Illustrated that an express train had been incorrectly routed. In a 'slight fog' on the evening of 7th February, the 6.10pm Paddington to Birkenhead found itself on the ex-GC line after reaching Ashendon Junction, about eight miles from Princess Risborough. It seems that the crew on the 'Castle' heading the train had travelled some six miles before realising they were on the wrong line and stopped at Grendon Underwood. In due course, an engine was sent to haul the express back to Haddenham so it could continue on its correct (ex-GWR) route to Banbury. Passengers travelling as far as Wolverhampton arrived, non-too amused presumably, a little after midnight, almost three hours late. It was suggested that the signalman may have forgotten that it was a Friday, which involved the running of a relief train, and set the points for what he thought was the 6.18pm from Marylebone!

As 1959 drew to a close, one of the worst periods for steam withdrawals took place. It was reported early in the New Year in the February issue of Trains Illustrated magazine:

'At the beginning of November the LMR attacked its lengthening lines of stored steam power and the outcome was the most massive list of withdrawals we can recall printing in one issue. The list is topped by 57 0-6-0s of Midland Type, followed by 43 0-8-0s, 32 2-6-2 tanks and 23 Class '2P' 4-4-0s; also notable is the condemnation of all but one of the nine Stanier 0-4-4 tanks at one blow.'

Trains Illustrated, February 1960, Motive Power Miscellany, p.115.

If one was needed, these withdrawals were a clear warning that steam's long reign was seriously under threat. Nevertheless, I doubt that anyone at this time could have predicted quite how quickly the process of dieselisation and electrification would be carried out.

1960 (The final steam engine is built for BR)

I made my first visit to Tamworth at the beginning of April, and spent the day in 'The Field' (a locally well-known viewpoint enabling one to note engines on both high and low level lines) with countless other spotters. Together with engines seen during the outward and return journeys, I logged a grand total of 106 steam representing 21 classes. Thirty-one express passenger locomotives were noted: 9 'Coronations', 10 'Jubilees', 7 'Royal Scots', 4 'Patriots', 1 'Princess Royal' plus 1 'Clan' and 1 'Britannia'. Even so, diesels were also well in evidence, with 13 English Electric Type '4's seen during the day, all from what I remember on the Trent Valley line. (See appendix 3)

As enjoyable as my first visit to Tamworth was, the real highlight of the year would come later in the summer, at the end of August. I can still remember waiting for what seemed to be an age for Derby Works Open Day to come around. I was now ten, and knowing that I would be going on this trip on my own would make it a very exciting and special adventure. It seemed 1960 was going to prove to be an eventful and thrilling year.

Tamworth was a favourite haunt for spotters during the 1950's and early 1960's. The view from 'The Field', to the right of this shot, would often see forty or fifty or more lads noting the movements of trains both on the High Level and Low Level lines. Taken in the 1950's, 'Princess Royal' class engine No. 46204 Princess Louise is seen heading north with The Red Rose, which operated between Euston and Liverpool Lime Street between 1951 and 1966.
R S. Carpenter collection.

Often seen at Tamworth from late 1956 until January 1959 when it was delivered to the Eastern Region for evaluation tests, Deltic is pictured here at Doncaster station in the summer of 1959. Following a severe oil leak, the locomotive returned to English Electric Company's Works at Newton le Willows, but the necessary repairs were never sanctioned and the engine was withdrawn in March 1960. Author's collection.

Glasgow Central station, summer 1959. Station pilot, standard 5MT No.73055, is passed by Fairburn 2-6-4T No. 42059 while diesel electrics No's 10201/2 head the up Royal Scot, again regularly seen at Tamworth. Designed by Bullied, they were transferred to Camden in April 1955, but by 1960 they would find themselves on secondary passenger and freight duties and, together with 10203, would be officially withdrawn at the end of 1963. Author's collection.

While waiting impatiently for the trip to Derby, I spotted regularly at Small Heath, and also made a number of visits to Tyseley shed. Following the closure of Chester (West), it had in addition to its two resident '8F's, received a further eight of this class, which I noted over a number of weeks following their arrival. Pocket money, having been put to one side over several weeks, was dipped into at the beginning of August, when I made my first visit to Wolverhampton, and Stafford Road shed. The day produced a total of 127 steam of 25 varieties, including 'Kings' (8), 'Castles' (15) 'Halls' (23) and for good measure two 'Royal Scots'.

One of the fifteen 'Castles' logged during my first visit to Stafford Road MPD was No. 5038 Morlais Castle. Built in June 1935 and pictured by the shed's coaling stage circa 1962, she would eventually be withdrawn in September 1963. (M.L. Boakes collection).

Built at Swindon in July 1927, Collett 'King' No. 6005 King George 11 is seen in the yard of Stafford Road shed about the time of noting the engine on my first visit to the depot mentioned above. The 4-6-0 would be employed for a further two years and complete 1,679,275 miles before withdrawal in November 1962. (M. L. Boakes collection)

'Modified Hall' No. 6944 Fledborough Hall, seen here at about the same time I noted the 4-6-0 on my first visit to 84A. The engine would move from Shrewsbury to Cardiff East Dock and finally to Severn Tunnel Junction, from where it would be withdrawn at the end of 1965. W.E.Cooper (M.L.Boakes collection).

The industrial holiday fortnight (last week in July and first in August) was, for my parents, synonymous with a much welcome break from work in the summer. It was also a time when a number of holiday expresses operating from both Snow Hill and New Street stations always featured regularly. I was over the moon when I found out that I would be going to New Brighton for a day out with my mum, aunt and cousin on one of these special trains. Needless to say, my agenda had nothing to do with the seaside. It was somewhere new to see different engines and collect their numbers. What a day it turned out to be! If I had been looking forward to a bright summer's day on the beach I would have been dreadfully disappointed. From what I recall, it rained continually: all the way there, all the time we were in the town and all the way home again. One thing we did do, undoubtedly at my insistence while at the fun fair, was to have a ride on the miniature railway. Owned and run by Tommy Mann's Enterprises, I still have the postcards of the railway that Mum bought for me on the day. And despite the awful weather I had a great time.

Now part of a much larger collection of railway post cards are the two (above) I returned home with after travelling on Tommy Mann's miniature railway at New Brighton. Summer 1960.

At last, after what seemed to be an inordinate length of time, Saturday 27th August finally arrived. Early on the morning Mum made sure I had plenty of sandwiches and drinks (and a few sweets) in my duffle bag before I set off for New Street station to catch the train to Derby. I had already found out that the Works were situated next to the station, and was confident I would find my way to the entrance without any difficulty.

On board a packed train, I arrived at the town's Midland station at about 10am and soon realised there were lots of other spotters getting off the train too. A few minutes later, after following the main throng, I was inside the Works.

I didn't comprehend its size at first, but as I began to explore the different buildings and workshops, including the machine and fitting shop, plating and welding shop and locomotive erecting shop, it appeared to be a huge place. Indeed, the Works covered an area the size of approximately 70 football pitches, and to a ten-year-old one can imagine the bewildering impression it gave. Disorientated at times, I took down the number of a few of the many engines I came across more than once, but I couldn't have been enjoying myself more. Derby had built its final steam engine, No. 73154, in the summer of 1957, and by now was involved in the construction of diesel shunters and engines of the 'Peak' class of which I noted in the very early stages of production No's. D19, D20 and D21. The repair and overhaul of steam would continue here for a further three years.

Bursting to tell of the day's adventure, and having spent the entire journey back to New Street with my head out of the carriage window, I arrived home many hours later with the mandatory bits of unburned coal in my hair and a much-blackened face. Mum and Dad were told of all that had happened and the different engines I had seen. Not quite so enthusiastically, I showed them a copy of the official programme I had bought as a souvenir. Expecting lots of information about the Works and at least pictures of the guest engines on display, all to be found were boring details about the different flowers being exhibited, the various competition categories for garden produce and who the judges were - what a disappointment! But the day itself had been far from that. In addition to the 43 steam engines recorded while travelling to and from Derby, I had logged a further 133 in the Works and on shed, including, the star of the show for me, standard '8P' No. 71000 Duke of Gloucester, which I hadn't seen before, and was on display in front of the Work's office block. By the time I arrived back in Birmingham, I had seen a total of 33 different varieties of locomotive, including several preserved engines (No's. 80, 118, 158A and 1000) during what had been a truly fantastic day out (See appendix 4).

Time spent fishing increased during the summer months and, although I often went with dad, I started going off on my own, especially during weekdays while he was at work. The local park was okay, but Lapworth and Stratford upon Avon were much different, and prospects at both of these venues a lot better. I would catch the local train from Small Heath and on arriving, to keep ahead of other fellow anglers to ensure I had a good spot, I'd run with my creel and rods to my favourite places to fish. I had the best of both worlds at Lapworth when I fished 'The Pound'. Here, I had to try and watch my float and, at the same time, note the numbers of the engines as they passed along the main line from Paddington to Birmingham. I'm sure some of the fish sensed what I was doing and new exactly when to bite and not get hooked!

Stratford was different. I couldn't watch any trains from where I fished the River Avon, but the prospect of an exciting return journey home more than made up for this. Although the river was little bit further away, my routine was the same as for Lapworth: weighed down with my rods and basket, I'd scamper from the station across the town and fish for roach next to an old mill. My favourite bait was hempseed, banned at this time because it was thought to grow on the bottom of rivers and pools, even though it had been boiled until the seeds burst open! The roach went crackers for this bait (cooked the night before) and I often caught fish up to 2 1/2 lb, which doesn't sound that remarkable, but for this particular species was pretty impressive. But enough of the tales of the riverbank; I had something else to look forward to at the end of the afternoon.

I would fish until about 5.30pm and then make my way back to the station. I should have started off about an hour earlier to catch the local service back to Small Heath, but there was a far more interesting and faster train that would take me directly to Snow Hill instead. It had started out from Penzance at 10.30am and was better known as 'The Cornishman'. At Bristol, a Wolverhampton Stafford Road-based 'Castle' would take over for the remainder of the journey; sometimes it would be double-headed with about 12 or more chocolate and cream carriages. I shouldn't really have caught this train, and on the one or two occasions I was asked for my ticket, I pleaded innocence and said I thought it would stop at Small Heath! Invariably, even when there were two engines in charge, the train would usually be late into Snow Hill and I'd miss the local service to take me back home. This meant a short walk to catch the bus - a small inconvenience considering the excitement of speeding back to Birmingham non-stop aboard a named express!

My favourite place for spotting at this time was from the road bridge next to Small Heath Station where I first used to watch the trains from my pushchair. Although it was quite a drop to the embankment, I would often sit with my legs dangling over the wall at the side of the bridge with what was a clear view of the line northwards towards the city centre. I remember vividly the sight of 'Kings' and 'Castles' appearing in the distance with southbound expresses, and the bets amongst fellow spotters as to which class of loco was heading the train. You needed a keen eye to be the first to tell the difference between these engines - the initial sighting would be just before it reached Small Heath Bridge about half a mile or so away!

Inevitably, we grew tired of regularly seeing some locos every day and, as a result, their familiarity led to various expletives being shouted out including 'scrap it', which really requires no further comment. One day I remember arriving at the bridge to find that things weren't quite the same. Invariably, one of a number of Tyseley-allocated 0-6-0 pannier tanks employed on Bordesley sidings shunting duties would be found resting directly below where we sat. But on this occasion, the normal sounds and smells emanating from one of these little locos no longer drifted up to our elevated position; they had been replaced by the dull, monotonous throb of an 0-6-0 diesel shunter, together with the unfamiliar and unpleasant whiff of diesel fumes drifting skywards.

Lengthy summer evenings brought with them the opportunity to trainspot after teatime. Sitting wearing short trousers on the wall at the side of the bridge by Small Heath station after a hot sunny day, one could feel the warmth being given up by the blue bricks, adding a little comfort to the otherwise hard and unforgiving surface. As it swiftly progressed towards Snow Hill, an express passenger train nearing the end of its journey would regularly be seen at about 7.30pm. What I didn't realise at the time was that the working was a historically significant one. Invariably with a 'King' in charge, the engine had one less carriage to haul than when it set off from London. At the start of the Western Region's summer timetable on 13th June, the service was the last example of the employment of the once numerous slip coaches used up and down the country. Departing Paddington at 5.10pm for Wolverhampton, the slip coach would have been detached at Blackthorn for Bicester. Three months later, on Friday 9th September, the practice ceased and 102 years of slipping coaches came to an end.

Above. The view from the middle of the road bridge next to Small Heath & Sparkbrook station looking towards Birmingham city centre as I remember it in the 1950's and early 60's. Slightly to the left from where the picture was taken is the spot where I first glimpsed what seemed like lots of pannier tanks hectically shunting in the sidings, while 'Kings' and 'Castles' intermittently rushed to and fro along the up and down main lines. Small Heath North signal box is in the foreground, and Small Heath Bridge can be seen in the distance. R.G. Nelson collection, courtesy of T. Walsh. Below. On 3rd August 2008, 'Hall' 4-6-0 No. 4965 Rood Ashton Hall is at the head of The Shakespeare Express. Together with the signal box, which was situated close to where the loco is, the many lines that once made up the busy Bordesley Junction sidings are now long gone.

Other changes had occurred during the year which were reflected in the pattern of my jottings: Chester (West) shed had closed in April and, as mentioned earlier, by the end of the month Tyseley depot had received no fewer than eight of its '8F's; nearer to home, Bournville shed had closed in February and its locos, staff and duties had been transferred to Saltley; in August the same depot found itself with further extra motive power to work the Redditch-Evesham-Aschurch branch in the form of six additional Fowler 2-6-4 tanks. On the diesel front, the Western Region blue Pullmans, their introduction postponed indefinitely earlier in the year because of the need to upgrade the signalling for the accelerated timings, finally entered service in September, while the first of the 'Westerners', would be usurpers of the 'Kings', were beginning to take shape in Swindon Works by the end of December.

1960 had also witnessed its fair share of significant incidents and accidents on the railways, too. As early as 22nd January, five people lost their lives when a freight train ran into the first three carriages of the 9.05pm Glasgow St Enoch to London St Pancras. After reaching Ais Gill, Polmadie 'Britannia' Pacific No 70052 Firth of Tay, at the head of the passenger train, started producing a knocking noise alerting the driver that there was something wrong. The driver stopped at Garsdale, and in a raging blizzard did his best in the pitch-blackness to examine his engine by the light of a small torch. Not finding anything wrong with the bearings or suspected left-hand big end, he decided to proceed at reduced speed. Unsurprisingly, considering the conditions, what he hadn't discovered was both right-hand slidebars were missing. Eventually, the piston rod fractured causing further stresses and fracture until the connecting rod, crosshead and piston rod came free and smashed into and badly damaged the adjacent track as the engine came to an abrupt stop. Most unfortunately, this in turn caused the derailment of a freight train headed by Kingmoor-based 'Crab' No. 42881.

In completely different weather conditions to those surrounding the above accident, and with the same number of fatalities, the Severn Bridge of the Western Region was partly demolished by two tank barges carrying petrol to Sharpness on the River Severn. On the night of 25th October, in thick fog, they missed the entrance to the docks and, carried along by the incoming tide, collided with one of the piers. As a result of the impact both tankers blew up, two spans of the bridge crashed down on to the barges and, sadly, five people lost their lives. The bridge would never be rebuilt.

A total of 1,181 team engines had been withdrawn by the year's end, with 0-6-0 and 0-6-0T types bearing the brunt of the changes with well over 600 being scrapped. Several of the express passenger varieties I was familiar with had also faced their first losses with seven 'Castles', two 'Patriots and the first 'Jubilee' being condemned during the year. Interestingly, the continuing practice of fitting double chimneys to members of the 'Castle' class didn't prevent No. 4097 Kenilworth Castle, becoming the first conversion (completed in June 1958) to be taken out of service. In the region of four hundred diesels and fifty electrics had entered service as main line locomotives together with three hundred or so diesel shunters built for the more humdrum duties of railway work. Three new steam engines had been completed, fulfilling the order for two hundred and fifty-one standard '9F' 2-10-0's. The last of these was appropriately named Evening Star and in true Swindon tradition fitted with a copper-capped chimney.

1961 (The diesel threat continues to grow)

At the beginning of 1961 British Railways still had approximately 13,000 steam locomotives in service representing about 200 different classes of engine. Some of these varieties may only have had a handful of surviving members but, even so, it represented a huge variety of steam motive power. Nevertheless, even though Evening Star, the final steam engine built by BR, had been out shopped only nine months earlier, waiting impatiently in the wings, were an ever-growing number of diesels that would all to soon push steam aside and take centre stage. Changes were on the horizon for me, too. I would see out the concluding few months at junior school before moving on to Pitmaston Boys' in Hall Green, about three miles from home. It would be the only school I would attend where the familiar sounds of the railway failed to reach.

One of the engines I recorded for the first time during my visit to 'The Field' on 15th April 1961 was Royal Scot No. 46154 The Hussar. Allocated to Edge Hill at the time, the 4-6-0 would move to Willesden and then Llandudno where it was based when this picture was taken while being turned in Patricroft shed in January 1962. The engine would soon be leaving the depot to head the return working of 'The Llandudno to Manchester Club Train.' J. Carter. (Author's collection)

Records of my forays both locally and further from home seem to have been lost for the period September 1960 to March 1961. I can't believe that I gave up spotting for nearly seven months! Consequently, the first entry I have is for a trip to Tamworth on 10th April 1961. A year had passed by since my first visit here, and I obviously enjoyed myself so much that I returned to 'The Field' a further five times before the month's end. The English Electric Type '4's were gaining an ever-increasing foothold, of course, and as a result expresses hauled by Stanier's 'Coronation' Pacifics were few and far between. On 10th April I recorded only three of these engines compared with fifteen Type '4' diesels. It was a similar picture on 29th April when four 'Coronations' and twenty-one Type '4's were noted. Other classes of steam seen working on this day included the odd 'Patriot' and 'Royal Scot' but, with a total of eight members of the class logged, the 'Jubilees', it appeared, were now the most prolific of the express passenger engines working along the Trent Valley line.

Snow Hill, my much-preferred station to spend a few hours watching the trains come and go. The fireman of 'Modified Hall' No. 7908 Henshall Hall looks back along the platform to see whether all the carriage doors are safely shut and for the guard's signal to get his stopping train under way, probably as far as Leamington Spa. New in January 1950, the 4-6-0 was first allocated to St Philips Marsh. Following a brief spell working out of Shrewsbury, it was transferred to Tyseley in September 1955 from where it would be withdrawn in October 1965. See colour section (page 34 and 35) for examples of this locos 'exam and repair' and 'daily exam' cards completed during October 1961. Author's collection.

Frequently putting my bike to good use, so that several places could be reached easily in a day, during the remainder of the year I continued to visit the city's local sheds, main stations (especially my favourite, Snow Hill - see above) and its popular line side locations. Trips taking me further away from home increased as the year slowly unfolded and Crewe, for instance, was visited on four occasions. My visit there on 23rd August was organised by the Warwickshire Railway Society and included a conducted tour of the Works. Steam was still much in evidence and a good number were in the process of being overhauled. Diesels, too, were noted, and being built at the time were twelve 'Peak' class locomotives (No's. D120 to D131), which would gradually enter service over the next two months or so. Other interesting engines that I hadn't seen before and were preserved in the Works included 'Pet', 'Lion' and 'Tiny' whose names seemed to me to be rather unusual for railway engines.

Steam locos noted in the Works on 23rd August included 'Patriots' No's 45501, 45528 and 45540, 'Jubilees' No's. 45587, 45601, 45622, 45623, 45624 and 45685, 'Royal Scots' No's. 46119, 46138, 46139 and 46170, 'Coronations' No's. 46221, 46223, 46225, 46238, 46239 and 46241 and 'Britannias' No's. 70047 and 70032.

I hadn't previously listed many ex-LMS locos whose numbers began with the numeral 5, but several were recorded on the day - 0-6-0ST's No's. 51412, 51444, 51446 and 0-6-0s No's. 52218, 52312, 52441 and 52456. These seven lovely old engines, originally of the Lancashire and Yorkshire Railway, had certainly seen many years of service, probably in the region of 500 years between them!

The visit to Crewe works produced quite a mixed bag of motive power, including four of J.A.F. Aspinall's 0-6-0's freight engines now used for shunting. Built in large numbers between 1889 and 1917 at Horwich Works, close to 250 were still at work in 1948 and over 70 by the beginning of the 1960's. No. 52322 would survive into preservation, but No. 52312 (above), built in November 1895, would be broken up by the end of the following month after its withdrawal at the end of September 1962. Author's collection.

On Saturday 26th August, three days after visiting Crewe, I was on my way again to Derby for its Works Open Day. Guest locomotives included the now famous standard '9F' No. 92220 Evening Star, 'Coronation' class No. 46254 City of Stoke-on-Trent and preserved three-cylinder compound No. 1000. Fully aware this time of its format and contents, I duly purchased the official programme as a souvenir. By the time I had completed my return journey home, I had seen no fewer than 40 different classes of engine amongst a total of 186 steam locos logged, and recorded 95 cops. Other visitors worthy of a special mention were Somerset & Dorset 2-8-0 No 53809 and 'K3' 2-6-0 No 61959. I cabbed Evening Star and one other engine while in the Works. The second loco was a good deal smaller than the 2-10-0 and required the normal, but not so high a climb up on to the footplate. Originally built in 1880 for use in the docks served by the North London Railway, No. 58850, after withdrawal the previous September had been put into store but, fortunately, within seven months would be delivered safely to the Bluebell Railway for a new life in preservation.

Earmarked for preservation from the day of its completion in March 1960, Riddles '9F' No. 92220 Evening Star graces Saltley MPD while resting in the shed's north yard, not too long after entering traffic. The 2-10-0 had a very brief life, and following a collision with buffer stops on 26th March 1965, rather than effect repairs estimated at a little over a £1,000, the loco was withdrawn and put into store. The Curator of Historical Relics refused to accept the damaged engine, but after rather protracted negotiations with prospective buyers, including a certain Mr J. R. Green whose deliberations with BR spanned well over three years, the engine's ownership was in the end given over to The National Railway Museum. (M.L. Boakes collection)

Recorded at Derby Works Open Day, 46254 City of Stoke on Trent is seen earlier in the year leaving Crewe, possibly about the time in June when I visited this always busy railway centre. The Pacific would continue working regularly for a further three years until withdrawal sometime in September 1964. Author's collection.

On 30th August I spent an hour or so at Small Heath station before making my way to Saltley and Aston sheds. By this time the latter had an allocation of nine 'Britannia' Pacifics and, judging by the spotless condition of these engines, it appeared the cleaning staff were still taking pride in their work. Always a difficult place to get into unofficially, every step down towards and then past the shedmaster's office was taken with an increasing sense of anxiousness and unease. There may have been an alternative way in, but I certainly didn't know of one. As I moved quickly past the point of no return, there was no response to my presence, and I now faced the problem of avoiding him as he would most likely be somewhere around the depot!

Fortunately, I managed to do just that and at the same time noted five 'Britannia' Pacifics, No's. 70017 Arrow, 70024 Vulcan, 70027 Rising Star, 70031 Byron and 70043 Lord Kitchener. Also present amongst the remaining motive power was Holyhead-based 'Royal Scot' No. 46134 The Cheshire Regiment and 'Jubilee' No.45647 Sturdee.

Saltley, also successfully negotiated, was home to several express passenger engines worthy of note, including 'Jubilees' No's. 45643 Rodney, 45649 Hawkins and 45569 Tasmania, 'Patriot' No. 45532 Illustrious and 'Royal Scots' No's. 46122 Royal Ulster Rifleman and 46157 The Royal Artilleryman. The last two locos were members of a seven strong batch the shed had received in June. Fascinatingly, and most likely down to a clerical error, the records show that sister engines No's. 46106 and 46137 were allocated to both Saltley and Trafford Park from 2nd September while 46118 was allocated to Saltley and Nottingham from 26th August. During the summer the 'Scots' were often employed on extra passenger trains on Saturdays, but for most of the time they could be found working through vacuum-fitted freights to such places as Banbury, Eastleigh and Basingstoke. The rest of the locos logged reflected the depots main purpose of supplying suitable motive power for freight, banking and shunting duties. Occasionally, an ex-GWR engine might find its way here, and so it proved on this visit with the presence of Churchward 2-8-0 No. 3821, allocated to Oxley. A total of 50 steam representing 12 different varieties were noted. (See appendix 5 for full compliment of steam engines on Aston and Saltley).

'Jubilee' No. 45579 Punjab standing in the yard of Saltley MPD on 24th April 1961. Transferred from Derby earlier in February, the 4-6-0 would spend nine months based here before moving to Burton, and finally in June 1963, back to Derby, from where it would be withdrawn at the end of August 1964. M.L. Boakes collection.

Hauled by English Electric Type '4' No. D337 on the morning of 2nd September, I was once more heading for Crewe. This would primarily be a shed bash, and luckily I managed to get round both North and South depots without any problems. Steam was still very much the main source of motive power here, and I recorded amongst many other classes of engine 'Britannia' (3), 'Princess' (3), 'Coronation' (9), 'Royal Scot' (15), 'Patriot' (4), and 'Jubilee' (21). Five engines belonging to these varieties (No's. 45623, 46170, 46221, 46238 and 70047) were back in traffic having been noted in Crewe Works a little over a week earlier. A total of 196 steam, 40 Diesel and 9 electric locomotives were noted during the day - a very enjoyable and satisfying end to the summer holidays.

September brought with it the need to travel by bus each day to my new school, and also the challenge of tackling more homework than I'd ever had before. Even so, it was to be the start of a very eventful period in my life, not only in terms of my interest in steam, but in lots of other ways too.

Earlier in the year, the August issue of Trains Illustrated confirmed what had been heard on the spotters' grapevine that Derby Works had built the 1,000th main line diesel locomotive. 'Peak' No. D34 had been completed on 20th June and had been allocated to the motive power depot literally 'next door'. By the end of the year, the number of diesels in service had climbed to almost 1,300. Further news in the same publication involving the class of diesel just referred to appeared before the end of the year. If any residents living near the Lickey Incline - generally accepted to be the steepest main line gradient in Britain at 1 in 37 1/2 for some 2 1/2 miles - had read the December copy of Trains Illustrated they would have been well pleased to find out that, following the successful testing of 'Peak' No. D40 on September 20th, a good many members of this class would replace steam on this route and be quite capable of tackling the bank unassisted. It appeared that in the not too distant future the direction of the wind would no longer be a major factor in deciding whether or not a successful washing day was to be had.

Not without its critics, another 'advance' that would affect far more people than the few residing next to the Lickey Bank, was the introduction, at the start of the new timetable on 11th September at York station, of the 24 hr clock. This was intended to make for easier reading of a station's numerous departure and arrival times, a system of course that had been in use on the continent for many years. Still, as my BR Principle Passenger Services timetable for summer 1963 demonstrates, the use of the 12hr clock would continue for a while before a complete network-wide changeover would be achieved.

With an ever-increasing number of diesels available, more and more steam engines were becoming surplus to requirements, resulting in approximately one thousand six hundred being withdrawn by the year's end. Of the express varieties, further 'Princess Royals', 'Patriots', 'Castles', 'King Arthurs' and 'Jubilees' had been taken out of service to name but a few. The net was widening, though, and 1961 also saw the first 'A3's, 'Schools' and 'Lord Nelsons' suffering a similar fate. Luckily these changes didn't really impact on the variety of engines seen locally on the ex-GWR main line or on the ex-LNWR route through New Street. The trickle of 'Castles' being modified with the fitting of double-chimney, blastpipe and four row superheaters to produce more power at higher speeds and also reduce coal consumption (BR locomotives consumed over 9,000,000 tons in 1960) had been sustained throughout the year and had brought the total converted to sixty-seven. Indeed, at the close of the year, there were still over eleven and a half thousand steam locos in capital stock. Withdrawals next year, however, would be more far-reaching and severe, and the next twelve months would generally be accepted to be the pivotal period in the process of eliminating steam from BR.

Only three of the Hughes-Fowler 'Crabs' (No's 42864, 42893 and 42930) were withdrawn during 1961, but the class would not escape so lightly the following year with almost a quarter of the 245 being scrapped. Shortly after becoming a Saltley engine in August 1962, No. 42707, seen above at St Andrews Junction with a mixed freight, would escape the mass withdrawals on the horizon and continue to work out of 21A for the next 22months. After its transfer to Birkenhead in June 1964, the 2-6-0 would be made redundant after only three months further service. Author's collection.

'Black 5' No. 44837 stands next to a Derby lightweight multiple unit in Manchester Piccadilly. Formerly named London Road, the station was altered to accommodate the L.M. Region's electric train services to London and re-opened in September 1960. During its lifetime the 4-6-0 would find itself allocated to a number of depots including Crewe North, Longsight, Barrow and Aston before moving finally to Edge Hill, from where it would be withdrawn in September 1967. Author's collection.

1962 (Farewell to the 'Kings' and 'Princess Royals')

My railway expeditions last year had taken me to such places as Wolverhampton, Tamworth, Derby and a new destination that little bit further from home, Crewe. This year would see this trend continue and I would visit a number of other well-known railway centres ever more distant. The first of these I want to mention, Nottingham, didn't seem to feature highly on many of the local trainspotters 'must go there' lists from what I recall, although it was quite an important railway centre. I have no date recorded for this trip, only a heading, well, two actually. The first, Wigston North, has one or two numbers underneath (including 'Britannia' Pacific No. 70010 Owen Glendower), indicating that I travelled to Nottingham via Nuneaton and Leicester. A little later, amongst further engines noted en-route (mainly '8F's, and 'Black 5's), is ED10 a small 3ft gauge service engine built by Ruston & Hornsby in 1958 and allocated to Beeston Sleeper Works, which was engaged in the production and creosoting of sleepers.

Following a reasonable walk from Midland station, I entered Victoria. Opened in May 1900 and once serving both the Great Central and Great Northern Railway companies, it was virtually unaltered since being built. It had two long island platforms with four bays for local traffic making a total of twelve platforms. If I'd have taken more interest in the building rather than heading straight for the nearest platform, I would have noticed how old the station looked, including its wood-panelled booking hall and waiting rooms, which would be retained until its closure in September 1967. When the station was pulled down only the clock tower would escape demolition.

Under the second heading, Nottingham Victoria, my notes reveal that during my brief visit here I recorded for the first and only time class 'L1' 2-6-4 tanks, of which there were three, together with a 'K3', a 'B1' and a '9F'. Returning home via Derby, and having checked the engines noted, shed codes, withdrawal dates, diesels entering traffic (for instance No. D133 seen on the way home entered service sometime in December) etc., I would suggest the above trip was made during the Christmas holidays, most probably at the end of December or beginning of January.

In spite of steams decline, my enthusiasm for trainspotting continued to grow. Anyway, things couldn't be that bad could they? After all, steam locomotives had only recently finished being built, and improvements and modifications to some locomotives were still taking place. And, even though early in February Monument Lane became the first of the City's sheds to close to steam, there were still three remaining. The next few entries in my notebooks are not dated, so using a similar investigative approach as before, approximate dates are given as necessary. With at least one missing notebook, resulting in a gap in my records of approximately three months, the story continues with visits to Crewe (station only) and York during the Easter holidays.

At Crewe on 21st April I noted a significant jump in the number of E3000 class electric locos in service since my previous visit in September 1961, with a total of 21 recorded for the day. Diesel and steam totals were 39 and 132 respectively, with 30 different classes of the latter represented (See appendix 6 for steam noted). It must be remembered, though, that on this occasion I didn't visit either of its two MPD's. Further visits to this trainspotters' Mecca followed in May and June with the first of these trips producing one or two engines of note, including the experimental English Electric Type '4' Diesel, DP2 (which, after a mishap at Camden shed, returned to the Vulcan Foundry for repair on 22nd May), No. D813 Diadem (my first sighting of a 'Warship' here) and, built specifically for the Somerset & Dorset Joint Railway, class 2P 4-4-0 No. 40634.

A few days later, before the Easter holiday came to an end, I left New Street for Sheffield behind 'Peak', No. D24. Here I changed trains and travelled on to York behind another 'Peak', No. D106. Between Sheffield and York a variety of motive power was noted, including 'A4's, 'V2's, 'B1's and 'Jubilees'. Nothing unusual about such an assortment, but then, somewhere along the route, I spotted class C2X 0-6-0 No. 32545 of the Southern Region. I later found out that this engine had been withdrawn sometime during the previous November or early December. On the return journey another Southern engine was noted, class 'H' 0-4-4T No. 31261, withdrawn the previous September/October. I could only think that they were heading for a scrapyard in the Sheffield area. Interestingly, the railuk.info website lists both engines being scrapped at Ashford Works, yet I would record seeing No. 32545 again within a few weeks (see footnote page 261).

York MPD was home to a total of 84 steam engines representing 13 different classes. Together with ten preserved engines in the museum, a grand total of 181 steam were recorded for the day. Once again I'd noted some locos that I'd only previously seen in photographs in my combined volume, including the fastest steam engine in the world, No. 60022 Mallard; this was one of my best days out since I'd started trainspotting and I didn't think it could get any better.

Half term was on the horizon, and I had the great news that my aunt Eileen, who had been on the trip to New Brighton for the day two summers earlier, had invited me to visit her during the weeklong holiday. My uncle, in between time, had left the Birmingham Post & Mail to take up a reporting/photography post with the Manchester Guardian and Evening News. This meant leaving Sparkbrook and moving to somewhere closer to his work, and they had chosen Marple, Cheshire, so that he could commute to Manchester each day. What this meant for me, of course, was the opportunity to see steam in an area I hadn't been to before and possibly visit some of the Manchester sheds! I must say I have a lot to thank my uncle for with regards to the provision of films when I started to take pictures of steam, but more of that later.

On the morning of 11th June I walked to Marple station to catch the local service into Piccadilly. I can remember a long covered footbridge serving the station, which was gas lit. I also recall the train crossing an impressive viaduct way above the River Goyt, then one of the most heavily polluted rivers in the country. From Piccadilly I caught the train to Sheffield Victoria, made the short walk to the old Midland Station and was soon on my way to Doncaster for a second visit here in the space of a couple of months. On this occasion I was determined to get around the Works, or 'The Plant' as it was known locally, but had no idea or plan as to how I would manage to do so. And what a grand day I thought it would be if I could bunk the shed, too! Confirming my sighting of the engine two months earlier, I once again noted 0-6-0 No. 32545.

I can't recollect exactly how I managed it, but my notebook confirms that I was successful on both counts! I can vaguely picture myself climbing over a wall to access the Works and immediately feeling very conspicuous once inside. While trying to pretend I had a valid reason to be wandering around alone, good fortune intervened and I came across and joined the tail end of a visiting party, luckily without drawing attention to myself. The look on my face, though, wasn't easy to disguise. My eyes must have resembled organ stops. I couldn't believe the engines I was recording in my notebook - seeing so many 'A4's alone had made it worth the effort! Fourteen of this class were noted during the day, together with seven 'A3's, six 'A2's, fifteen 'A1's, oh yes, and ten 'V2's! (See appendix 7 for all steam seen during trip). Regrettably, my notes fail to delineate between those engines logged in the Works and those on shed. After returning home, I discovered that I had seen the first member of the 'K1' class to be withdrawn, No. 62034, which I think was in 'The Plant'. Steam cops for the day totalled 129 - unbelievable!

Looking as smartly turned out as when I first saw it forty-eight years earlier in August 1960 at Derby Works Open Day, standard '8P' Pacific No. 71000 Duke of Gloucester approaches Carmarthen with RTC special, The Pembroke Coast Express, on 5th May 2008. Also noted at the works with the 'Duke' was the equally impressive Midland compound No. 1000, seen below at Shildon in 1975 during the 150th anniversary celebrations of the opening of the Stockton and Darlington Railway.

BRITISH TRANSPORT COMMISSION
BRITISH RAILWAYS

"X" EXAMINATION & REPAIR CARD 7908 B.R. 87268

DATE 30 OCT 1961 Date of last "X" Repair 18 10 61 ENGINE No. —

84 E Depot TENDER No. —

Item No.	PARTS TO BE EXAMINED	Date Completed	Examiner's Initials	Check No.	Time Occupied H.	Time Occupied M.
	Examine in Steam—All repairs to be booked on reverse side.					
1X	Steam cocks & joints in cab & steam manifold	30 OCT 1961	[illegible]	628		45
2X	Brake system	30 OCT 1961	—	628		—
3X	All joints in smokebox	30 OCT 1961	—	628		—
4X	Cylinder cocks & gear.	30 OCT 1961	—	628		—
5X	~~Steam sanding apparatus~~					
6X	~~Condenser gear~~					
7X	Injectors & pipe joints	30 OCT 1961	—	628		—
8X	~~Compressed air controlled regulator gear~~					
9X	~~Coal pusher~~					
10X	~~[illegible]~~					
11X	All flexible pipes, other than lubrication system	30 OCT 1961	—	628		—
12X	~~Graduable steam brake valve~~					
	Examine out of Steam—All repairs to be booked on reverse side.					
13X	General examination by Examining Fitter with special reference to the following items:—					
14X	~~Axlebox wedges~~					
15X	Oil pipes and oil pipe clips	30 OCT 1961	—	628		—
16X	Springs and spring gear	30 OCT 1961	—	628		—
17X	~~Nose snow ploughs~~					

Item No.	The following items to be examined and receive attention as laid down in the "Schedule of 'X' Examinations."	Date Completed	Fitter or Boilersmith Check No.	Fitter or Boilersmith Time H.	Fitter or Boilersmith Time M.	Fitter's or B'smith's Mate Check No.	Fitter's or B'smith's Mate Time H.	Fitter's or B'smith's Mate Time M.	Repair Code No.
18X	Tender tank, ~~side and saddle tank~~				45				1/8
19X	~~Combined external water feed valve and sieve~~								
20X	Tender ~~[illegible]~~ water pick-up apparatus	30 OCT 1961	628	—					
21X	Blast pipe, blower ring, exhaust pipe from ejector ~~or Westinghouse pump~~	30 OCT 1961	628	—					
22X	~~Compressed air controlled regulator gear~~								
23X	~~Coal pusher~~								
24X	Axlebox underkeeps with drain plugs, ~~filling holes or removable covers~~	30 OCT 1961	628	—					
25X	Axlebox trimmings and oil boxes. Piston and valve spindle swabs	30 OCT 1961	628	—					
26X	~~Grease nipples, except on Skefko roller bearing axleboxes~~								
27X	~~Vacuum controlled regulator gear (Push/Pull locomotives)~~								
28X	~~Mechanically controlled regulator gear (Push/Pull locomotives)~~								
29X	~~Timken roller bearings~~								
30X	~~Motion oil bath~~								
31X	~~Caprotti, Lentz and other poppet valve gears~~								
32X	Smokebox internal deflector plates								
33X	~~Rocker grate and drop grate~~								
34X	~~Hopper~~ ashpan and damper gear fittings								
35X	Gravity sanding apparatus	30 OCT 1961	628	—					
36X	A.W.S. apparatus (~~other than ex G.W.R.~~)	30 OCT 1961	628	—					
37X	~~[illegible]~~								
38X	~~Speed indicator~~								
39X	~~Graduable Steam brake valve~~								
40X	Brake gear	30 OCT 1961	628	—					
41X	Whistle chain	30 OCT 1961	628	—					

P.T.O.

7908

B.R. 87268
Back

REPAIRS REQUIRED One item only to be entered on each line	Date Completed	Fitter or Boilersmith Check No.	Fitter or Boilersmith Time H.	Fitter or Boilersmith Time M.	Fitter's or B'smith's Mate Check No.	Fitter's or B'smith's Mate Time H.	Fitter's or B'smith's Mate Time M.	Repair Code No.
[illegible]	30/x.	674	-	15	672	-	15	
[illegible]		674	-	15	672	-	15	
[illegible]	[illegible]	674	-	15	672	-	15	N15.
[illegible]		674	-	30	672	-	30	
[illegible]								
[illegible]		674	-	30	672	-	30	
[illegible]		674	-	15	672	-	15	[illegible]
[illegible]								
[illegible]		674	-	15	672	-	15	[illegible]
[illegible]		674	-	30	672	-	05	
[illegible]		674	1	30	672	1	30	
Examination of engine and tender and steam test after "X" repairs.	[illegible]	628		45				

MATERIAL USED

DATE	DESCRIPTION OR CATALOGUE No.	QUANTITY
30/x.	[illegible]	1
	[illegible]	1

SIGNATURE OF MECHANICAL FOREMAN OR LEADING FITTER [illegible] DATE 31/10/61

Between visits to the works for more involved and extensive repairs, the day-to-day upkeep of locos was carried out at the motive power depots. Indeed, there existed quite thorough practical and administrative mechanisms to ensure that an engine was available for work as often as possible. This meant reporting any mechanical problems as well as requisitions for oil, water, coal and of course servicing and maintenance work. The E & R card relating to Tyseley's Modified 'Hall' No. 7908 Henshall Hall dated 30th October 1961, gives an idea of the checks and repairs needed to keep a steam loco in good running order and hence revenue earning service. Such a procedure was carried out every two to three weeks, and the information recorded in this example shows both what and when various parts of the engine should be checked, the repairs required and the date these were completed. When all necessary work had been concluded to his satisfaction, the Foreman Fitter or his equivalent, would date and sign the bottom of the form, which would then be kept as part of the engine's maintenance history.

Derailed

BRITISH RAILWAYS DAILY EXAMINATION B.R. 87319/1

DATE 15 OCT 1961 TIME DRIVER DEPOT PAY No. 625 ENGINE No. 7908 SHED No. 84E

REPAIRS REQUIRED—ONE ITEM ONLY TO BE ENTERED ON EACH LINE	TO BE FILLED IN BY REPAIRING STAFF CHECK No.	HOURS	REPAIR CODE No.
Driving & Trailing Brake Beams Bent	630665	3.30	
Both Brake Rod Bent	630665	2.	
L Driving & Trailing Brake Hangers Bent	630665	6.30	
R Leading Sand Pipe Broken & R Trailing	630665	7.30	
Sand Pipe Made [illegible]	630665	1.30	
Tender Leaking Bad. over Brake Service	630665	2.30	
New Coupling Links Wanted	630665	2.30	
NAME OF SHED WHERE ENGINE WAS LEFT (IF RELIEVED, ENTER "RELD." AND STATE WHERE)	TENDER No.		

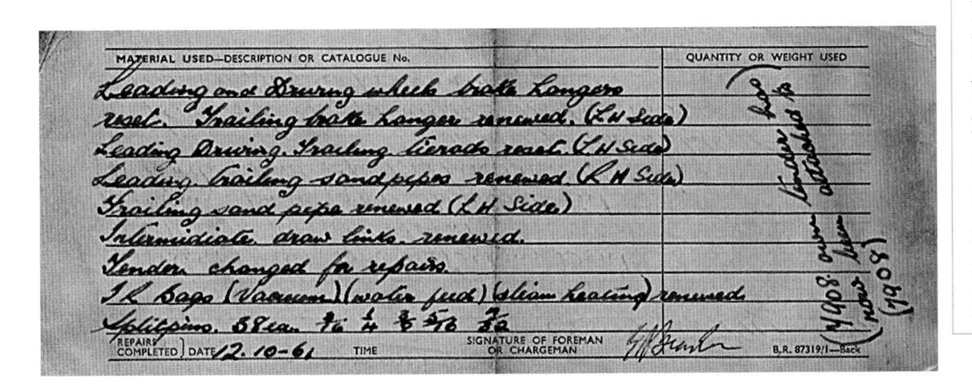

MATERIAL USED—DESCRIPTION OR CATALOGUE No.	QUANTITY OR WEIGHT USED
Leading and Driving wheels brake hangers	
reset. Trailing brake hanger renewed. (LH Side)	
Leading Driving. Trailing tierods reset. (LH Side)	
Leading. Trailing sandpipes renewed. (RH Side)	
Trailing sand pipe renewed (LH Side)	
Intermediate draw links renewed.	
Tender changed for repairs.	
IR bags (Vacuum) (water feed) (steam heating) renewed.	
Splitpins. 58 ea. 3/16 1/4 3/8 5/16 7/32	

Tender from 4908 was attached to (4908) 7908

REPAIRS COMPLETED DATE 12.10-61 TIME SIGNATURE OF FOREMAN OR CHARGEMAN [illegible] B.R. 87319/1—Back

In addition to the extensive checks mentioned above, each day the driver, fitter or foreman would list anything on the loco that needed attention on a daily examination card like the one shown left. Interestingly, the necessary repairs recorded on 6th October 1961 for 7908 were a direct result of the engine having been derailed.

Fresh out of Crewe works, Fairburn 2-6-4T No. 42119 is seen standing in Crewe North shed in the summer of 1961. Built at Derby in 1949 and initially allocated to Watford, she is ready to return to her home depot of Barrow where she would continue to be based until withdrawal in August 1965. A. Thomas.

The crew of 'Princess Royal' class 4-6-2 No. 46210 Lady Patricia wait for the 'right away' so they can start their journey from Crewe to Euston, some time in the Summer of 1961. This loco, together with sister engine No. 46207 Princess Arthur of Connaught, was employed to work on the Paddington to Birkenhead services when all but three of the 'Kings' were withdrawn for remedial work on their front bogies at the end of January 1956. A. Thomas.

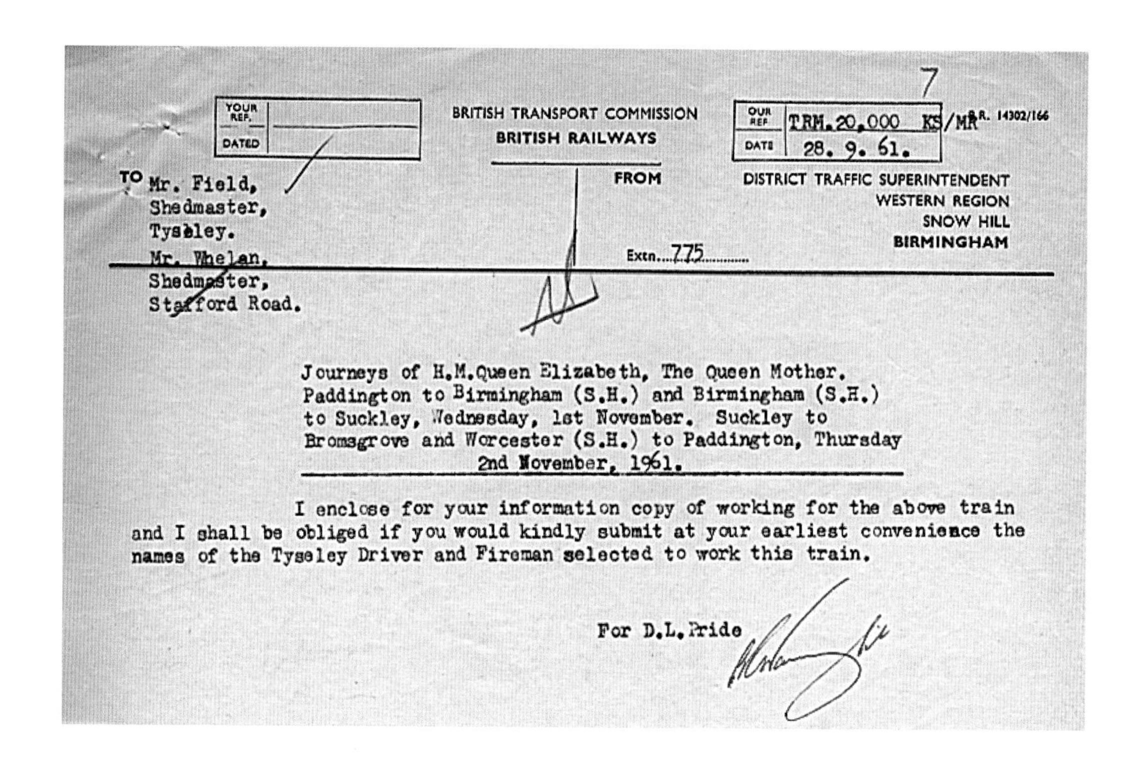

YOUR REF. | DATED

BRITISH TRANSPORT COMMISSION
BRITISH RAILWAYS

OUR REF. TRM.20,000 KS/MR
DATE 28. 9. 61.

B.R. 14302/166

TO Mr. Field,
Shedmaster,
Tyseley.
Mr. Whelan,
Shedmaster,
Stafford Road.

FROM DISTRICT TRAFFIC SUPERINTENDENT
WESTERN REGION
SNOW HILL
BIRMINGHAM

Extn. 775

Journeys of H.M.Queen Elizabeth, The Queen Mother.
Paddington to Birmingham (S.H.) and Birmingham (S.H.) to Suckley, Wednesday, 1st November. Suckley to Bromsgrove and Worcester (S.H.) to Paddington, Thursday 2nd November, 1961.

I enclose for your information copy of working for the above train and I shall be obliged if you would kindly submit at your earliest convenience the names of the Tyseley Driver and Fireman selected to work this train.

For D.L.Pride

C O P Y

Journeys of H.M.Queen Elizabeth, The Queen Mother. Paddington to Birmingham (S.H.). and Birmingham (S.H.) to Suckley, Wednesday, 1st November.
Suckley to Bromsgrove and Worcester (S.H.). to Paddington, Thursday, 2nd November, 1961.

Further to my letter of the 18th instant, and subsequent telephone conversation between our representatives, I give below details of eht engine working, together with the selected engine numbers:-

5/25p.m "Deepdene" Train Birmingham (S.H.). to Bransford Road Junction - November 1st (4/55p.m empty stock ex Tyseley.)

Worcester "Castle" Class Locomotive No.7007 will work 8.0a.m Worcester to Birmingham on this date then stable for "Deepdene" Train. A Tyseley 49xx Class Locomotive to take up the working of 8.0a.m Ex Worcester i.e. 5/45p.m ex Birmingham Snow Hill.

6/38p.m "Deepdene" Bransford Road Junction to Suckley.

Worcester Locomotive No.6989, 5/10p.m light engine ex Worcester Shed work train to stabling point and stand on train throughout night period returning light engine to Worcester after departure of "Deepdene" Train.

10.18a.m "Deepdene" Suckley to Bromsgrove November 2nd.

This train will be worked by Locomotive No.7007 to leave Worcester Shed at 8.5a.m and return 11.40a.m empty stock Bromsgrove to Worcester, thence to Shed for servicing prior to working continuation of the 4/5p.m Hereford to Paddington forward from Worcester on the same day. Stafford Road "Castle" Class Locomotive No. 5031 will act as standby engine at both Birmingham (S.H.) and Worcester on November 1st and 2nd.

Will you please arrange for these locomotive to be specially examined by the Mechanical, Boiler and A.W.S. Inspectors.

Tyseley Enginemen will work the train from Birmingham (S.H.) to Bransford Road Junction thence light engine to Worcester Shed and Worcester Enginemen will be responsible for the remainder of the working. Will Mr. Pride please let me have at his earliest convenience the names of the Enginemen working the 10.10a.m Pullman ex Paddington on November 1st, also the names of the Tyseley Driver and Fireman selected to work the "Deepdene" Train. Mr. Powell to kindly let me have the names of the Worcester Enginemen who will be in charge of Locomotive No. 6989 at Suckley (2 sets of men), the Driver and Fireman who will work the "Deepdene" Train from Suckley to Bromsgrove and the Driver and Fireman who will work the 5/10p.m Worcester to Paddington, November 2nd.

Towards the end of September 1961, Mr Field, Tyseley shedmaster, received the communication (shown previous page) concerning the visit of H.M. Queen Elizabeth, The Queen Mother, to the Midlands on 1st/2nd November. Initially, two Drivers and two Firemen from Tyseley were subsequently proposed for the workings listed in the rosters shown left.

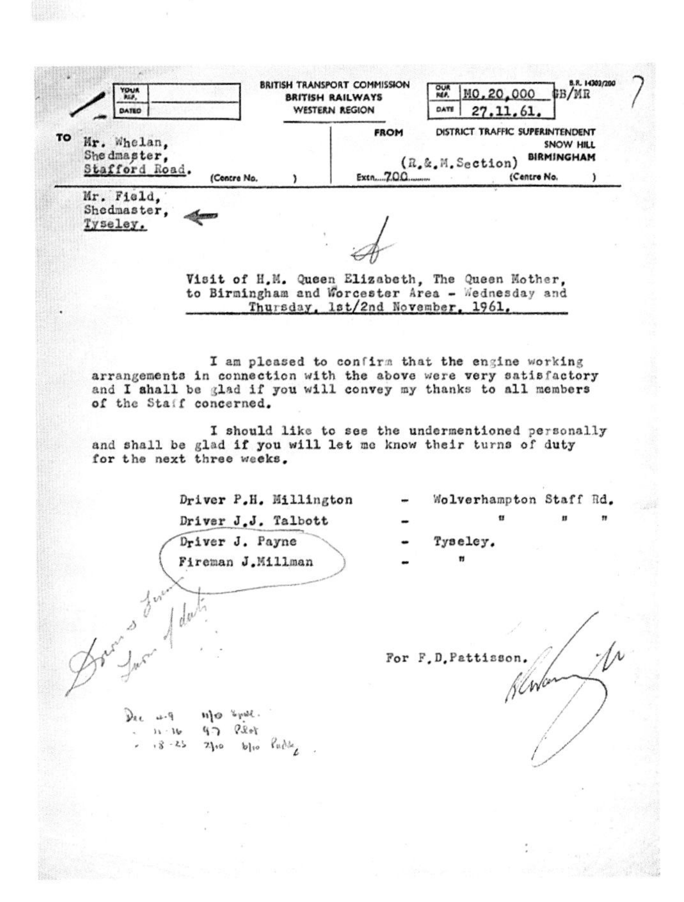

BRITISH TRANSPORT COMMISSION
BRITISH RAILWAYS
WESTERN REGION

B.R. 14303/200

YOUR REF.
DATED

OUR REF. MO.20,000 GB/MR
DATE 27.11.61.

TO Mr. Whelan,
Shedmaster,
Stafford Road. (Centre No.)

FROM DISTRICT TRAFFIC SUPERINTENDENT
SNOW HILL
BIRMINGHAM
(R.&.M.Section)
Extn. 700 (Centre No.)

Mr. Field,
Shedmaster,
Tyseley.

Visit of H.M. Queen Elizabeth, The Queen Mother, to Birmingham and Worcester Area - Wednesday and Thursday, 1st/2nd November, 1961.

I am pleased to confirm that the engine working arrangements in connection with the above were very satisfactory and I shall be glad if you will convey my thanks to all members of the Staff concerned.

I should like to see the undermentioned personally and shall be glad if you will let me know their turns of duty for the next three weeks.

Driver P.H. Millington	-	Wolverhampton Staff Rd.
Driver J.J. Talbott	-	" " "
Driver J. Payne	-	Tyseley.
Fireman J.Millman	-	"

For F.D.Pattisson.

In the final communiqué shown opposite, District Superintendent, Mr F. D. Pattisson, makes it known how satisfied he was with the way things had gone, and was seeking to thank footplate crews, Drivers Millington and Talbott of Stafford Road and Driver Payne and Fireman Millman of Tyseley, personally for their successful endeavours over the two days.

Railtours involving steam locos would continue to be ever more popular as the 1960's progressed. Unrebuilt 'Patriot' No. 45543 Home Guard is about to carry out such a duty and head the Derby to Northampton Bridge Street leg of the LCGB 'The Midland Ltd. Railtour'. The 4-6-0 is seen standing in the yard of Derby MPD on 14th October 1962. Author's collection.

After being withdrawn from service on 25th April 1963, No. 60022 Mallard began a new life in preservation. Seen above leaving Stratford upon Avon on 2nd November 1986 with the first of two specials travelling up to Marylebone, she has been given her original number 4468. Not having a camera when I first saw this engine twenty-four years earlier and, as I write, she hasn't worked for a similar number of years since seeing her at Stratford, I decided to include this picture as a reminder of where many would like to see her - gracing the mainline once more.

Collett 4-6-0 No. 6018 King Henry VI is seen resting in Swindon MPD after working the Stephenson Locomotive Society (Midlands Area) special 'Farewell to the Kings' from Birmingham to Swindon Works on 28th April 1963. The return journey would see the 'King' take the train via Swindon, Didcot North Junction, Oxford, Banbury, Leamington Spa and Tyseley to Snow Hill. After being serviced at Tyseley MPD, the loco would return once again to Swindon but, sadly, this time to eventually face the cutter's torch later in September. Author's collection.

Locomotive Drawing Office,
SWINDON.

D/L/03026

7th February, 1963.

Statement concluding outstanding experiments on steam locomotives on the Western Region. This advice replaces the usual individual copies of Concluding Report Form 'D' in this instance.

Experimental Ref. No.	Locomotives fitted.	Nature of Experiment	Remarks
W/SW/L/66	4936	Manganese steel liners fitted to coupled axleboxes and horns for comparison with W.R.std. bronze liners on "Hall" class locomotives.	Experimental discontinued after fitting of one locomotive.
W/SW/L/105	75001 75002 82005 82043 82044	Piston head carriers to be eliminated on certain B.R. std. locomotives to study affect on cylinder, piston head and piston ring wear.	Comparison with standard arrangement over a 5 year period showed little advantage gained. Slight decrease in cylinder wear associated with greater increase in piston wear.
W/SW/L/108	5035 (Tender No.2889)	To increase efficiency of lagging on train heating pipe under tender use 3 layers of felt and 1 of canvas.	Experimental arrangement of lagging found lacking in durability. Tender No.2889 has been scrapped.
W/SW/L/116	4088 5091	Pinnacle Metal Diaphram Self Locking Nuts on front cylinder covers, air pumps and anti-vacuum valves.	Experiment indeterminate.
W/SW/L/123	4153/KDR 4155/TYS 5164/65 5166/89 6118/34	'BC' brand high tensile steel tyres on the coupled wheels of tank engines in the Wolverhampton district in connection with loose tyre problem.	Tyres remained tight on wheels while under observation for 5 years, but several of the locomotives, viz.5165, 5166 & 5189 have been scrapped.
W/SW/L/124	4299 (Boiler No. 6017.) 7227 (Boiler No. 6385.)	To overcome loose boiler keys fit certain locomotives with a key locking device.	Key locking device effective, but not adopted, as incidence of missing boiler keys was found to be not so high as originally thought.
W/SW/L/126	6156	Coupling rod and motion bushes majufactured from "Main Metal" (Aluminium - Zinc Base Alloy.)	Material proved unsatisfactory for coupling rod bushes and very satisfactory for small motion bushes. Std. bronze bushes now fitted on No. 6156.

Cont'd.........

-2-

Experimental Ref. No.	Locomotives fitted.	Nature of Experiment	Remarks.
W/SW/L/130	6024 6025	Overheating detectors in coupled axleboxes of "King" class locomotives.	All locomotives of this class now withdrawn.
W/SW/L/135	75003 75025/Nos.	Firebar elements to Southern Region drawing No. W.11468 to improve steaming qualities and to make cleaning of elements easier.	No noticeable improvement in steaming but cleaning of elements was considered to have been made easier. Both locomotives now fitted with std. firebar elements.
W/SW/L/145	6024 6025	Overheating detectors to the inside connecting rod big-ends of "King" class locomotives.	All locomotives of this class now withdrawn.
W/SW/L/149	5626 5696 5699 6623/60	Empire '75' brand high tensile steel tyres on coupled wheels to combat excessive flange wear.	Wearing qualities found to be satisfactory, but tyres difficult to re-turn. Not extended to further locomotives.
W/SW/L/179	6112	New pattern trip cock gear apparatus.	Satisfactory, but not proceeded with because of high cost involved.

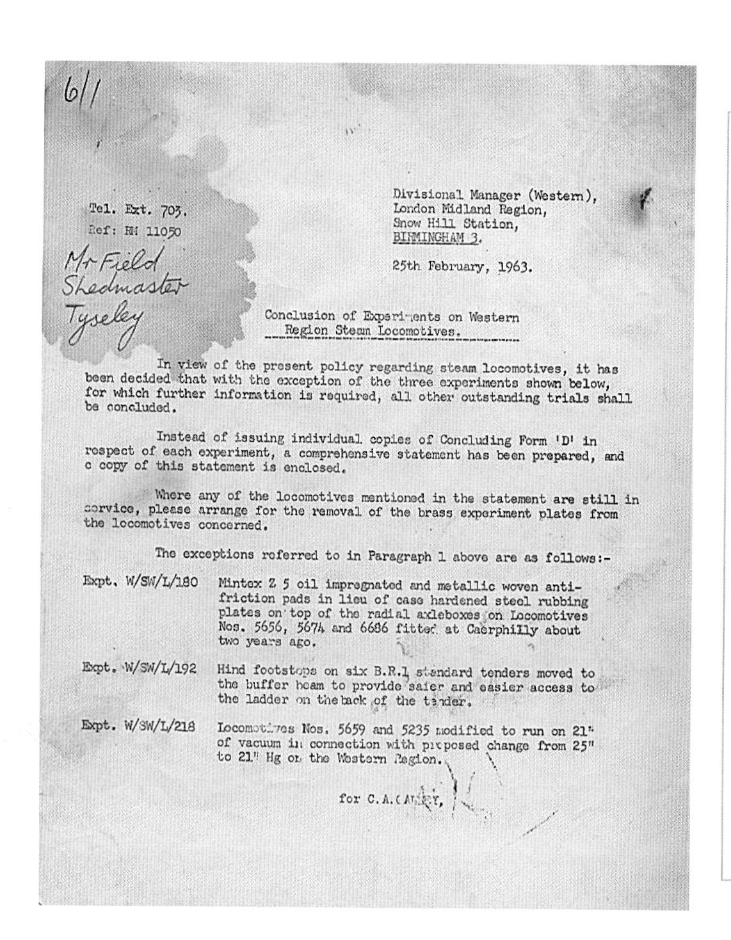

6/1

Tel. Ext. 703.
Ref: RM 11050

Mr Field
Shedmaster
Tyseley

Divisional Manager (Western),
London Midland Region,
Snow Hill Station,
BIRMINGHAM 3.

25th February, 1963.

Conclusion of Experiments on Western Region Steam Locomotives.

In view of the present policy regarding steam locomotives, it has been decided that with the exception of the three experiments shown below, for which further information is required, all other outstanding trials shall be concluded.

Instead of issuing individual copies of Concluding Form 'D' in respect of each experiment, a comprehensive statement has been prepared, and c copy of this statement is enclosed.

Where any of the locomotives mentioned in the statement are still in service, please arrange for the removal of the brass experiment plates from the locomotives concerned.

The exceptions referred to in Paragraph 1 above are as follows:-

Expt. W/SW/L/180 Mintex Z 5 oil impregnated and metallic woven anti-friction pads in lieu of case hardened steel rubbing plates on top of the radial axleboxes on Locomotives Nos. 5656, 5674 and 6686 fitted at Caerphilly about two years ago.

Expt. W/SW/L/192 Hind footsteps on six B.R.1 standard tenders moved to the buffer beam to provide safer and easier access to the ladder on the back of the tender.

Expt. W/SW/L/218 Locomotives Nos. 5659 and 5235 modified to run on 21" of vacuum in connection with proposed change from 25" to 21" Hg on the Western Region.

for C.A.C[illegible],

Early in 1963, Tyseley shedmaster, Mr Field, received correspondence concerning experiments on steam locos allocated to the Western Region shown left and previous. With regard to motive power policy at the time, their content held no surprises and the details would have been much as expected. With the exception of those experiments listed in the circular dated 25th February (left), all such trials would cease forthwith. Interestingly, it appears that the fitting of a brass plate identified the locos in question so that shed staff and footplate crews would be fully aware of the modifications made to each particular engine.

I first visited Stewarts Lane on 28th September 1963 (see page 63), three weeks after it closed its doors to steam. One 'Schools' class engine, No. 30928 Stowe, was still present and would be preserved. Sister engine No. 30926 Repton, seen on Stewarts Lane shed above on 6th June 1962, would also escape being cut up, and would eventually be based at the North Yorkshire Moors Railway. Author's collection.

Destined to survive: Hawksworth 0-6-0PT No. 1501, now based at the Severn Valley Railway, is seen leaving Bridgnorth with the 12.30pm for Kidderminster on 17th February 2006. Together with sister engines No's. 1502 and 1509, which were used for spare parts, the three locos were purchased by the SVR from the NCB in 1970.

Crewe station 11th October 1964: Dennis makes a note of English Electric Type '4's No's. D374 and D306 (next to platform). The latter engine would be preserved, and would appear as the infamous D326 in 'Buster' the film about one of the leading members of the gang involved in 'The Great Train Robbery'. No. D374 would be withdrawn in May 1984 and No. D306 in April 1983.

Fortunately, I have had the opportunity to make amends for my only disappointing photograph of a 'Coronation' Pacific in BR days (see page 98) The images opposite portray chameleon-like No. (4)6233 Duchess of Sutherland sporting three different liveries since being preserved. Top. In Crimson Lake livery, near Morpeth, East Coast Mainline, on 1st October 2005. Centre. In LMS lined black near Hexham, 18th September 2010 and bottom in early Brunswick green shortly after leaving Bridgnorth, SVR, on 21st September 2013.

My first opportunity to photograph Evening Star didn't occur until well after it had been preserved. The engine is seen taking part in the Cavalcade celebrating the 150th anniversary of the opening of the Stockton & Darlington Railway on 31st August 1975. Note the sun glinting off its copper-capped double chimney.

Someone with unquestionable skill, experience, and an eye for detail (not to mention a steady hand) was needed to produce the result that is evident in the two photographs, left. With the combination of paint supplied by the oldest, and arguably the best company in the world specialising in railway paints and coatings, T & R Williamson's of Ripon, North Yorkshire (founded in 1775), and the indubious ability of Ian Matthews (centre), the Gresley Pacific's appearance can only be described as stunning. Seen inside the workshop of Locomotion, NRM Shildon, work on Dominion of Canada had not quite been completed when these pictures were taken on 14th May 2013.

Still gleaming two months after hauling the funeral train of Sir Winston Churchill, the 'Battle of Britain' Pacific of the same name is seen resting at Bournemouth West on 4th April 1965.
Author's collection.

'Warship' No. D841 Roebuck stands next to Locking Road station, Weston-super-Mare, on 14th August 1965. On entering traffic in December 1960, the diesel hydraulic was allocated to Laira. Withdrawn on 3rd October 1971, after eleven years of service, disposal would take place at Swindon the following February.

'Terrier' 0-6-0T No. 32678 and 'Coronation' Pacific No. (4)6229 Duchess of Hamilton are seen on display at Butlins Holiday Camp, Minehead, on 13th August 1965. Both had been withdrawn from BR service the previous year, the 4-6-2 having completed over one and half million miles when taken out of service in the February. Eventually, the two engines would be removed from the camp and restored to working order, ready to begin a new life in preservation.

Above. Named after the Brush works where it was built, No. D0280 Falcon (one of the forerunners of the Brush Type '4' class) stands in Bristol Temple Meads station on 18th August 1965, not long after returning to traffic after a spell in Swindon works. The engine would continue to see service until October 1975, by which time it would be based at Newport Ebbw Junction MPD working Llanwern iron-ore trains.

Work-stained 'Black 5' No. 44777, recently transferred from Saltley to Tyseley during week-ending 2nd October 1965, makes a spirited entrance into Snow Hill station with a southbound mixed freight. The fitting of a shed plate would not be bothered with and 2A has been painted on the bottom of its smokebox. Photographed again on 14th November 1965 at Bordesley Junction (see page 191), the 4-6-0 would move on to Oxley the following April. Further re-allocations would take place to Shrewsbury, Edge Hill and, finally, Patricroft from where it would be withdrawn in June 1968. Author's collection.

Above. Looking clean and refreshed, but with time definitely not on their side, 'Granges' No's. 6853 Morehampton Grange (nearest the camera) and 6861 Crynant Grange, both allocated to Tyseley, are seen leaving the shed in the late summer sunshine on 18th September 1965. Both engines would be withdrawn at the end of the following month and taken to Cohen's, Kettering to be broken up. I had planned to visit Wolverhampton on this day, but decided to give it a miss in favour of travelling to Gloucester in a week's time. If the visit had materialised, I would probably have noted standard 5MT No. 73025 seen on Oxley MPD (below) on the same day. Looking very presentable, the 4-6-0 had been overhauled about four months earlier at Cowlairs works and had been seen on running-in turns locally during June. What is interesting, however, is the fact that it is carrying a 6A shedplate and the depot's name, Chester, on the buffer beam. Records show that the engine was once allocated to 6E Chester (GWR) in 1958, but there is no indication that it was ever a 6A loco. Author's collection.

Both 'Kings' languishing in Barry scrapyard (see page 188) would be purchased for preservation, although No. 6023 would not leave until December 1984. No. 6024, pictured above on 9th June 2007 at Lapworth with the RTC Cambrian Coast Express, was more fortunate. Bought for about £4,000 in 1974 by the King Preservation Society, there followed sixteen years of hard work on its restoration and, after moving under its own steam on 2nd February 1989, it eventually found itself back on the main line in April 1990.

Hauled by sister engine No. 31618 to Barry in June 1964, No. 31806 (above) departed Barry scrapyard for the Mid-Hants railway in October 1976. Following an extremely quick restoration lasting eighteen months, the loco was back in service on 24th April 1981. Originally built as a 2-6-4T, the 'U' class 2-6-0 is seen descending Erdington bank on the Severn Valley Railway on 22nd September 2012.

Built in February 1932 and originally numbered 9303, this loco spent a short while based at Tyseley in the 1950's. Following design alterations by Charles Collett, including the provision of side cab windows and outside steam pipes, it was one of twenty engines introduced with such modifications. These attractive locos were appreciated for their versatility, being able to handle many types of duties. The 2-6-0 is seen in Bridgnorth station after arriving with the 1.00pm departure from Kidderminster on 23rd September 1999.

Recorded and photographed while in store deep inside one of the many building comprising Stratford Works on 10th April 1966 (see page 229), ex-LNER 'Super D' No. 49395 was returned to working order after an involved and costly restoration. The 0-8-0 is seen shortly after leaving Bridgnorth on 24th September 2006 with a train for Kidderminster during the SVR Autumn Gala weekend.

1962 continued.

The following day, 12th June, I spent spotting at the four main stations in Manchester - Piccadilly, Central, Victoria and Exchange. In charge of the train from Marple into Central station was standard 4MT 2-6-0 No. 76089, a Trafford Park engine. This route included a stop at Stockport Tiviotdale a striking station in the heart of the town and which only six years later would be razed to the ground after closing in January 1967. Manchester Central was an imposing building, too, with its single span roof of over 200 feet and seemed very grand and spacious to a twelve year old. It would continue to provide a passenger service until 4th May 1969.

One of the more significant steam cops of the eighteen recorded during the day was 'Black 5' (the name given to these engines in contrast to the red 4-6-0's known as 'Jubilees') No 45212, seen while sitting on Victoria station. She would prove to be a rather special engine and have a most welcome surprise in store for me on 4th August 1968, the day steam ceased working on British Railways. Quite a lot more will be said about this loco later, and indeed her driver on that day, in part two of my journey following steams fortunes from July 1966 to the end of steam on BR. Some of the other classes noted during the day included 'Jubilee', 'Royal Scot', WD, Fowler 0-6-0, and Fairburn 2-6-4T.

Before heading home, I plucked up the courage to visit several of the Manchester MPD's, and was lucky enough to safely make my way round three steam sheds - Trafford Park, Longsight and Newton Heath. Unfortunately, Gorton, the ex-Great Central Railway depot, proved too difficult and I only managed to list fourteen engines before being asked in none too polite terms to leave! At the end of 1961, this shed had an allocation of approximately 75 engines, half of which were ex-LMS and half ex-LNER and, from what I could see, there were a good few engines that I failed to record. The number of steam locos recorded on the three depots I managed to bunk was 18, 14 and 31 respectively. A total of twenty different classes were seen during the day, including 'J11', 'J39', 'O4', 'G2', 'Jubilee', 'Royal Scot' and 'Patriot'.

The end of the summer term was fast approaching and with it the normal activities one would expect at this time of the school year. Sports day was an event I was looking forward to particularly and, of course, the class trip, which for my form would be a visit to the Elan Valley, Wales at the end of June. Water issuing forth out of the tap at home was not something I'd thought about too much, and part of the reasoning behind this trip was for us to see exactly where our supply came from and how it was managed using a system of reservoirs. I'm sure there were lots of other reasons, too, but for me it presented the possibility of visiting the seaside town of Aberystwyth, and the opportunity (if we were let loose for long enough!) to visit its railway station. Here I would be able to see standard gauge locos alongside the narrow gauge (1' 11 1/2") 2-6-2 tank engines of the Vale of Rheidol Line (V of R).

After seeing the impressive Elan Valley reservoirs, from where our water began its long journey, and being reminded once more of the engineering feat involved to transport it to our homes in Birmingham, we set off for Aberystwyth, and I couldn't wait to get there. Fortunately, the teachers involved agreed that we could have one hour to look around the town on the understanding that we did so in pairs. I didn't realise it at the time, but it would prove to be the start of a life-long friendship with fellow classmate, Dennis Perfect.

While sitting next to Dennis on the coach, who I didn't know that well, he asked me what I planned to do. I told him I was heading straight to the railway station and that he could tag along if he wanted to. In the short time we were there, we recorded five steam engines: V of R 2-6-2T

No.7, 2251 class 0-6-0 No. 2217, Mogul No. 7312 and 'Manor' class 4-6-0's No's. 7800 Torquay Manor and 7810 Draycott Manor, all ex-GWR locos. Since that day we have remained close friends, and Dennis, after becoming a fully-fledged trainspotter, went on to work as an engineer at Derby Loco works and finally Doncaster Works where he completed his railway career. Towards the end of our secondary education, we were both determined to become engine drivers, but Dennis discovered that he was slightly colour blind and I found out that my short sightedness was so bad I had no chance of passing the necessary medical exam!

Two views of the old standard gauge steam shed at Aberystwyth on 22nd July 1972. The depot had been converted for use by the Vale of Rheidol loco fleet during 1967-8, following its closure in 1965. The picture below, looking from inside the shed towards the station, has 2-6-2T No.8 Llywelyn standing in the yard. A short while later sister loco No.7 Owain Glendwr arrived on shed and is seen taking on water.

Once the end of term arrived the long summer holiday meant the opportunity to go fishing and trainspotting more often. Visits to the local sheds and favourite spotting places around the city continued with occasional expeditions further from home. The new 'Western' class diesel hydraulics had begun to establish themselves on the Paddington - Birmingham - Wolverhampton expresses and the 'Kings' were now finding work in short supply. During a days fishing at Lapworth in July, I didn't record a single turn for any of these engines. Needless to say, the 'Westerners' were much in evidence with six noted at the head of various expresses.

Further days during July and into August were spent at Snow Hill, the 'Button Factory' and Small Heath, with the 'Kings' noticeable by their absence. During this period I have only two of Collett's 4-6-0's noted in charge of Paddington - Birmingham - Wolverhampton Expresses: No. 6018 King Henry V1, allocated to Old Oak Common, and 6016 King Edward V working out of Stafford Road.

The log of my third annual visit to Derby Works on 25th August shows 115 steam engines noted for the day, representing 21 different classes. Special guests included 'Britannia' Pacific No. 70048 The Territorial Army 1908-1958 and 'Coronation' class No. 46256 Sir William A. Stanier, F.R.S. Diesels were well in evidence with a batch of 'Peak' class locos, No's. D179-D193, under construction.

Derby Works Open Day, 25th August 1962. One of the two guest steam locos for this special occasion was 'Coronation' Pacific No. 46256 Sir William A. Stanier, F.R.S., seen above on display at the front of the work's offices. Many a young (and older) trainspotter enjoyed the opportunity to wander freely around the works during this special event each year. J. Hewitt. Author's collection.

Before the end of the summer holiday I travelled to Wolverhampton to witness what for all intents and purposes was the end of the 'Kings'. My train on the outward journey from Snow Hill was hauled by diesel hydraulic No. D1005 Western Venturer, and after arriving at Low Level I made straight for Stafford Road shed. I hoped I might see one or two of the remaining 6000 class engines actually in steam, but not one of the eight on shed - No.'s 6002, 6007, 6012, 6014, 6017, 6019, 6021, 6026 - looked remotely ready for any further work and all appeared to be in store. While avoiding piles of randomly deposited ash, as well as keeping a careful eye on all manner of obstacles lying abandoned between the tracks, I also logged twelve 'Castles' - No's. 5018, 5019, 5031, 5045, 5046, 5047, 5082, 5089, 7014, 7015, 7019, and 7032 - with several of these being noted in store too.

Ex-GWR 4-6-0 No. 6019 King Henry V stands in the yard of Stafford Road MPD about two or three weeks before I noted the engine cold on shed at the end of the summer holidays. Following official withdrawal on 21st September 1962, the engine would be delivered to Cashmore's, Newport for breaking up. M. L. Boakes collection.

Seen adjacent to the coaling stage of Stafford Road MPD, Collett 'Castle' No. 5031 Totnes Castle is ready to move into the yard to await its next turn of duty. The photograph was taken at about the time I logged the engine at the end of the school summer holidays when a total of twelve of these engines were on shed. Except for a brief period allocated to Chester (GWR) from November 1954 to February 1955, the 4-6-0 remained an 84A loco from January 1948 until its transfer to Oxley in September 1963 when Stafford Road closed. This would prove to be its final move, but residency at its new home would be short lived, however, and its withdrawal would take place virtually immediately. The 'Castle' almost made 'Royal Train' status in November 1961 - see page 37. M.L. Boakes collection.

I was off to Shrewsbury a few days later to experience the mix of ex-GWR and ex-LMS steam locos that could still be seen here. I knew this railway centre would be a lot more vibrant and interesting than Wolverhampton had proved to be, not least because of the variety of motive power that would be on view. Its shed had previously served both the GWR and LNWR and its allocation still reflected its dual identity. A year after my visit, in September 1963, the LMR would take control of the depot and under its auspices would continue to service steam locos until March 1967.

I couldn't have planned the journey better in terms of the trains I decided to catch. I didn't note departure times, but from Snow Hill my train was hauled by soon to be withdrawn No. 5047 Earl of Dartmouth and on the return journey by No. 7915 Mere Hall. Fifty six steam locos were recorded during the outward and return journeys, and Shrewsbury shed had a total of 88 steam in residence, representing 23 different classes, including 'Hall', 'Grange', 'Castle' 'County', 'Manor', 'Patriot', 'Jubilee' and 'Coronation'. Oh! How I wish I'd had a camera!

Immediately recognisable as 'King' class 4-6-0 No. 6000 King George V, the engine is seen slowly coming to a halt in Birmingham Snow Hill with an up express for Paddington in the late 1950's. Built in June 1927, the 'King' visited the USA shortly afterwards and was presented with the bell above the front buffer beam. When withdrawn in December 1962, the engine had completed nearly 2,000,000 miles.

The start of the winter timetable was only days away and would mean the culling of many more steam engines. The full extent of the withdrawals would not become apparent to me until they were reported in the December issue of Modern Railways. In the Motive Power Miscellany section the Western Region Report began:

'There was a massive slaughter of W.R. steam power at the conclusion of the summer timetable. In all, 169 locomotives were condemned. The total included the first three 'County' 4-6-0s to be withdrawn (Nos. 1004/18/26), 25 'Castles', 33 'Halls', and nine 'Kings'.

Modern Railways, December 1962, Motive Power Miscellany, p.425.

In fact, by the beginning of October, only six of the 'Kings' were still in service. Soon after 21st December, when No. 6011 King James 1 worked the 10.50am Paddington to Shrewsbury throughout, and No. 6018 King Henry V1 the 1.25pm Paddington to Penzance relief, they were withdrawn together with the other four remaining class members. But that wasn't quite the end, or so it appeared. It had been reported that four 'Kings' would be reinstated for the summer service as 'stand-by' engines - two at Old Oak Common and two at Stafford Road. As it turned out this news was inaccurate and was possibly down to the wishful thinking of a steam enthusiast who couldn't come to terms with their demise! Nevertheless, the story wasn't quite done and dusted. The Stephenson Locomotive Society put in a request for a 'King' to head a farewell special from Snow Hill to Swindon in the New Year and, if granted, would mean that at least one of the stored engines (other than No. 6000) would have a brief reprieve from the cutter's torch.

Ex-GWR 'Castle' No. 5015 Kingswear Castle is about to leave Stratford upon Avon with 'The Cornishman'. The driver and fireman are looking back along the train awaiting the guard's signal to get the train underway. Out of picture is a 'Hall' ready to move to the rear of the train and help the 'Castle' on its climb away from Stratford. This is the service I would often catch after a day's fishing on the River Avon. Its next stop would be Birmingham Snow Hill. Author's collection.

The year had witnessed the end of the 'Kings' heading daily expresses on the Western Region and similarly the 'Princesses' on the London Midland Region. The 'Streaks', too, had not escaped the diesel threat. By the end of December the 'Deltics' had been put in charge of many of the express services out of Kings Cross and five of the 'A4's had been withdrawn. At eight years of age, Class '8P' No. 71000 Duke of Gloucester, had been taken out of service in November and, of some significance, too, was the withdrawal of the last '2P' 4-4-0 No. 40670 which, together with the downfall of the SR 'Schools', meant the end of the regular employment of steam locos with this wheel arrangement.

Numerous classes of engine had disappeared altogether or had been greatly depleted in number. If not being withdrawn, some engines were being stripped of their nameplates, like 'Royal Scot' No. 46101 whose name Royal Scots Grey was given over to 'Deltic' No. D9000. On a more personal note, August had turned out to be the last month that I was able to catch 'The Cornishman' after a day's fishing at Stratford-upon-Avon. From September, it had been re-routed and travelled via Gloucester and Birmingham New Street; this in turn meant that I had to be satisfied with returning home on the ordinary, unexciting local 'stopper'.

Letters from enginemen concerning their working conditions had been arriving on the desks of the editors of the popular railway magazines during the year. Footplate-men were becoming more and more disillusioned with the inadequate maintenance of steam locomotives, which were still expected to put in respectable performances and keep to timings. One such letter (adding weight to a previous letter of complaint) came from a Doncaster fireman who wrote to the editor of Modern Railways saying:

'The condition of about 90 per cent of steam locomotives at Doncaster is poor and neglected. After works overhaul, it is not many months before they are in the same poor condition. They say you can't do a job right unless you have the proper tools. How can we as locomotive-men do our job properly, efficiently and with enthusiasm, when our tools are in this hopeless condition?'

Modern Railways, April 1962, Letters to the Editor, p.287.

While the number of complaints about poorly maintained engines was steadily growing, the most significant statistic to try and comprehend was that which highlighted the fact that during the preceding twelve months nearly three thousand steam locomotives had been withdrawn from service. Coming at a time when the last steam locomotive to be built was not yet three years old, it would prove to be the highest figure during the process of purging steam from British Railways. Even modified engines like No. 5078 Beaufort of the 'Castle' class, withdrawn in November, had only managed to survive a further 11 months after the expense of its conversion to double-chimney, although as fate would decree, this particular engine would be put back into service briefly at the beginning of the New Year. Coupled with the news that three of Stanier's 'Coronation' Pacifics (No's. 46227, 46231, and 46232) had been condemned in December, it was no surprise that many enthusiasts like myself wondered what on earth was going on. If the culling continued at such a pace it begged the question: would there be any steam left to see by the beginning of 1966?

As 1962 came to an end, what was to prove to be a very severe winter started to take hold. My remaining notebooks show that my jottings once again petered out once autumn had passed. One of the reasons for the apparent lack of spotting activity from this time on may have been down to the misplacing of a logbook or two, but I have a feeling that it was most likely because of the extremely cold weather. It might have been a great time for tobogganing, but standing around in sub-zero temperatures whilst waiting for the next steam engine to appear would definitely not have been quite such an enjoyable prospect.

Only comprising ten in total, half of the 'Clans' (No's. 72000-72004) were taken out of service in December. Just shy of her eleventh birthday, No. 72003 Clan Fraser, a Polmadie engine, is seen near Shap. Disposal would take place at Darlington works. Author's collection.

1963 (Steams winter resurgence)

The winter was to prove to be one of the worst in living memory, and the rail system had its fair share of problems, not least with the route I lived next to. As a result of heavy snowfalls blocking the line between Banbury and Princess Risborough, trains from Paddington to Birmingham were diverted via Reading and Oxford during much of January. Many services were cancelled, including the diesel-electric Pullmans. Steam power was frequently called upon either to replace or double-head with the 'Westerners' so that carriages could be heated adequately. A particular combination of note occurred on 11th January 1963 when 'Jubilee' No. 45699 Galatea, being piloted by diesel hydraulic No. D1049 Western Monarch, was seen leaving Snow Hill with the up 'Inter-City'.

Steam would have a little more to say than expected as the beginning of the year unfolded. With the UK in the vice-like grip of what was often described at the time as an Arctic winter, the availability of diesel power continually failed to meet the everyday requirements of the system. On the Midland main line, for instance, as a result of the Type '4's being plagued by frost damage, train-boiler failures and other mechanical problems, they couldn't even meet 50% availability. The reinstatement of withdrawn engines was the only option, and a number of 'Jubilees' stored at Burton were put back into traffic, some of which were in questionable condition. Diesel multiple units were having their fair share of difficulties, too, with Fowler '4F's regularly substituting on the Birmingham to Derby and Nottingham services, and on 14th January, there was witnessed quite a change in motive power when 'Britannia' Pacific No. 70011 Hotspur found itself sitting in New Street at the head of the 9.18am to Ely, normally a Monument Lane dmu turn.

Most other parts of the rail system were also suffering from the snow and freezing conditions, and stored steam locomotives were being brought back into service up and down the country. Carlisle Upperby, for example, reinstated several 'Royal Scots' and two 'Coronation' Pacifics. In London, because of the shortcomings of diesel train heating equipment, the empty stock movements into and out of Kings Cross were put into the hands of several 'B1's. The West Country suffered badly as well and, on 23rd January as a consequence of improvisation, the former Polmadie 'Britannia' Pacific No. 70052 Firth of Tay was seen arriving with the 12.5pm Manchester to Plymouth throughout from Shrewsbury. It was reported as failing on Dainton but not, fortunately, with the same disastrous consequences as happened when almost three years to the day its loss and disconnection of parts of its right hand motion caused the derailment of a freight train as revealed earlier.

The Southern Region pressed into service previously withdrawn engines, too, including a small number of the sixteen 'Schools' that had been withdrawn only a few weeks earlier. Similarly in Scotland, several of its stored 'A3s' were reported active again in January, among them No's. 60043 Brown Jack, 60057 Ormonde, 60087 Blenheim, 60096 Papyrus, 60098 Spion Kop and 60100 Spearmint, which would continue in traffic for a further 2 1/2 years and not be condemned until June 1965. Returning closer to home, Snow Hill witnessed an extraordinary event on 28th January when 'Western' class diesel, No. D1001 Western Pathfinder, headed a ten-coach train made up of corridor stock in place of the three-car dmu normally found on the 5.5pm service to Stratford upon Avon.

Out in the freezing cold: 'A3' Pacific No. 60107 Royal Lancer, having worked north from Kings Cross, finds itself exposed to the elements in the yard of Doncaster MPD in January 1963. The 4-6-2 would be transferred from 'Top shed' to Grantham in June where it would spend three months before being withdrawn. It would then visit Doncaster one further time - to be cut up at the works where it was built in May 1923. Author's collection.

After the closure of the S & D line during the first week of January 1963, standard 5MT No. 73052 is seen with an up train heading towards 1,829 yard Combe Down tunnel, sometime shortly after sufficient snow had been cleared to allow services to resume the following week. The tunnel would eventually be reopened for cyclists and hikers in April 2013. The 4-6-0 would be withdrawn in December 1964. M. Burch. Author's collection.

Stanier '8F' No. 48468 eases its way towards Bath Green Park with a mixed freight off the Somerset & Dorset line in January 1963. The 2-8-0 had been transferred from Shrewsbury to 82F in January the previous year and would be one of a batch of these locos to take over the work of the S & D class '7F's (see page 69). In May 1964 the engine would be withdrawn only to be re-instated a few weeks later to work initially out of Stourbridge shed. In July 1966, it would be transferred to Lostock Hall and, following a further re-allocation to Rose Grove in June 1967 the 2-8-0 would be withdrawn in March 1968. M. Burch. Author's collection.

Closer to home, a solitary trainspotter makes his way along the platform at Bromford Bridge. The wintry scene is quite dismal with little snow lying to add a little brightness to an otherwise dull and depressing day. Meanwhile, '8F' No. 48640, allocated to Nottingham, makes its way south with a coal train. The 2-8-0 would be transferred to Northwich in March 1964 and would work out of this shed until withdrawal in May 1967. Author's collection.

From Christmas Day until the beginning of March the country was either experiencing freezing temperatures or raging blizzards. In January the Thames turned to ice across its width in places and half a mile from the shoreline at Herne Bay even the sea froze! In February a blizzard hit the west of the country and lasted 36 hours creating snowdrifts up to 20 feet high. When all the statistics were gathered in, it was found by the Met Office to have been the coldest winter for 200 years. It is not surprising then, that I have nothing recorded until the spring, when I travelled to Bristol on 17th April 1963.

Both St Philips Marsh and Barrow Road motive power depots were visited, and a total of 121 steam locos were noted during the day representing 26 different classes, including 'Castle' (3), 'Hall' (10) and 'Jubilee' (9) (See appendix 8). Quite where I was ten days later on 27th April I don't know, but I missed a great opportunity to see the influx of Southern Region motive power that was employed to bring in supporters' specials from the south for the FA Cup semi-final between Manchester United and Southampton at Villa Park. Eight of the specials hauled by Bullied Pacifics headed for Birmingham via Banbury. Terminating at Snow Hill, one of these was hauled by Battle of Britain No. 34052 Lord Dowding, which I would photograph, and be photographed in the cab of, while on my last visit to Salisbury shed four years later.

Meanwhile, the SLS request for a 'King' to head a farewell to the class special from Snow Hill, mentioned previously, was given the go ahead, and earlier in March, after being in store at Old Oak Common since 18th November, No. 6018 King Henry V1 was moved to Swindon Works. After repairs and a repaint, she departed the Works on 18th April and set off for Stafford Road MPD, only for the crew to be told on arrival that she should have been delivered to Tyseley!

Journey's end: having completed the task of heading the Stephenson Locomotive Society's 'Farewell to the Kings' special on 28th April, 'King' No. 6018 King Henry VI finds itself back at Swindon for the last time. Seen above on 26th May 1963, the loco was never officially a Tyseley engine, but someone decided to paint the shed's pre-1950 shedcode, TYS, on the side of the engine's buffer beam. Perhaps it was thought that the brief time the loco worked out of the depot in late April was sufficient to merit Tyseley being designated as its final home shed. Author's collection.

The following day No. 6018 was duly despatched to the correct depot, presumably light engine. The special train she would be in charge of was booked to run on 28th April (a month after The Re-shaping of British Railways - 'the Beeching Plan' - was published), and it appears, from information sent to the Railway Magazine by an observer, someone must have decided that, rather than sit around idling the time away, she could continue to earn her keep for a few days. So, from 22nd - 25th April she was employed on local passenger duties, and at least one of the workings was the Birmingham to Leamington local and back. I didn't get to hear about this at the time, otherwise I'm sure I would have been off to see her on shed at Tyseley, or indeed travelling through Small Heath Station.

About two months later, sometime in June, I decided to see if I could succeed in carrying out an unofficial visit to Wolverhampton Works, Stafford Road. Recorded in pencil in one of my school notebooks, the numbers are now much faded. But I can clearly remember the visit, not least for the excitement of trying to bunk the Works without getting into trouble. I had been told about a side entrance in Gorsebrook Road and it proved to be a useful access point. It may well have been a Sunday, as once inside the building, I recall how quiet it was and with little apparent activity.

Obviously anxious about being caught, I decided to conclude my visit as quickly as possible. As a result I recorded several engines more than once. Locomotives present (without the duplications) were: No's. 2211, 2237, 2257, 2855, 3620, 3625, 3666, 3677, 3802, 3834, 3836, 4147, 4939 Littleton Hall, 5568, 6101, 6140, 6169 6336, 6616, 6655, 6830 Buckenhill Grange, 6873 Caradoc Grange, 7443, and 9798. Not all of these engines were in the Works for repair, however, several (No's. 2237, 2855, 4939, 5568, 6101, 6336 and 6616) had already been taken out of service, but the prospects for Collett 2-8-0 No. 3802 were much better as she would ultimately be rescued from Barry scrapyard and be preserved.

Wolverhampton Works would continue overhauling steam until 11th February the following year when ex-GWR 2-8-0 No. 2859 of Pontypool Rd (86G) was out shopped. She was built at Swindon in May 1918 and cost in the region of £6000.00. What the bill for her overhaul turned out to be I don't know but, after entering traffic again, she would only remain in service for a further ten months and would be withdrawn at the end of December 1964. People employed in the Works had been informed through an internal report that the Modernisation Programme would provide new hope for its future, with the prospect of repairing mainline diesels. But this would not come to fruition and the overhaul of the Collett 2-8-0 would prove to be its last.

Stafford Road MPD had only about three months left before closing on 9th September, but I decided to give it a miss, most likely because of the absence of the 'Kings'. So, from the Works I made my way to Oxley to see what was on shed there. No diesels were noted amongst the 38 steam present, representing a number of varieties, including 'Hall' (10), 'Grange' (5), 'Manor' (1), 'Castle' (3) and Churchward 2-8-0 No. 4707. During my journey back to Snow Hill four 'Western' class diesels were logged.

At the beginning of the summer holidays, I started a part-time job working for my uncle, Stanley Wheeler, who was a cobbler and had a shop in Bordesley Green, Birmingham. I took over from my cousin, Derek Spilsbury, who had moved to Nottingham with his parents. Twice weekly I had the task of taking a large sack of shoes prepared ready for new soles to be sewn to the uppers to the Forward Leather Company, Digbeth, returning each time with the newly stitched ones left there previously. This meant that I could now combine my earnings and the pocket money, which Mum continued to give to me, to pay for railway journeys to more distant locations.

At this time there were some delightful little engines still busy working between Gloucester and Chalford and Berkley Road and Sharpness, so during the first week of August I splashed out and bought a return ticket from New Street to Gloucester to see, amongst other varieties of motive power, these Collett 0-4-2 tanks. And I wasn't disappointed: Horton Road, the ex-GWR shed, had amongst the 37 steam present four of these appealing little locos - No's. 1440, 1453, 1455 and 1472 and, sharing equally in the spoils, Barnwood, Gloucester's old Midland Railway Depot, also boasted four - No's. 1409, 1420, 1421, and 1474, plus a further 23 steam. I logged a grand total of 87 steam during the day, with no fewer than twenty-four different classes represented. On the way home I noted several engines prepared for banking duties at Bromsgrove, including Standard '9F' No. 92223 and B.R. built 0-6-0PT's No's. 8403, 8405, 8418 and 8430.

After visiting railway centres further away from home, it was always difficult to settle back into the routine of local spotting, bringing with it the recording of familiar locos that had been seen many times before. After the Gloucester trip, I was soon thinking about where to travel to next to see different engines in other more distant and different surroundings. During a visit to the 'Button Factory' various venues for my next outing came to mind: perhaps London, or York or Manchester, and then about somewhere completely new, somewhere I hadn't been before. As elsewhere, the continuing influx of diesels was rapidly influencing steams distribution in south Wales, so I decided I would travel down to Newport and Cardiff before the month's end. My notebook reminds me that during the three hours or so watching both the main lines into the city and thinking about further possible journeys, I logged amongst the numerous diesel locos and dmu's a total of 30 steam workings with seventeen different classes represented, including 'Castle', 'Hall', 'Grange', 'Jubilee' and 'Britannia'.

On 7th and 9th August I cycled to both Bromford Bridge and Bordesley and recorded a total of 87 steam workings (37 and 50 respectively) involving twenty various classes of engine, including 'Britannia', 'Jubilee', 'Hall', 'B1', and 'Castle'. On 8th and 10th I made visits to 'The Field' at Tamworth knowing only too well that steam would not be as prevalent as it had been during previous trips here. A total of 90 steam representing seventeen different classes were noted over the two days. Expresses with 'Coronation' Pacifics in charge were again few in number with just two noted each day. With only one of each class seen during the two days, the 'Royal Scots' and 'Patriots' were also scarce.

The trip to South Wales was duly made towards the end of August and took in visits to Pontypool Road, Newport Ebbw Junction, Newport Pill and Cardiff Canton sheds. Including those seen en-route, a total of exactly 100 steam locos representing nineteen different classes were noted. Following hard on the heels of this excursion, I decided to make the relatively short journey to Nuneaton, a location I hadn't been to before. The town had two stations, Trent Valley and Abbey Street and, close to the former, an engine shed too. The journey from New Street took about forty minutes and as well as spending time watching the trains on the London to Crewe line, I was hopeful that at some point during the day I would be able to get to see what steam the depot was playing host to.

The shed used to regularly service locomotives running in after repair at Crewe, and during the winter of 1960/61 five 'Patriots' had been transferred to the depot for light duties, but these engines had long gone. Nevertheless, I was confident that there would still be one or two express passenger engines to be seen on shed. Once again I was fortunate enough to bunk another new depot, and although there were only 25 steam present, including three 'Jubilees' No's. 45599 Bechuanaland, 45624 St Helena and 45643 Rodney, the variety was reasonable, with eight classes represented. By 1966 Nuneaton would be the most southerly steam shed on the West Coast Main Line. During the final few months leading up to its closure on 6th June that year, there would be little or no work to be found for its steam allocation of 31 engines.

Thinking about travelling further afield to see steam the previous month while spotting at the 'Button Factory' must have persisted at the back of my mind, and on 14th September I set off from Snow Hill for London hauled by a 'Westerner'. My intention was to focus on spotting at Paddington, Kings Cross, Liverpool Street and Waterloo stations, which I did for most of the day. But I couldn't resist the temptation to visit at least one steam depot. So, after an hour or so at Waterloo, I made my way to Nine Elms and successfully bunked the shed. A total of 58 steam were noted, with the following Southern Region classes represented: 'M7' (2), 'Merchant Navy' (8), 'Battle of Britain' (5), 'West Country' (11), 'U' (5), 'S15' (4), 'Schools' (4), '0298' Beattie Well Tank (1) and 'Q1' (1). Except for an ex-GWR 0-6-0PT (No 4672) the remaining varieties were of various standard designs.

By the time my train to take me home was leaving Paddington, a grand total of 107 steam had been recorded, representing 28 different classes. I had thoroughly enjoyed the day out; bunking Nine Elms had given me the confidence, and indeed the desire, to return to the Capital to visit some of its other sheds and see more of their diverse motive power on offer as soon as I could. With my pocket money, wages from my part-time job (not to mention a small income from a scam returning empty beer bottles collected from the rear of The Marlborough Public House, near where I lived, to various local 'outdoors' to receive a return of deposit!) I knew I wouldn't have to wait too long before I would be on my way to Paddington once more.

Indeed, my earnings from working for my uncle, and the usual generous help from Mum, enabled me to return to London sooner than I could have wished for. Two weeks after my visit on 14th September, I was once again heading south to Paddington, this time with Dennis. We had worked out an itinerary that, if everything went smoothly, would enable us to bunk several depots during the day. The 'Westerners' were now fully in charge of the express passenger trains on this route, and it was behind No. D1004 Western Crusader we departed Snow Hill at 7.30am on 28th September.

My notes confirm that we arrived at Paddington on time at 10.00am and immediately set off for Willesden. The first shed visit of the day provided a substantial mix of diesel and steam locos. Worthy of note amongst the 69 steam present were the following: 'Coronation' Pacific's No's. 46222, 46225, 46230, 46235, 46239, 46254; 'Royal Scots' No's. 46101, 46114, 46156; 'Jubilees' No's. 45664, 45623, 45620, 45735, 45736; 'Patriot' No. 45529 and 'Britannia's' No's. 70001, 70004, 70010, 70012, 70018, 70024, 70031, 70032, 70034, and 70043. Also on shed was LMS Type '3' diesel No. 10001.

The next depot on our itinerary, Old Oak Common, was still harbouring a couple of withdrawn 'Kings', No's. 6005 King George 11 and 6010 King Charles 1, together with 25 'Castles', 10 'Halls', 3 Churchward 2-8-0s (No's. 4701, 4703 and 4704) and 'County' No 1010 County of Caernarvon. Allocated to Cardiff East Dock, '9F' No. 92241, presumably having worked a freight turn, was also availing itself of the depot's facilities. Altogether we noted 73 steam locos on shed.

Rebuilt 'Patriot' No. 45529 Stephenson standing in the yard of Willesden MPD around the time of my visit to the shed on 28th September 1963. The 4-6-0 would shortly become an Annesley engine and would be withdrawn from this depot a few months later in February 1964. Built at Crewe in 1933, it would return to its birthplace to be broken up. Author's collection.

Cricklewood, the third depot we successfully bunked, was home to 27 steam representing 7 different classes. Well evident were the shed's standard 4MT 2-6-0s, several of which would soon become Saltley and Oxley engines. From here we proceeded to Waterloo and then via Battersea to Stewarts Lane. The shed appeared to have closed to steam perhaps only days before and seemed lifeless. I later found out that the depot had in fact ceased servicing steam on the 9th September, just under three weeks prior to our visit.

Except for two, all the engines noted were in store waiting to be removed for cutting up. These locos, I discovered later, had all been withdrawn between November 1962 and January 1963 and were as follows: No's. 30534, 30537, 30540, 30928 Stowe, 31305, 31542, 31822, 31893, 31894, 31896, 32337, 32340, 32343. The two locos that appeared to be still in service and not quite ready for the cutter's torch were 'Battle of Britain' class No. 34090 Sir Eustace Missenden, Southern Railway and standard 2-6-2T No. 82023. 'Schools' class engine, No. 30928 Stowe, would be bought for preservation and so be spared the humiliation of being cut up. The 16 steam on shed represented eight different classes. A flavour of the shed in steam days is provided in the photographs that follow and one on page 40 of the colour section.

Not surprisingly, Nine Elms, our next destination, seemed a hive of activity after Stewarts Lane. Fifty-three steam were on shed, including preserved Beattie Well Tank No. 30585 and Drummond class 'T9' 4-4-0 No. 120. Excluding the preserved locos, 12 different classes of steam engine were present. Once back at Paddington, we logged four steam locos - three 0-6-0 PT's (including No. 8459 see pic. page 65) all of the '9400' class and 2-6-2T No. 6163. A grand total of 276 steam engines were noted during the day representing 50 different varieties! (See appendix 9 for list of all steam noted on the five sheds).

Standing next to an unidentified 'Schools' class 4-4-0, 'Battle of Britain' class 4-6-2 No. 34082 615 Squadron rests in the yard of Stewarts Lane MPD sometime during the summer of 1960, about three years before the above mentioned visit. Allocated to Ramsgate when new out of Brighton Works in September 1948, the Pacific would be withdrawn in April 1966 after completing a little less than 273,000 miles. Author's collection.

Standard 2MT No. 84024 at rest in the yard of Stewarts Lane MPD on 22nd August 1961. Built at Darlington Works in April 1957, the engine was one of thirty in the class, which were all motor fitted for push-pull trains. Shortly after this photograph was taken the engine would be transferred to Warrington Dallam. Withdrawal would come in September 1964 while allocated to Crewe Works. Author's collection.

Hawksworth 0-6-0PT No. 8459 doing what it does best - carrying out the important but tedious job of moving empty stock into and out of Paddington. The 'Westerner' in the background could well be the locomotive ready to head the line of carriages being moved into the station. Summer 1963. Author's collection.

'Castle' class 4-6-0 No. 5056 Earl of Powis is seen standing in Paddington's platform 1 at the head of an evening express to South Wales around the same time when noted during my visits to London in September and October. Allocated to Cardiff East Dock, the engine would be transferred first to Hereford and then Oxley, from where it would be withdrawn in November 1964. Author's collection.

A further nocturnal scene at Paddington featuring another 'Castle' recorded when visiting London during the autumn of 1963. No. 7010 Avondale Castle would continue to eke out a living for another five months before being withdrawn from service in March 1964 while allocated to Reading MPD. Author's collection.

Routine visits to Saltley and Aston following the London trip continued throughout October. The former depot by this time had an allocation of 102 steam locos, exactly the same number as in January. Its allotment now, though, included a small stud of eight 'Jubilees' - No's. 45584 North West Frontier, 45617 Mauritius, 45631 Tanganyika, 45647 Sturdee, 45653 Barham, 45674 Duncan, 45676 Codrington and 45709 Implacable. Saltley was primarily concerned with providing motive power for freight work and a few suburban passenger turns, but I soon discovered that they had been brought in to work the Birmingham New Street to Bristol and Sheffield express passenger services.

An interesting visitor to Saltley early in the month was an extremely clean 0-4-0 tank engine, No. 41535, which I cabbed. I later found out that she was fresh from overhaul at Derby Works and was on her way to Swansea East Dock shed as a possible replacement for 0-4-0ST No. 47003. However, her journey to south Wales would not be without incident, several incidents in fact, mostly concerning hot axle boxes. Almost seven months would pass before the tank would reach her new home. Indeed, trying to piece together the amount of time she spent firstly getting to Swansea (reportedly in the middle of May), and then in revenue earning service is not at all easy but, suffice to say, the engine seemed to spend the majority of its time being repaired rather than working. East Dock shed would close in June, and by the following August the 0-6-0T was stored out of use in Neath Shed. The loco would be officially withdrawn in early October 1964.

Built at Crewe in January 1935, 'Jubilee' No. 45653 Barham stands in the yard of Saltley MPD on 7th April 1963. Used on the Bristol to Sheffield expresses, the 4-6-0 arrived at Saltley during the first few days of the previous month from Blackpool and, although only officially on loan, someone had decided she would be around for a good while and should therefore carry a 21A shed plate denoting her new home. After returning to Blackpool at the beginning of May 1964, the loco would move to Newton Heath the following month and continue working from here until withdrawal w/e 3rd April 1965. Author's collection.

Seen on the same day as sister engine No. 45653 (above), another member of Saltley's stud of 'Jubilees', No. 45709 Implacable, rests in the yard of her home shed. Also built at Crewe, the loco would be allocated or on loan to Saltley four times during her lifetime. After five months in store, she started her third stint as a 21A engine w/e 9th March 1963. Officially a Crewe North loco at this time, she would briefly return to 5A during w/e 16th November 1963, only to be withdrawn a week later.
Author's collection.

Stanier'Jubilee' No. 45647 Sturdee in the yard of Saltley MPD on 15th August 1963. The loco was officially a Crewe engine, but had been on loan to Saltley for about five months by this time. The 4-6-0 would return to Crewe North shed the following February, only to be immediately despatched to Farnley Junction. The loco's final move, in November 1966, would see it allocated to Holbeck from where it would be withdrawn on 26th April 1967.

The lure of London and the diversity of steam power that could be found there was difficult to resist and on 30th October 1963 I was once again heading for 'The Smoke'. I left Snow Hill at 7.50am hauled by D1065 Western Consort and arrived Paddington at 10.05, five minutes late. Camden, Finsbury Park, Hornsey, Stratford, Hither Green and Nine Elms Motive Power Depots were on my itinerary, and I managed to get round each one without being apprehended. My notes reveal that considerably fewer steam were logged compared with my previous visit a month earlier but, of the sheds visited, only Nine Elms could still be described as being a fully operational steam depot.

Closed to steam over twelve months earlier on 9th September, Camden had not quite rid itself of this form of motive power, and I noted three steam locos on shed: Speke Junction allocated 'Black 5' No. 45034; 'Coronation' Pacific No. 46240 City of Coventry and 'Britannia' Pacific No. 70032 Tennyson both belonging to Willesden shed. The EE Type '4' diesels that had ousted steam from their passenger duties on the West Coast Main Line, over thirty of which were now based here, would soon follow in steams footsteps and be driven out as a result of electrification. The shed, having already been partly pulled down, would close completely on 3rd January 1966.

From Camden I made my way to Kings Cross and caught the local train to Hornsey, noting York-based 'A1' No. 60120 Kittiwake en-route. The depot was now a diesel stabling point, but I was fortunate enough to record another 'A1' in steam here. With the safety valves reluctantly allowing the odd wisp of steam to escape, I can still visualise No. 60156 Great Central standing proud in the yard quietly waiting to return north and to her home depot of Doncaster.

The next shed on my schedule, Stratford, had had a staggering allocation of 383 steam in 1950 and still boasted almost 200 in 1959. Three years later, in September 1962, it had closed its doors to this form of traction for good. Nevertheless, on this my first visit to the depot, I was pleased to find steam still evident in the form of three stored engines - 'J15's No's. 65464 and 65469 and class 'N7' No.69621.

Nine Elms, the old LSWR depot, was my final shed visit of the day. This produced a total of 58 steam locos, including 'Schools' class No. 30902 Wellington and sister engine No. 30921 Shrewsbury. Withdrawn the previous December, both had been noted here earlier on 14th and 28th September. A grand total of 96 steam were seen during the day representing a total of 30 different classes.

As the Christmas holidays approached, I decided to return to Bristol. This time, though, I would make the short journey from Temple Meads to Bath Spa station and then, hopefully, bunk Bath (Green Park) MPD. I didn't record the date of the trip; it was possibly late December or early January when I departed New Street behind 'Peak' No. D153. During the journey south I recorded 26 steam engines, including several pannier tanks on banking duty at Bromsgrove, 'Castle' No. 7025 Sudeley Castle and two 'Jubilees' No's. 45641 Sandwich and 45690 Leander all heading passenger trains.

After spending a brief period on Temple Meads (noting nearly all diesel movements), I left the station and hurried round Bath Road noting one steam engine, 'Castle' No. 5002 Ludlow Castle, amongst the many 'Hymeks' and 'Peaks' on shed. From here I set off for St Phillips Marsh MPD where I knew I would find a reasonable number of steam locos present, if of course, I could make my way round the depot without my presence being called into question. Well, unnoticed (or ignored) I was, and a total of 42 steam representing 12 different classes were duly logged. Most evident were 'Halls' (21) and 'Castles' (7). Also worthy of note was the presence of Churchward 2-8-0 No. 4704.

Barrow Road, the former Midland Railway shed, was next on my itinerary and I was lucky enough to get round the depot without difficulty. Twelve different designs of engine were represented amongst the 49 noted, with no fewer than seventeen locos belonging to the 0-6-0PT variety. Three 'Jubilees' were present: No's. 45561 Saskatchewan, 45641 Sandwich, allocated to Derby and Burton respectively, and 45647 Sturdee allocated to Saltley. Also in residence was Fowler 2-8-0 No. 53809, one of the eleven members of the class specifically designed for the S & D, and which I would have expected to come across during my next shed visit - Bath Green Park. Barrow Road would see its allocation of ex-GWR locos increase gradually during the next two years or so, and would be the last of the Bristol sheds to close to steam.

The ultimate shed visit also went well, with 23 steam noted representing 8 different classes on Bath Green Park. The Stanier '8F's that were present, No's. 48431, 48468 (picture page 58), 48660 and 48737, had virtually taken over all the freight duties normally handled by the S & D 2-8-0's two of which, No's. 53806 and 53808 were also on shed. The day had been an enjoyable one with a grand total of 141 steam representing 26 varieties entered in my logbook. Darkness had fallen by the time my train pulled out of Temple Meads. With no spotting possible on the way back home, I remember sitting in the warm carriage and working out how many cops I had made during the day and then, with my well-travelled 6" ruler in hand, carefully underlining the newly seen engines in my Combined Volume.

Before the Stanier '8F's had made inroads into the duties of the S&D.J.R. Fowler 7F's, No. 53810 is seen leaving Bath Green Park with the 6.20pm freight to Avonmouth in May 1962. A member of the second batch of these engines built by Robert Stephenson & Co. Ltd, the 2-8-0 would be withdrawn in the December of the following year (1963) and disposed of by Cashmore's, Newport. M. Burch. Author's collection.

On 28th July 1962, Saltley-based Hughes-Fowler 2-6-0 No. 42790 is seen leaving Bath with the 12.30pm to Bristol Temple Meads. It would appear that the 'crab' had been in the area for a while, so may well have been on temporary loan to Bath Green Park MPD. Built at Crewe in October 1927, the loco would remain allocated to 21A throughout its time working for British Railways. M. Burch. Author's collection.

As the last day of the year drew closer, 1963 had witnessed the continuing implementation of The Modernisation Programme and, as a consequence, further fundamental changes to many aspects of the running of British Railways had come in to practise. Derby Works, which I so much enjoyed visiting, had out shopped its last steam overhaul on 20th September in the form of standard 4MT 4-6-0 No. 75042; Doncaster Works, too, had overhauled its last revenue-earning steam engine, 'A4' Pacific No. 60009 Union of South Africa, which was returned to traffic on 6th November. However, the 'streaks' had succumbed to the 'Deltics' and other diesels now working out of Kings Cross and were no longer welcome in the capital; their stamping ground was now north of the border.

In February, Tyseley shedmaster, Mr Field, received two statements concerning experiments on steam locos allocated to the Western region (see pages 39/40). Considering the motive power policy with regard to steam at the time, neither held any surprises and the information was much as expected. With the exception of those experiments listed in the circular dated 25th February 1963, all such trials would cease. Interestingly, it appears that the fitting of a brass plate identified the engines in question so that shed staff and those on the footplate would be fully aware of the modifications to each particular engine.

Relatively close to home, but somewhere I never visited: Willesden-based '8F' No. 48624 passes underneath 'Birdcage Bridge' of the Great Central line at Rugby during the winter of 1963-64. The 2-8-0 would be withdrawn in September 1965 on the closure of 1A, its home depot, where it resided for at least seventeen years of its life.
Author's collection.

The ever-growing number of the now not so new forms of motive power had continued to ensure the unrelenting displacement of many more steam locomotives during the year. Altogether 1,717 had been withdrawn: the 'A4's now totalled nineteen, the 'A3's twenty-six; fifty percent of the 'Castle's remaining at the beginning of the year had been condemned and the class was now down to forty-nine members. Dislodgement of the 'Jubilee's had gathered pace and a further 31 had had their services dispensed with. The less glamorous freight and shunting engines had also been hit with no fewer than one hundred and thirty five LMS class '4F' 0-6-0's being sold for scrap. The remaining five members of the GW '15XX' 0-6-0PT variety suffered a similar end, although No. 1501, sold to the NCB in 1961, would in time be preserved (see pic. page 41). Indeed, one hundred and seventy one ex-GWR pannier tanks had been removed from capital stock, including the last three of the '54XX' Class.

Even so, there were still occasional reports of steam engines being recalled to duty after being retired. Before the year was out, three Stanier '8F's, No's. 48773-75, after withdrawal in December 1962, while allocated to Polmadie MPD, Glasgow, were overhauled at Norwich Works and returned to traffic based at Carlisle Kingmoor. All three had been War Department stock and had returned to BR ownership after the Suez crisis in 1957. However, by September 1965, No 48774 would once again be withdrawn, but sister engines No. 48775 and 48773 would remain in stock until the end of steam in August 1968. No. 48773 was to be the luckiest of the three of course; not only did she survive service abroad, working on six railways in three continents, she would then avoided the cutter's torch for possibly the seventh time during her lifetime when she was bought for preservation by The Stanier '8F' Locomotive Society.

Removed from capital stock twice in 1963, Fowler '4F' No. 44198 (built at St Rollox Works in October 1925) stands next to the shed building of Muirkirk MPD, a sub-shed of Hurlford, during the winter of 1963-64. In the middle of the 1950's, half of the shed was demolished and the other half extensively rebuilt. One of well over a hundred (see above) to be condemned during the year, the 0-6-0 had been withdrawn for the first time in January 1963, but was reinstated the following month. The '4F' was finally removed from capital stock three months later at the end of May and its disposal at T.W. Ward's, Langloan, Airdrie would take place in February 1964. The engine in the background is an unidentified Caledonian class '812' loco. Author's collection.

While a few engines were unexpectedly called out of retirement, frequent reports were made of the need for steam locos to cover for either diesel shortages or failures. Such events followed the sad news that the 'Castles' used regularly on the Hereford-Worcester-Paddington expresses would finish work at the start of the Winter Timetable. This was confirmed in the November issue of Modern Railways (Motive Power Miscellany) which informed its readers that engine No. 7023 Penrice Castle had taken charge of the last rostered steam turn on 7th September with the 11.10 Worcester-Paddington and 7.15pm return. By the time I read this account, however, the situation with regard to the dieselisation of this route, and indeed onward from Worcester to Hereford, hadn't gone quite as smoothly as anticipated.

If a poll amongst steam enthusiasts was carried out to find the most fitting name for Stanier '8F' No. 48773, it would be no surprise if 'The Great Houdini' came out top of the list. On the misty morning of 18th February 2006, forty-four years after being originally withdrawn by BR, the 2-8-0 is seen on the Severn Valley Railway shortly after leaving Bridgnorth with the 11.05 am to Kidderminster.

The world's fastest steam engine, No. 60022 Mallard, was one of ten 'A4's withdrawn during the year. Seen above at the head of an LCGB Tour on 24th February 1963, the well-known Pacific would be preserved after withdrawal the following April (see colour picture page 38). Author's collection.

Fortunately, for those steam enthusiasts much preferring to see steam at the head of the passenger services from Hereford and Worcester to London, there was welcome information to follow this announcement. After barely three weeks of Winter Timetable operation, the number of diesel failures (mainly 'Hymeks') had climbed to over seventy, with regular steam substitutions being required to ensure continuity of service. 'Penrice Castle' was taken out of store at the rear of Worcester goods shed before Christmas and returned to traffic. Indeed, the regular use of steam to cover the non-availability of diesels or their failure would see this route to London having to rely on steam power for months to come.

Ex-GWR 'Castle' No. 7004 Eastnor Castle emerges from Ledbury Tunnel with a Paddington - Worcester - Hereford express and is about to stop at Ledbury station. A small number of these elegant Collett engines would, after the route had been dieselised, find themselves being called upon more and more to deputise for mainly, but not exclusively, failed 'Hymeks'. January 1963. Author's collection.

Inevitably, despite such resurgences, the dispersal of steam power would carry on changing. With the ever increasing supply of alternative motive power, it was plain to see the that the switch from steam to diesel and/or electric traction, witnessed once again in many areas of the country during the last twelve months, would be unlikely to falter or diminish during the coming year: steams involvement in the daily running of BR and its boundaries of operation would inexorably continue to contract as time moved on.

The 1955 Modernisation Plan predicted that BR would be back in profit within seven years, but this had not proved to be the case, and losses had increased from £68 million in 1960 to £104 million in 1962. The Government's forbearance had come to an end and it decided to look for a more drastic solution.

Working to a brief provided in 1960, Dr Beeching's report on the future of our railway, 'The Reshaping of British Railways', had been published on 27th March 1963. The reduction by about one third of the existing route mileage, the closure of 2,300 stations and 800 freight depots, and the loss of around 70,000 jobs over three years, were just some of the proposals. If accepted and acted upon, a tidal wave of change lay ahead.

1964 (Farewell to Stanier's 'Coronation' Pacifics)

Trainspotting at the start of the New Year followed much the same pattern as before. The local depots of Saltley, Tyseley and Aston were visited regularly, as was Bordesley, Bromford Bridge, Small Heath and 'The Button Factory' for mainline action. As the year wore on, expeditions further from home would take me again to Crewe, London, Doncaster and York, but the most exciting trip would occur during the first two weeks in August, and would involve, quite unexpectedly, the taking of my first few pictures of steam while on holiday in Devon.

By the beginning of 1964 BR standard gauge steam motive power had been reduced to approximately 7,000 locomotives representing over 100 different classes. More than 6,000 engines had been taken out of service and scrapped since the beginning of 1961. If the stripping of the railway of its steam power continued at such a rate, there wouldn't be any left by the middle of 1967, or so I thought when I recorded my forecast in the back of the logbook I was using at this time.

Steam specials were on the increase. Arranged by a wide variety of railway societies and clubs, and even individuals such as Alan Pegler of Flying Scotsman fame, they would happen regularly throughout the coming year. By the time the last of these, organised by the Stephenson Locomotive Society (Midland Area), entitled Farewell to L&NWR Steam had taken place on 12th December, the total number had reached in excess of ninety. Featured below is the first such special of the year.

Discovered amongst a number of family pictures many years ago, there was no information accompanying this or indeed the following three photographs. However, after a little research, it became clear that they were taken during a Warwickshire Railway Society special rail tour to York and Darlington on 18th January 1964. Standard Pacific No. 70000 Britannia was in charge of the train on what was obviously a very misty and miserable day, and is seen being prepared by the driver for the return journey from Darlington (3.50pm) to Birmingham New Street.

A member of an extraordinary class of steam engine: 'J72' No. 69020, withdrawn the previous month after completing thirteen years service, stands in Darlington shed yard. The 0-6-0 was one of a further 28 engines built between 1949 and 1951, the first 'batch' of the class being built between 1898 and 1925. With very little alteration to Worsdell's original design, all of the surviving later arrivals would be condemned by the end of the year.

Seen earlier on the same day in York MPD, 'V2' No. 60929 is shrouded in mist and steam. The engine would turn up at Saltley shed on 16th April next year, and I would photograph it in much warmer and brighter circumstances (see page 117).

Built at Doncaster in July 1934 and named after the thoroughbred racehorse Colombo, 'A3' No. 60036 sits surrounded by thick grey mist next to Darlington MPD's turntable. The horse was often spoken of as having a 'raking, effortless stride' and the portrayal would, for many enthusiasts, equally fit this and the other engines of the class. In August 1958, after running into platform 12 buffers at York with the 7.32am Sunderland-York, the engine was repaired and put back into service. Withdrawal would come ten months after this picture was taken, sometime in November.

February

The first trip of note was on 8th February when Dennis and I visited Shrewsbury and Oswestry. Leaving Snow Hill behind No. D1033 Western Trooper, we recorded 8 steam during the first leg of our journey. As soon as we alighted at Shrewsbury we made straight for the shed and, once inside, found a wide variety of engines present, including 'Halls', 'Granges', a 'Castle', a 'Patriot' and a 'Manor'. A total of 50 steam locos were recorded representing 15 different classes.

Checking the numbers noted against those in my Combine while walking back to the station, I discovered that I had copped twelve steam, almost a quarter of the total seen on shed. The booking office was our next port of call to buy return tickets to Oswestry, a place neither of us had been to before. The station wasn't particularly busy, and after noting the numbers of a dmu, we caught the train for Gobowen, pulled by Brush Type '4' No. D1682. With Ivatt 2-6-2T No.41285 in charge, our next train was already waiting to take us the further two and a half miles to Oswestry. This shuttle service would remain operative until November 1966.

Originally belonging to Cambrian Railways, Oswestry MPD had an allocation of around fifty engines through the 1950's, including several 'Manors'. The last of these, however, had been transferred to Machynlleth at the end of December 1963, and by the time of our visit the depot's steam allocation had fallen to around 23. On this visit we noted 26 such engines representing a surprisingly wide variety of types totalling 16 in all. The shed would continue to service steam for a further eleven months before closing on 18th January 1965.

Our short return journey back to Gobowen was again courtesy of No. 41285, and from here to Shrewsbury we were delighted to have Chester-based 'Black 5' No. 45305 in charge of our train. This engine would continue in service right up until the end of steam on Sunday 4th August 1968, and would head a BR special departing from Manchester Victoria commemorating the historic day. By the time we had completed the next stage of our trip, I had checked and carefully underlined a further fourteen steam cops in my Combine. One or two steam workings were noted at Shrewsbury station while we watched the 4-6-0 move off our train and be replaced by Brush Type '4' No. D1701, which would take us forward to Snow Hill. A grand total of 97 steam had been logged during the day representing 25 different varieties. (See appendix 10 for steam recorded on shed).

March

The 'Western' class diesel hydraulics had all but disappeared from the Paddington-Wolverhampton passenger workings by this time. Brush Type '4's were now the dominant form of diesel power and it was behind one of this class, No. D1712, I found myself on the morning of Saturday 7th March, heading once again to London. Several steam locos were recorded en-route to the Capital, including No's. 3825, 5975 Winslow Hall, 6857 Tudor Grange, 6933 Birtles Hall, 7806 Cockington Manor, 7013 Bristol Castle, 42082 and 44810.

Sufficient time was spent at Paddington to note pannier tanks No's. 3763 and 8743 on empty-stock duties before setting off for Willesden, the first depot on my itinerary. Twelve different classes of engine were evident amongst the 56 steam present here. A few minutes later I was making my round Old Oak Common, logging in the process 44 steam on shed representing 9 different types, including 'Castle'(14),'Hall'(9), 'Grange' No.6818 Hardwick Grange, 'County' No.1024 County of Pembroke, and three class 47xx 2-8-0's (No's. 4701, 4704 and 4706).

Diesel prototype No. 10000 was by now in store at Derby Works. However, sister engine No. 10001, recorded at Willesden MPD during my previous visit on 28th September1963, was not on shed on this occasion. No longer employed on express passenger duties, it was most likely working a north London freight turn similar to the one seen above at Willesden later in the year on 24 October. Author's collection.

The last shed bunked, Nine Elms, was home to 58 steam engines representing a wide variety of classes totalling 15 in all. An interesting visitor, in fine external condition, was 'Britannia' Pacific No.70020 Mercury, seen earlier on Willesden MPD. I didn't have the cheek to stop and ask the fitter attending to the engine why it was on shed, but later discovered that she was being prepared to take charge of 'The South-Western Rambler' steam special, organised by the Southern Counties Touring Society, the following day.

Once back at Paddington, six steam locos were noted - No's 6110, 8743, 9435, 9470, 9495 and 9710, all of which seemed to be involved with empty-stock duties. As expected, a Brush Type '4' was in charge of my train home, with No. D1710 of Bristol Bath Road fulfilling the roster. Soon after leaving Paddington, I began adding up the number of engines I had seen during the day. Bearing in mind the massive withdrawals suffered during the previous three years or so, the variety of steam power, with 36 different classes noted, was not inconsiderable. Altogether 185 steam had been logged during the trip.

Saltley and Aston were visited the following day, 8th March, with the former boasting fifteen classes of steam present, including 'Britannia', 'Hall', 'Jubilee', Fowler 0-6-0 and 2-6-4 tanks, together with various other mixed traffic and freight varieties. Amongst the 18 locos on Aston were four 'Britannia's'- No's 70005 John Milton, 70029 Shooting Star, 70042 Lord Roberts and 70052 Firth of Tay, and 'Jubilee' No. 45567 South Australia.

While spending the following Saturday, 14th March, at Bromford Bridge, on the main line from Birmingham to Derby, Dennis and I made plans for a trip to Doncaster and Leeds during the forthcoming Easter holidays. Doncaster MPD, now familiar territory for us, would be visited first, followed by Leeds sheds Copley Hill, once of the ex-Great Northern Railway, Holbeck of the former Midland Railway and lastly Neville Hill also originally a GNR shed. Holbeck's allocation had changed significantly since the start of the 1960's when it had numerous 'Jubilees' together with a small number of 'Scots' and 'Britannia's'. Even so, there were still about ten 'Jubilees' on its books and, although a number of them would be a busy at work, we hoped we would see one or two of these express engines on shed.

Two weeks later, on Saturday 28th March, we departed New Street Station (8.25am) for Sheffield Midland behind 'Peak' No. D96. We kept good time, and after about a ten-minute wait at Sheffield we caught our connection to Doncaster, pulled by Brush Type '2' No. D5684. By the time we arrived at Doncaster (10.55am), I had logged 45 steam of 17 different types. We now had about two hours in which to make our way to and around the shed and be back again in time to catch the 1.10pm to Leeds.

We managed to bunk the depot without any problems, and in the process noted 9 different classes of locomotive amongst the 64 steam present. Varieties recorded included 'A3', 'A1', 'V2', 'B1', 'O4' and 'K1'. Once back at the station, we tucked into our sandwiches and pop while waiting to catch our train to Leeds Central. I can't remember whether it was on time, but my notebook reminds me that the yet to be named 'Deltic', No. D9006 was in charge of our train.

Attempts to bunk Copley Hill failed miserably, so we hurriedly set off for Holbeck. Seemingly unnoticed, we made our way round this shed successfully and found 29 steam present, which, for a busy Saturday, was a reasonable total. Our hopes of seeing a few 'Jubilees' were realised with No's 45697 Achilles, 45568 Western Australia and 45573 Newfoundland on shed. One 'Britannia', No 70052 Firth of Tay, was also noted plus representatives of seven other steam varieties. Conscious of the time in hand - we could not afford to miss our train (5.06pm ex-Leeds City) otherwise we would arrive back at New Street in the early hours of Sunday morning, something I don't think our parents would have been too happy about - we decided for some reason to head for Stourton, rather than Neville Hill as originally planned.

Well, Stourton wasn't chosen because we thought it might be catering for a substantial number of engines, steam or otherwise! It produced a variety of 5 different classes amongst a total of 13 steam on shed and was far from the highlight of the day. On a more positive note, however, it must be said that I did cop ten of the steam logged which, on reflection, seems to suggest that we decided to forgo the visit to Neville Hill because of the number of engines we needed off this shed.

With less than an hour left before our train was due to leave for Birmingham, we waited impatiently for the bus back to the centre of Leeds. Fortunately, one turned up after a few minutes and, much relieved, we were on our way to City Station. We had not been quite as successful as expected in terms of shed visits, although during the day we had seen a total of 173 steam locos representing 24 different designs; we would be back to visit Neville Hill and Holbeck sheds, but Copley Hill would not be attempted again before it closed later in the year on 7th September.

It was business as usual the following day (Sunday 29th): I was up early and cycled to the three local sheds. Saltley had 68 steam in residence representing 15 different classes, including 'Jubilee' (2), 'Hall' (3) and 'V2' No. 60982 a York-based engine. Two of the 'Halls', No's 6935 Browsholme Hall and 6950 Kingthorpe Hall, had most likely worked freights up to Lawley Street Goods depot from Newport and Cardiff respectively, with Saltley crews taking over from Worcester. Aston had 5 different varieties amongst 13 steam noted, but Tyseley excelled itself by producing 13 classes out of a total of 21 steam present.

April

A visit to Oxley MPD, Wolverhampton, on 19th April revealed a total of 41 steam engines, thirty of which were ex-GWR locos. Amongst the 15 classes noted were 'Hall', 'Grange', 'Castle', 'Manor' and Churchward 2-8-0, represented by No. 4704, which appeared to be in store.

By the time I set off for Crewe at the end of April, I had made a total of twelve visits to Saltley, eight to Aston and a similar number to Tyseley since the start of the year. I was now looking forward to a change from these familiar sheds and other regular local spotting haunts and, needless to say, although I had by this time been to Crewe several times before, it was always with a sense of anticipation that I made the journey to this busy railway centre.

Disappointingly, I didn't record the exact date I made the trip, but my notebook does reveal all the locos I saw during the day. North shed had 10 classes of engine present amongst the 33 engines listed, and South shed had 76 steam present with 19 different varieties represented, including 'Coronation', 'Patriot', 'Jubilee' 'Hall' and 'Grange'. Also stabled there was ex-LNWR 0-8-0 No. 49407, which had been transferred in December 1963 to carry out snowplough duties as required. The highlight of the day came when I discovered that my train back to New Street would be hauled by steam in the form of 'Britannia' Pacific No. 70042 Lord Roberts, which I had noted earlier on North shed.

One of two 'Coronations' recorded on Crewe North shed during my visit at the end of April was No. 46235 City of Birmingham. Seen above two months earlier on a wet and miserable 16th February, she would be withdrawn later in September. After spending time stored in Nuneaton shed, the Pacific would eventually return to Crewe Works for a makeover in readiness to be put on display in the Birmingham science museum. Hauled by 'Black 5' No. 45039, her final journey to Birmingham would be made on 19th May 1966. H. W. Robinson. Author's collection.

May

May came and went with little trainspotting activity recorded. Saltley and Aston sheds were each visited twice, but with nothing out of the ordinary to report. No unusual visitors were seen, although the gradual influx of British Railways Type '2' diesels into Saltley's pool of motive power was becoming more apparent. The 'Jubilees' by contrast were less in evidence, with only two now officially allocated to the depot. As at 16th May, its steam allocation had fallen to 79, yet it still had quite a variety of engines. Classes continuing to see service here were as follows: Fowler 2-6-4T (1), 'Crab' 5MT 2-6-0 (3), Ivatt 4MT (2), Fowler 0-6-0 (3), Midland 0-6-0 (7), 'Black 5' (25), 'Jubilee' (2), Ivatt 2MT (4), Stanier '8F' (10), standard 2-6-0 4MT (6) and '9F' (16).

The planned reconstruction of New Street station was now under way, and the news that it would be able to cater for all Snow Hill's traffic, except for some peak-hour workings, would mean its eventual closure. Moor Street station would remain open to ensure extra capacity was available for the city's commuters. Once completed, I always found New Street to be a dismal, gloomy and uninviting place to have to wait for a train. Despite the introduction of electrification some two and a half years later, an estimated 300-400 diesel trains would continue to pass through each day and, even though all the platforms were fitted with an elaborate induced extractor system (only duplicated in Montreal station according to BR), the fumes seemed to be able to evade all attempts at their removal. During the times I waited for a train here, I felt as if I was in a rather large and draughty underground station, and often wondered whether any real improvements had been made at all.

June

As far as I can ascertain, it was about the beginning of June when I set off once again from New Street to Doncaster and York. There's no date written in my notebook but, considering the engines listed, including newly introduced diesels, I think this point in time to be reasonably accurate. By the time I had reached Sheffield 22 steam had been noted, all of which were either freight or mixed-traffic design. Included in these, seen near Bescot, was No. 49173, one the few remaining ex-LNWR 0-8-0's. Sheffield to Doncaster produced 5 steam two of which were express passenger engines - 'Jubilee' No. 45739 Ulster and 'A1' Pacific No. 60114 W.P. Allen.

With a number of '9F's, 'WD's and two 'A1's, No's 60119 Patrick Stirling and No. 60149 Amadis, all out of service, Doncaster seemed to have a good many more stored engines than when I previously visited the shed at the end of March. A total of 8 varieties of locomotive were represented amongst the 47 steam present.

York had its fair share of stored/withdrawn engines, too, with several of the last surviving 'B16's, including No's 61421, 61434, 61448, 61454, 61457, and a number of 'V2's - No's. 60833, 60855, 60856, 60925, 60932, 60942 and 60975 all apparently now unemployed. I recorded a total of 68 steam on shed with the different types represented as follows: '9F' (4), '8F' (2), 'Crab' (1), 'WD' (9), 'K1' (11), 'A1' (5), 'A3' (1), 'B1' (10), 'B16' (5), 'J27' (1), 'O4' (1), 'V2' (15) and Ivatt 4MT (3). With the addition of a further 34 steam locos seen on the way home, another thoroughly enjoyable day out had produced a grand total of 177 belonging to 21 different classes.

Interestingly, about three weeks later at the end of June, I made a visit to Oxley and witnessed something that, as far as my records show, I hadn't experienced before. There were no steam engines present other than those of ex-GWR design. In all previous visits there had always been the odd ex-LMS or standard engine noted too. The following is a list of locos and classes present: 57xx 0-6-0PT's No's 3605, 3631, 3778, 4635, 8767, 9610 and 9661; 5101 2-6-2T's No's 4148, 4165, 4179; 47xx 2-8-0 No.4706; 56xx 0-6-2T No. 5684; 'Castle' 4-6-0's No's. 5089 Westminster Abbey, 7012 Barry Castle, 7014 Caerhays Castle, 7019 Fowey Castle and 7026 Tenby Castle; 'Hall' 4-6-0's No's 5936 Oakley Hall, 5983 Henley Hall, 6907 Davenham Hall, 6917 Oldlands Hall, 6925 Hackness Hall, 6933 Birtles Hall, and 6947 Helmingham Hall; 'Modified Hall' No. 7928 Wolf Hall; 'Grange' 4-6-0's No's 6803 Bucklebury Grange, 6825 Llanvair Grange, 6827 Llanfrechfa Grange, 6831 Bearley Grange, 6833 Calcot Grange, 6839 Hewell Grange, 6851 Hurst Grange, 6864 Dymock Grange and 6871 Bourton Grange; 'Manor' 4-6-0's No's 7806 Cockington Manor and 7824 Iford Manor.

It was around this time that Mum and Dad started talking about where we might go for our summer holidays, which, as normal, would be during the Midlands Industrial Holiday fortnight (25th July - 8th August). They seemed keen to visit the south coast of Devon and mentioned a particular place near Teignmouth. No prizes for guessing my reaction to this news! As soon as possible, I was looking at Dad's road maps (which showed railway lines too) to see exactly where about on the coast we might be heading for. I realised straight away that the area had a lot to offer with regard my railway interests, and from then on, without trying to sound too keen, every opportunity was taken to say how good an idea I thought it was!

July

By the beginning of July everything had been confirmed, and as I had hoped, we would be off to the south-Devon coast to a caravan park next to Labrador Bay. A few pages in the notebook I was using at the time serve to remind me how I had spent time listing the engines allocated to Newton Abbot, Laira (Plymouth), Exeter and, the best depot in the area for steam, Exmouth Junction. With a bit of luck, I would attempt to get round all of these sheds while on holiday. As to how successful I would be? Well, I would just have to wait and see.

Early in the month I took myself off to Wolverhampton and managed to make my round Oxley and Bushbury Depots without any problems. Out of a total of 41 steam on the former shed 35 were ex-GWR varieties and included 'Castles' (6), 'Halls (6), 'Granges' (10) and a solitary 'Manor'. The latter produced 16 steam of 11 different classes. Only a handful of the ex-LNWR 0-8-0's were still active, so to come across two here came as a bit of a surprise. When I got close enough to see their numbers, 48895 and 49452, I realised that the latter wasn't listed in my Combine and had in fact been withdrawn while still a Bushbury engine at the end of 1963.

A Sunday visit to Saltley during the middle of July proved to be most interesting. It produced the most wide-ranging variety of locomotives that I had ever recorded there. A total of 17 different classes of engine were present amongst the 68 steam noted: '8F' (13), Ivatt 4MT 2-6-0 (2), 'Black 5' (19), standard 2MT 2-6-0 (1), Fowler 0-6-0 (3), Fairburn 2-6-4T(1), 'Hall' (2), Stanier 2-6-4T (1), 'Jinty' (1), 'B1' (1), 'Jubilee' (2), 'Crab' (1), Ivatt 2MT 2-6-0 (4), standard 5MT (2), Midland 0-6-0 (4), standard 4MT 2-6-0 (4) and standard '9F' (7).

Before heading south to Devon on Sunday 26th, my jottings reveal that I was out and about trainspotting regularly during the previous week. Small Heath, Bordesley and Bromford Bridge were visited over a three-day period 22nd - 24th July and produced 23 different classes of engine amongst a total of 76 steam workings noted. Saltley on Saturday 25th July was home to 39 steam, including, 'Jubilee' No. 45611 Hong Kong from Derby, and 'B1' No. 61315 from Canklow. Standard 2-6-0 No. 76048, which I also a thought was an interloper from Cricklewood West, was in fact a new addition to Saltley's allocation.

Even though we were in our faster and more comfortable 'new' car, a second-hand Hillman Minx, the journey, as many journeys do when you are young, seemed to last forever. Before reaching the caravan site and the particular caravan that was to be our home for the next two weeks, no doubt Mum and Dad were asked umpteen times 'how much further is it?!

Dad's previous car, a Morris Eight, affectionately known in the family as 'Nellie', had given him ample opportunity to practise his mechanical expertise (developed while in the R.E.M.E.) and, despite every problem it had thrown at him, he had managed to keep it going. But, earlier in the summer, the dreaded knocking noise from the bottom of the engine had told him it was time to throw in the towel. So, reluctantly, he decided to take it to the breakers yard close to where we used to live in Bordesley Green, hopeful of at least getting a pound or two for its scrap value.

Dad parked the car outside what looked like an office-cum store with a sign outside informing people of how many parts were available to be bought 'off-the-shelf'. We picked our way through all manner of bits and pieces not having yet made their way on to the said shelves and, once inside, the man standing behind the counter was asked what he would pay for 'Nellie'. He looked outside, turned around, and without saying a word reached carefully behind a partly open door. As if by magic, he produced two balloons in one hand and a goldfish in a water-filled plastic bag in the other, and then asked Dad which he'd prefer! I saw the funny side of this, but I don't think Dad was very amused at the time, although we laughed about it lots of times afterwards.

Looking somewhat bruised and battered, the family's first car was affectionately referred to as 'Nellie'. This was the Morris Eight that managed to take us all on holiday to south Devon and Somerset on a number of occasions. Posing next to it, my grandfather has the confidence to lean on the headlight. What it would be worth restored today would be a significant sum, but one can see why its scrap value back then wasn't worth pursuing. Beer, S. Devon. Circa 1959.

During the first week away I managed to go along with the normal things that families do on holiday: spending time on the beach, visiting other local places of interest and as is necessary with self-catering the need to go shopping, which no doubt all of us found a chore. After four days, I was finding it more and more difficult to show any real enthusiasm for these things, all I could think about was visiting the nearby railway centres and seeing some steam. Nevertheless, my patience was eventually rewarded. Dad said I could go trainspotting at the weekend and, much to my surprise, he would show me how his camera worked so I would be able to take a few photographs too! My railway exploits were about to take on a whole new dimension.

August

On Sunday 2nd August Dad dropped me off at Newton Abbot station and arranged to pick me up again few hours later. Needless to say, I didn't see any steam workings and noted as expected a mixture of diesel-hydraulics (with the 'Warship' class being most evident) either in service or resting on shed. However, I couldn't resist trying out the camera, so my first few pictures featured 'Hymeks', 'Westerners' and 'Warships'. As it turned out, I am pleased that my impatience meant it was these locomotives rather than steam that were the subject of my first efforts, as the results left more than a little room for improvement.

The following day, 3rd August, Dad gave me a lift to Teignmouth station. From here, my records show that I caught the 10.47 am to Plymouth hauled, initially, by 'Warship' No. D835 Pegasus as far as Newton Abbot, and for the remainder of the journey by Hymek No. D7076. As the train entered Plymouth station, I caught a glimpse of the first steam locomotive of the holiday, an Ivatt 2-6-2T No. 41230, light engine. Allocated to Salisbury, she was probably one of the locos rostered for working the passenger trains on the Callington branch line.

Excited at the prospect of visiting another shed for the first time, I waited outside the station for the bus that would take me to the city centre. By now it was very warm and the sky was an uninterrupted expanse of uniform blue. After changing buses, I was on my way to the shed at Laira. A few months earlier I would have been attempting to get round the old steam depot, but it had closed in the spring and its last few remaining locos had been transferred to Taunton in April. By the end of October Taunton, too, would cease to have a steam allocation.

Moving quickly around the new depot, it was soon evident that the 'Warships' were by far the dominant class, with a total of 21 members noted. Not expecting to see any steam here, I was pleasantly surprised to find two in residence - Ivatt 2-6-2T No. 41308, an Exmouth Jnct. engine, and ex-GWR 0-6-0ST No. 1363. The latter loco, last allocated to Laira, belonged to a class constituting only five members, and was designed for shunting in areas with severe curves such as docks. This saddle-tank, which had been withdrawn by the end of 1962, would have the good fortune to be preserved.

Once back on Plymouth station, I again recorded amongst the many diesel hydraulics one steam working - a passenger train with unrebuilt 'West Country' pacific No. 34023 Blackmore Vale in charge. This engine would remain in service until steam finished on the Southern Region and would appear in countless camera viewfinders, including my own, before she was withdrawn. No steam were noted during my trip back to Teignmouth, which featured being hauled initially by D1070 Western Gauntlet to Newton Abbot, and then by 'Warship' No. D830 Majestic (the only member of its class rated at 2,400 b.h.p.) for the remainder of my journey.

After arriving back at the caravan, I kept thinking about the photographs I had taken with my father's camera. It wasn't anything grand and expensive, and I must confess that I can't recall the make, although I do remember that it had bellows and unfolded and could possibly have been a No. 2 Folding Autographic Brownie. With each roll of 120 film I could take eight photographs measuring 3 1/4" X 2 1/14". I do recall, however, how impatient I was to discover how successful I had been; I couldn't wait until we got back home to take my films to the local chemist to be developed and printed and to see the results of my efforts.

Pictured just prior to leaving Newton Abbot on 5th August 1964, diesel hydraulic No. D1029 Western Legionnaire is seen at the head of its train for Paddington, which I would take as far as Exeter St. David's. Built at Swindon earlier in the year, but retained by the works' Research and Testing Section, D1029 had been the last of the class to enter revenue-earning service the previous month. The loco would be withdrawn in November 1974, but prior to this would be renamed Western Legionaire in September 1967.

On Wednesday 5th August, following a day of typical holiday routine, I caught the 9.49am from Newton Abbot to Exeter St David's headed by 'Western' No. D1029 Western Legionnaire. Close to the signal box, two ex-GWR pannier tanks, No's 4692 and 4694, were waiting to greet me while they rested between banking duties. I made my way to the end of the platform to get as close to them as I could and took my first photograph of the day. Remaining on the station for a while, the next steam engine I recorded was 'West Country' class No. 34015 Exmouth, followed in quick succession by two 'N' Class 2-6-0's No's 31845 and 31859 heading mixed-freight trains both of which I also captured on film.

Ex-GWR pannier tanks No's 4692 and 4694 are found resting next to Exeter Middle signal box while waiting for their next banking duty. In the foreground is Red Cow crossing situated at the north end of St. David's station. 5th August 1964.

With only a few weeks of its working life remaining, 'N' class 2-6-0 No. 31845, allocated to Exmouth Junction, leaves Exeter St David's with a mixed freight train. 5th August 1964.

As No. 31845 accelerates away from St David's, fellow classmate No. 31859, also based at Exmouth Junction shed, arrives with a passenger train. The gentleman in the white shirt greeting the driver with a salute is the Red Cow level crossing keeper. Both engines would be withdrawn by the end of September.

A roofless Exeter shed (closed the previous October) was home to five stored steam engines on 5th August 1964. Amongst these was ex-SR 'Battle of Britain' class 4-6-2 No. 34075 264 Squadron. Her final journey would be to South Wales and Bird's scrapyard in Bridgend. Withdrawn earlier in April, after about sixteen years service, she had completed almost 650,000 miles.

From the south end of the station I could see a number of stored steam engines on shed, and couldn't resist the temptation to get a closer look. Access was via a boarded crossing from the platform end, which meant I would easily be spotted as I made my way across the tracks. After finally summing up the courage, I set off and soon found myself, presumably unobserved, walking along the yard of the now closed depot. Standing in the middle of what was once the shed building (its roof had been removed) I noted the following locos: 'N' class No's 31812 and 31854, Collett 0-6-0's No's 2214 and 3205 and 'Battle of Britain' No. 34075 264 Squadron. The two ex-GWR engines would be transferred to Exmouth Junction MPD and No. 3205 would be bought and preserved. The ex-Southern Region locos would not be employed again and would shortly be removed for cutting up.

An unidentified 'Western' class diesel passes South signal box and enters Exeter St. David's from Newton Abbot. The lines veering away to the left are to Exeter Central, and the warning sign states that a bell will sound when engines are approaching from here, or indeed South Devon sidings a little further to the left of the picture. 5th August 1964.

Before catching the bus to Exmouth Junction to try and bunk the shed there, comprising sandwiches, biscuits and pop, lunch was had while spending a little while longer on St David's station. As I tentatively made my way round the depot, I hoped that I would not be asked to leave before making a note of all the engines present and, of course, taking one or two photographs. My apprehension proved to be unfounded, and I successfully recorded the 39 steam present and also took several pictures. A total of 18 'Battle of Britain' / 'West Country' Pacifics were noted plus 7 other different classes of engine. As much as I was enjoying myself, I didn't linger at the shed. I wanted to spend some time on Exeter Central to see what it had to offer in the way of Southern Region steam so I caught the first bus back to the city.

Central station was busy and in a relatively short space of time, I logged a total of 14 steam as follows: No's 3759, 4610, 4692, 4694, 31802, 34013, 34030, 34059, 34107, 35019, 35028, 41206, 41284, and 82040. I would have happily stayed a lot longer if time had permitted. It was a lovely summer's day with lots of steam still to see and make note of. But I had to meet up with Mum and Dad, which meant leaving Central station to catch what would be another diesel-hauled train from St David's back to Teignmouth. Without doubt, this had been the best day of the holiday and, as well as taking a few more photographs, I had copped 42 steam. (See appendix 11 for steam noted during holiday).

North British Type '2' diesel hydraulic No. D6321 standing in Exmouth Jnct. shed on 5th August 1964. Introduced in 1959, a total of 58 were built. They were intended for use in Devon and Cornwall, but were not very successful, the first of the class being withdrawn in December 1967. Condemned at the same time steam finished on BR in August 1968, D6321 would have a brief life of only eight years and four months.

On the same day, the fireman of 'West Country' Pacific No. 34017 Ilfracombe spreads the newly deposited load of coal in the engine's tender. In the background, waiting its turn to move under Exmouth Junction's coaling stage, is 'N' class 2-6-0 No. 31837.

Above. 'Merchant Navy' class 4-6-2 No. 35003 Royal Mail rests in the yard of Exmouth Junction MPD about a month before my visit. The loco would move to Nine Elms shortly after this picture was taken and have its western region shed plate changed from 83D to 70A. Author's collection.
Below. Unrebuilt 'West Country' No. 34030 Watersmeet stands in Exeter Central station on 5th August 1964. Before the end of the following month, and after completing a little over 744,000 miles, she would be withdrawn and despatched to Bird's scrapyard near Swansea to be broken up.

Exeter Central, 5th August 1964. Top. Ivatt 2-6-2T No. 41206, allocated to Exmouth Junction, on empty stock duty and above, 'Battle of Britain' class No. 34059 Sir Archibald Sinclair has its nameplate photographed by an admirer. Named after the wartime Air Minister, the engine would be withdrawn in May 1966 after completing a little over 877,000 miles. Sold to Woodham Brothers of Barry shortly afterwards, the loco would be rescued from the scrapyard some thirteen years later and would begin a new life in preservation at the Bluebell Railway.

The holiday was almost over, but before leaving the caravan site another highlight would unfold. The following morning after my trip to Exeter and Exmouth, I recall watching for the first time a school of dolphins making their way towards Teignmouth, keeping quite close to the shoreline of Labrador Bay. It was another grand day, and the sighting of these wonderful mammals moving effortlessly through the water was something special, and one I will always remember. On 7th August I trainspotted at Newton Abbot; I couldn't meet the cost of going to Exeter again, which I would have much preferred to do. Anyway, I'd run out of film and would have had to face the frustration of not being able to take any more pictures. Still decipherable amongst the rain spots which had smudged the numbers in my notebook, I recorded a total of 22 diesels with exactly half of them belonging to the 'Warship' class.

On the Monday morning after returning home, I took my three rolls of film to the local chemist's shop. With no same-day service available as in time there would be, I think it was about a week before I collected the white card wallets, which held the negatives and prints. I couldn't wait until I reached home before looking inside to see the results. As soon as I was outside the shop, I mentally crossed my fingers and hoped that at least a few pictures I had taken would be worthy of placing into an album with the desire to look at them again. Well, about a third of them had come out reasonably well, both in terms of composition and clarity, and a few are included here.

For some time I had considered visiting Hereford and its steam depot. Spurred on after discovering in July that things were on the turn - the depot had lost its four 'Castles' by the end of the previous month - I set off for this small but interesting railway centre on Friday 14th August. Situated near to Barton Goods Yard, the shed was a good walk from the station. Fortunately, I made my round the depot without any hitches and noted the following fifteen engines representing nine different varieties: No's 1420, 1613, 1631, 1667, 2242, 2286, 2896, 4135, 4161, 4623, 7318, 48347, 48525, 48534 and 90330. Also present was Brush Type '4' No. D1700, which had entered traffic at the beginning of the year. The shed would close three months after my visit, on 2nd November, with most of its twelve strong steam allocation being transferred and finding further work at Gloucester Horton Road (2242 and 2247), Severn Tunnel Junction (4107 and 4157), Worcester (4161), Cardiff Radyr (1613, 3728 and 4623) and Pontypool Road (4668). Pannier tanks No's 1631, 1657 and 1667 would not be so lucky and would be withdrawn.

Spurred on by the enjoyment of taking my first photographs while on holiday, I was eager to capture more images of steam as soon as possible. However, only being able to achieve just eight exposures per film, I was always conscious of the cost and wondered after each click of the shutter how well each of my pictures would turn out. Fortunately, a few days after visiting Hereford, my uncle gave me a couple of rolls of film, and on 17th and 18th, with much enthusiasm coupled with a great deal of photographic naivety, I found myself on New Street station taking more pictures of steam and diesel hauled trains. The station at this time resembled a building site: cranes, trucks and huge piles of materials and debris were now to be found in areas where locomotives once moved freely to and fro. Taken on 18th, the photograph of standard 4-6-0 No. 73021 gives some idea of the rebuilding taking place and a reminder, if one was needed, of all the changes our railway was experiencing during this period.

On 18th August a fast-changing New Street sees standard 5MT 4-6-0 No. 73021 ready to head a Gloucester-bound passenger train. This engine would end its days while allocated to Oxford MPD, and would be withdrawn twelve months after this picture was taken. The rebuilding of the former LNWR and Midland Railway station would continue for a further three years before completion.

Looking every bit like a bomb site rather than a building site: two trainspotters, from behind what barrier remains at the eastern end of platform 6, watch 'Jubilee' No. 45622 Nyasaland leaving New Street station on 18th August 1964. Three weeks after this photograph was taken, the Derby-allocated 4-6-0 would be withdrawn.

Before catching the train back home, I spent some time on Snow Hill with the intention of finishing the second roll of film in my camera. Determined to only photograph steam, I didn't quite succeed, and luckily had one shot left when I reached Small Heath (see picture of 'Castle' No. 5091 Cleeve Abbey, page 96).

Compared to New Street, I always thought the ex-GWR station was a far more pleasing place both to look at and to be on while watching the trains coming and going. It did have its quiet periods and almost felt as though it was a country halt at times. But, even during its busier periods, it always seemed to have an air of calmness, composure and organisation about it. It was tidy and clean, too, which New Street never seemed to be, even before all the building work had begun.

Resting in the sidings at the north end of the station was the station pilot on this day, 'Modified Hall' No. 7915 Mere Hall. She wouldn't be sitting there for long - the crew would be kept busy with a rescue mission soon after I arrived, and would be required to continue their duties in charge of a relief passenger train that had an engine struggling to keep going. While watching what was happening and the coming and going of the 'Hall' I forgot to note the number of the failed 'Manor'! Nevertheless I managed to take the couple of photographs shown below.

On 18th August 1964, acting as Snow Hill station pilot, 'Modified Hall' No. 7915 Mere Hall moves out of Northwood Street sidings ready to come to the rescue of a failed 'Manor'.

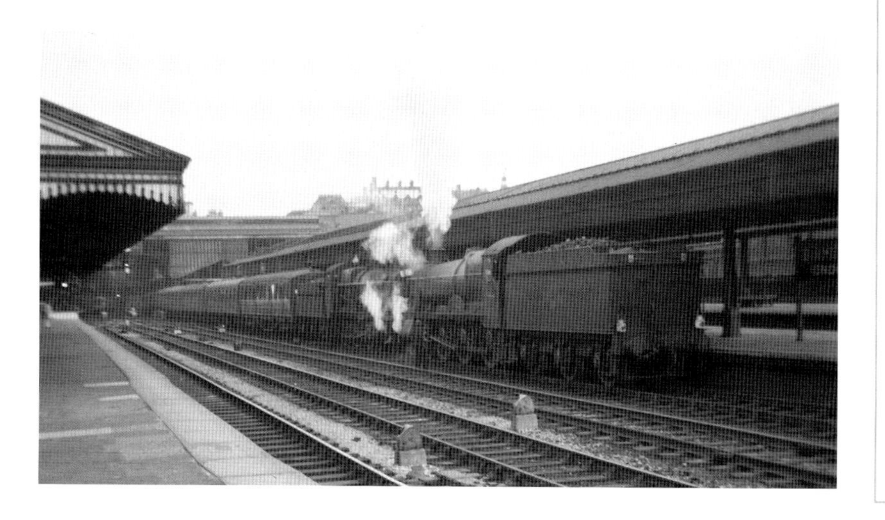

With the express passenger lamp arrangement displayed on her tender, No. 7915 leaves Snow Hill for Wolverhampton Low Level. To minimize the time taken to take the train forward from here, it must have been decided not turn the engine and to proceed tender first instead.

Shortly after the 'Hall' had completed its rescue assignment, Oxley-based 'Castle' No. 7019 Fowey Castle appeared with a northbound relief passenger train. The 4-6-0 would continue working for a further six months before being withdrawn.

Approximately three months before being condemned, Worcester-based 'Hall' class 4-6-0 No. 5962 Wantage Hall, moves slowly through Snow Hill with a northbound mixed freight. If any cleaners were still employed at its home shed, none, it would appear, could even be bothered to attend to the dirty last digit of its front number plate. Both above 18th August 1964.

With one picture left to finish my roll of film, I photographed Gloucester (Horton Road) allocated 'Castle' No. 5091 Cleeve Abbey speeding through Small Heath towards Snow Hill. The terraced houses to the right ran all along Armoury Road and housed the key workers of the BSA, situated on the other side of the street. Built originally as No. 4071, a 'Star' class 4-6-0, by the time of its rebuilding in December 1938, it had already completed 825,000 miles. When finally withdrawn two months after this photograph was taken, the total had increased to 2,000,000 miles. Interestingly, after ten years as a 'Castle' the engine was temporarily converted to oil firing in 1946.

By now Dai Woodham's Barry Scrapyard had developed a reputation for storing a considerable number of condemned steam engines. Instead of being cut up as expected, their ranks were continually increasing and, although it would not be a pretty or indeed satisfying sight to see so many dilapidated engines, I decided like many other spotters to see them before the cutter's torch was let loose on them. And besides, there were a few locos I hadn't managed to see while they had been working.

So, on 27th August, before the school holidays came to an end, I caught the train from New Street to Cardiff General. For some reason as the train reached the foot of the Lickey incline it slowed appreciably and gave me the opportunity to note several of the 0-6-0PT's (No's 8400, 8402, 8403, 8405 and 9453) used for banking duties. Also noted were two English Electric Type '3' diesels, No's. D6922 and D6938. Within the matter of a few days these locomotives, once crew training had been completed, would take over from the pannier tanks and render both them and the steam depot defunct.

Although the times aren't clear in my notebook, it must have been late morning when I arrived in Cardiff. By early afternoon, I was making note of row upon row of steam engines left open to the elements in Barry. Amongst a total of 92 locos ready to be reduced to more manageable lumps of metal, I recorded a total of 19 different classes represented. Little did I realise that, rather than being their final resting place, this scrapyard would turn out to be a safe haven not only for the locos present on the occasion of my visit (except for two that were cut up in 1980), but also for many others still to arrive.

From Barry I caught the train to Radyr and visited its four road MPD, a few minutes walk from the station. Here I found 6 classes of engine amongst the 28 steam on shed. Including locos seen while travelling during the day, a grand total of 207 steam of 31 different types had been recorded. With a total of 114 cops (56 of which were seen in Barry) it would take me a while to underline them all in my Combined Volume!

September

At the start of September it was back to school, which in turn would mean tackling lots of regular homework again. The month would also bring with it the prospect of ever shortening summer evenings, which in turn would result in less time for trainspotting. But that didn't stop Dennis and me planning our next trip after catching up with each other's news. I also showed him the pictures I had taken while on holiday in Devon, and subsequently at Snow Hill and New Street stations. Within a few days of the start of the new term, we had decided on another visit to Crewe (including the Works) early in October and that Dennis would write off for a permit.

Due to the progress of the electrification programme north from London, it was decided that as from 1st September several ex-LMS classes would be banned from working south of Crewe. This would negate the need to raise the height of certain bridges and tunnels to provide the clearance under the wires that would have otherwise been necessary for these engines to safely work. The classes involved were: 'Coronation', 'Royal Scot', 'Jubilee', 'Patriot', '4F' 0-6-0 and the ex-LNWR '7F' 0-8-0. There was some discussion, indeed confusion some might say, with regard to the '4F's and the height of their chimneys, but the main factor, or so it seemed, was the need for the fireman to climb up and into the tender safely (there being no doors) to enable him to move the coal forward when needed. All surviving members of these classes would be required to have a broad yellow band painted diagonally across their cab sides to denote that they were prohibited south of Crewe.

One evening during the second week in September, Dennis and I hurried home from school, met up at my house and cycled to Saltley and Tyseley. Amongst the 37 steam on shed at the former were 'Britannia' Pacific No. 70014 Iron Duke, 'Jubilee' No. 45674 Duncan, 'Hall' No. 6935 Browsholme Hall and Stanier 2-6-0 No. 42966. A further 8 classes of engine were noted during the visit. Tyseley had 10 different types of locomotive amongst the 14 steam on shed, which included two 'Castles' No's 7013 Bristol Castle and 7026 Tenby Castle.

October/November/December

I have nothing further recorded in my surviving notebooks until our visit to Crewe on Sunday, 11th October. Dennis had received our permit for an afternoon visit to the Works, and as we had time to try and bunk North Shed we made for there first. As luck would have it, we managed to get round without any problems. We noted 48 steam on shed, including 12 'Britannias', 9 'Coronations', 6 'Jubilees' and stored '8P' Pacific No. 71000 Duke of Gloucester. The shed's allocation of 'Britannia' Pacifics would continue to grow and by the following April would amount to just over half of the class.

Taken on 11th October, this poor photograph of No. 46256 Sir William A. Stanier, F.R.S., in Crewe North MPD represents the only picture of a 'Coronation' Pacific taken by myself in BR days. Luckily, two of these magnificent engines would be preserved in working order and grace our railway network in the future - see colour section page 42. Two weeks earlier, the 'Pacific' had been engaged on an RCTS special 'The Scottish Lowlander on 26th September and still had the now faded 1X75 route indicator fixed to its top lamp bracket. As the time had drawn closer for the final withdrawals of these magnificent engines, a number of specials had been organised, which either featured or used throughout several of the remaining members of the class. Seen below is No. 46256 in charge of such a train sometime earlier in the year. Author's collection.

After taking as disappointing picture of No. 70000 Britannia in Crewe North MPD on 11th October as I had managed to achieve with No. 46256 on the same day, a more successful outcome would unfold fourteen years later when the standard Pacific visited the Severn Valley Railway. She is seen here in Bewdley station on 9th September 1978.

Our afternoon tour of the Works was as enjoyable as ever. Ninety-four steam were noted in the process, with Stanier '8F's being the most prolific, accounting for over a third of the total steam seen. Six 'Britannia' Pacifics were in for repair - No's 70002 Geoffrey Chaucer, 70011 Hotspur, 70022 Tornado, 70033 Charles Dickens, 70034 Thomas Hardy and 70053 Moray Firth. Including two allocated to the works, several standard class 2-6-2 tanks were logged - No's 84015, 84022(CW), 84024(CW), 84025 and 84028. The two home-based engines appeared to be in store. Altogether, 11 different classes of steam locomotive were recorded during the visit.

No need to guess where we were off to next! Although having nowhere near its early 1959 allocation of 117, Crewe South still had a reasonable number of steam engines to call upon, totalling 69 at the time of our visit. Normally, a good number of visiting locos would be present, too, and so it proved on this occasion. A total of 84 steam were found on shed, representing 16 different classes. Worthy of note were the following guests: 'Granges' No's. 6813 Eastbury Grange, 6829 Burmington Grange, 6831 Bearley Grange, 6839 Hewell Grange, 6849 Walton Grange, Collett 2-8-0 No. 3861, 'Patriot' No. 45527 Southport and 'Jubilee' No. 45563 Australia.

Once back on the station, while tucking in to the last of our sandwiches and pop, we checked the numbers we had noted against the engines still to be marked in our Combined Volumes. The day had gone really well. We had logged a grand total of 247 steam belonging to 26 different classes, and by the time our train pulled into New Street, I had carefully underlined another 51 that I had seen for the first time.

Noted on Crewe South shed on Sunday 11th October 1964, Collett 2-8-0 No. 3861 with a headlamp arrangement suggesting it is heading an empty ballast or coal train, is seen in the Newport area of south Wales. From January 1948 until August 1960 the engine was allocated to such depots as Banbury, Hereford, Shrewsbury, Stourbridge and Oxley. Following its transfer to Pontypool Road, the locos final move, to Ebbw Junction, had taken place in August 1964. Eleven months later it would be removed from capital stock and sent to Bird's of Morriston to be cut up. Author's collection.

Before the year's end, Saltley shed was visited on 29th October, 8th November and 13th December. Steam totals and number of varieties present for each visit were 25/10, 55/14 and 51/11 respectively. There was little to report of any significance except that on the 8th November there was quite a variety of steam power once again, including two 'Halls', No's. 4929 Goytrey Hall and 6918 Sandon Hall, three 'WD's, Fairburn tank No. 42106 and sporting yellow cab side stripes withdrawn 'Jubilee' No. 45674 Duncan. Also present next to the 'Jubilee' was Leamington Spa-based standard 5MT No. 73069 receiving attention to its front end. Two weeks later Michael Mensing, the well-known railway photographer, captured both engines on film, and in his picture a fitter can clearly be seen engaged in welding work on the standard. The repairs necessary must have been quite extensive but worthwhile - the 4-6-0 would continue in service until steam finished on BR and would be the last member of her class to be withdrawn.

Aston was also visited on 8th November, about a month after all five of its 'Britannia's' had been transferred to Carlisle Kingmoor early in October. Its main stock of steam power now comprised the versatile but less striking 'Black 5's. Following the normal 'heart in the mouth' creeping past the shedmaster's office, I logged a total of 17 steam of 5 different classes: 'Black 5' (11), Stanier 2-6-0 (1), Ivatt 2-6-0 (3), '8F' (1), and '9F' (1).

Throughout another year the continuing implementation of the now ten-year-old Modernisation Plan had ensured that changes in many aspects of railway operation had proceeded, seemingly with little pause for reflection. With regard to BR motive power, the previous twelve months had witnessed a sustained flow of new diesel-electrics - 190 Brush Type '4's, 95 BR Type '2's, 51 EE Type '3's and 44 Clayton Type '1's - resulting in the stock of steam locomotives being further reduced to fewer than 5,000. This meant that on average 170 steam engines had been withdrawn each month with a number of classes becoming extinct, including Hawksworth's 'County' 4-6-0, ex-GWR '45XX' 2-6-2T, '47XX' 2-8-0, ex-LNWR '7F' 0-8-0, ex-LNER 'B16' 4-6-0, and also Sir William A. Stanier's elegant and powerful 'Coronation' Pacifics. Bullied's Merchant Navy class suffered its first withdrawals (7) and subsequent to the scrapping of a further 37 of Collett's Castle's only 12 remained in service. With 64 'Jubilee's having been made redundant their numbers had plummeted from 114 at the beginning of the year to leave 48 working members. Freight classes had been hit, too. Amongst many others, another 152 LMS '4F' 0-6-0's and, more remarkably, 16 of the much more recently built '9F's had also been withdrawn.

The allocation and concentrations of steam power had once again been shifting throughout the year. Rumours heard months earlier that the London Midland Region was to ban steam working south of Crewe from the start of the New Year had become official news, although pockets of steam would survive well into the following year. With more and more classes disappearing completely, I realised that I would have to travel more widely, and sooner rather than later, if I was going to see, record and photograph as many of the survivors as possible.

The 1965 Locospotters' Annual, a book always available well in time for Christmas, discussed the precarious position of the remaining express steam locomotives and alerted its readers to the fact that 'the British Railways Board had recently issued an order that any steam locomotive requiring such heavy repairs as to need a new boiler or surgery to main frames or cylinders is to be scrapped'. Other factors, such as line closures and decisions concerning the possible electrification of other routes, would also influence how long different classes of steam locomotive might remain in service. But as bad as the overall picture might be, there was occasionally some good news about the use of steam power and indeed how it could still be depended upon to haul certain express passenger trains.

Further details of the fate of the 'A4's had been revealed in the locomotive notes section for the Scottish Region in the August issue of The Railway Magazine and relayed the following news:

'At present the fate of the "A4" Pacifics is important news in the Scottish Region. No. 60026, Miles Beevor, was taken out of store at Bathgate recently, and was transferred to Aberdeen Ferryhill. On May 16th No. 60034, Lord Faringdon, was also taken from store and travelled light to St. Margarets, from which shed it is working meantime. This means that No. 60023 Golden Eagle, is the only "A4" in store at Bathgate and it is believed that it is due to be steamed. On May 11th No. 60006, Sir Ralph Wedgwood, was removed from store at Dalry Road, and the following day was sent north to Ferryhill. No. 60016, Silver King, is working from Kittybrewster, leaving No. 60019, Bittern, still in store. No. 60027, Merlin, is working from St. Rollox'.

The Railway Magazine, August 1964, Locomotive Notes, p.667.

All in all this was heartening news, and by the autumn six of the above locomotives could be observed regularly working the Aberdeen-Glasgow expresses. Furthermore, by the end of the year, it was rumoured that some of the remaining 'A4's would be overhauled at Darlington works. Although I may not have realised it, I think these developments provided the encouragement and incentive to seriously consider seeking out these engines before they finished for good. However, common sense, bringing with it as it does a degree of reality, was telling me that Scotland was not only a bit too far away, but to get there and back would cost more than I could possibly afford. As the winter progressed, I kept picturing the 'streaks' hard at work, doing exactly what they had been built for - hauling express passenger trains - and, before the year was out, I came up with an idea.

1965 (Gresley's 'A4's swansong in Scotland)

January/February

At the first opportunity on returning to school, I asked Dennis how he felt about seeing the last few 'streaks' working in Scotland (by the beginning of the year there were 12 remaining in stock) before they finally faced the end of their days. He thought it was a great idea, although straight away questioned how we could possibly afford such a trip. I suggested that if we saved as much money as possible and travelled by the cheapest means, we would get to see these very special engines before they retired from their last express passenger duties. I think he thought I was going to suggest travelling by coach, which, of course, would have been the cheapest alternative using public transport, yet nothing could have been further from my thoughts. Except for the mode of transport, I explained what I had in mind and, although he didn't fall about laughing, I had the distinct feeling his enthusiasm wasn't quite on par with mine.

Saving for a possible trip to Scotland would be briefly interrupted if our idea of visiting London during February half term materialised. My birthday fell during the holiday, and I had asked Mum and Dad if I could go to London as a treat again on Saturday 27th before returning to school. Luckily my request was granted, and Dennis managed to persuade his parents to allow him to go as well and to have the trip as his birthday present two weeks early!

During January and February we made our usual visits to the local sheds, Bordesley junction and New Street and Snow Hill stations. Saltley was visited on 17th, 24th and 31st January and 7th, and 28th February. Totals for steam present and number of different classes represented on these days was 68/14, 46/10, 36/9, 37/7 and 63/11 respectively. Interestingly, amongst the 63 steam noted on shed on the last day of February were two visiting 'B1's from York, No's 61049 and 61319 (both of which I cabbed), and no fewer than six 'WD's - No's 90024, 90136, 90139, 90211, 90243 and 90697, all Eastern Region locomotives.

Sir Winston Churchill's State funeral took place on Saturday 30th January, and was watched by millions on television. Salisbury-allocated 'Battle of Britain' class Pacific No. 34051 Winston Churchill hauled the funeral train from Waterloo to Handborough, a few miles northwest of Oxford, for his burial service at Bladon, near Woodstock. Thousands stood in silence along the trackside to pay their last respects while millions watched on television. Earmarked for preservation, the locomotive would continue in service for a further seven months.

On 31st January, Tyseley was home to 27 steam, twenty-four of which were ex-GWR engines, representing 13 different classes. Four members of the 'Castle' class were present, No's. 5014 Goodrich Castle, 7014 Caerhays Castle, 7026 Tenby Castle and 7034 Ince Castle. Between them these engines had clocked up over 3.5 million miles with Goodrich Castle having well surpassed 1.5 million since its introduction in June 1932. By the end of July, except for No. 7029 Clun Castle, which would be bought privately for preservation, the few remaining at work would have their services dispensed with and be condemned; the former GWR shed would not play host to as many 'Castles' again. Before visiting Tyseley on Monday 22nd February, I spent a few hours at Bordesley and noted nineteen steam workings including 'The Pines Express' double-headed by No. 6930 Aldersey Hall and No. 6823 Oakley Grange. Eventually arriving at the depot late in the afternoon, I found 22 steam in residence. Eleven different classes were represented, including three 'Manor' class 4-6-0's - No's. 7805 Broome Manor, 7818 Granville Manor and 7820 Dinmore Manor.

Above. Having brought in a passenger train from Birmingham Snow Hill, 'Castle' No. 7014 Caerhays Castle remains with the now empty stock as the carriages and loco are hauled out of Paddington station. Previously attached to such depots as Bristol Bath Road, Old Oak Common, Landore, St Philips Marsh and Oxley, the Collett 4-6-0 had been recently transferred to Tyseley, its final home depot (see comments regarding visit to 2A above). The 4-6-0 would continue to earn its keep for a further four months after this photograph was taken and would be withdrawn at the end of February 1965. Below. Destined to be preserved: Bullied Pacific No. 34051 Winston Churchill is now part of the National Collection and can be found at the National Railway museum. Both Author's collection.

Well prepared for its next turn of duty with a bunker full of coal, a rather scruffy looking ex-GWR 0-6-2T No. 6667 is seen resting in the south yard of Tyseley MPD. The engine would take on a much smarter look when called upon to head an SLS special later in the year (See page 187). Jan/Feb. 1965.

At long last the day arrived for our trip to London. On the morning of 27th February, having met up on the same local train into Snow Hill, Dennis and I hurried down the steps to platform 7 to wait for the 8.15am to Paddington. It was a typically cold and frosty February morning, and we wandered up and down the platform to help us keep warm while noting any movements within the station confines. Indeed, several steam locos made their way through the station, including 'Black 5' No. 44776 and 'Hall' class members No's. 5983 Henley Hall and 6926 Holkham Hall. Time was moving on, however, and the large clock on the platform next to the refreshment room confirmed that our train was running late.

Brush Type '4's allocated to Old Oak Common and Oxley were still the dominant force on the Wolverhampton to Paddington expresses and we began to wonder if the one of these had failed to fulfil its roster. In anticipation of something appearing soon, we slowly moved further along the platform towards its northern most point. For several minutes we stood and gazed past the signal box until, eventually, and much to our delight, a 'Britannia' pacific burst out of Hockley tunnel and up the 1in 47 climb towards the station... hauling passenger stock! We both looked at each other in disbelief - it couldn't be our train, could it? The fireman had done his job well; with steam to spare the safety valves had lifted and her exhaust was as clean and white as he could have hoped for as she entered the station.

Dennis and I sprinted the 400 yards back along the platform until we were standing next to what we confirmed was No. 70051 Firth of Forth. I looked inside the cab and asked the driver how far she would be taking the train. 'All the way to Paddington', came the reply. With grins from ear to ear we must have looked the happiest passengers on the train that morning and we probably were!

The run to Paddington was memorable for two reasons: firstly, because we were being steam-hauled when all express passenger duties on this route to London had been in the hands of diesel power for some time and, secondly, because of the spirited effort she made to make up for the late departure from Snow Hill. As far as I remember neither of us hardly sat down during the entire journey; we remained in the vestibule for the most part, with the windows down, and either looking at or listening to the engine working hard as she made her way southwards.

A fast-disappearing scene: 'Modified Hall' No. 6980 Llanrumney Hall finds itself in Paddington at the head of an express early in 1965. Allocated to various depots after entering traffic in December 1947, including Shrewsbury, Tyseley and Oxley, the 4-6-0, now a Banbury engine would be withdrawn before the end of the year. Author's collection.

The arrival of our 'Britannia'-hauled train was mentioned in the April issue of Modern Railways (traffic report) as being an excursion from Wolverhampton rather than a scheduled service, which may have been the case, and could therefore explain the reason for using steam power. Also noted in the same report was another 'Britannia' working out of Paddington two days later on 1st March, when 70053 Moray Firth took charge of the 16.20 to Banbury via Didcot normally diagrammed for a dmu. This engine remained in service for a further two years, but No. 70051, after being involved in a tragic incident later in June, which I will come back to later, would be one of twelve of the class to survive until the end of December 1967.

As soon as we stepped on to the platform at Paddington, we ran to the front of the train to have a closer look at the 'Britannia'. The roar of the steam escaping from the safety valves and the bright red glow and accompanying heat from the partly open fire-doors are still vivid in my memory. Our plan to visit several sheds during the day meant we needed to press on, so we didn't wait to see her reverse out of the station after the removal of the empty stock. I took one final look at her before disappearing amongst the mass of people heading towards the underground - what a great start to the day it had been!

Only two of the six sheds to be visited during the day had steam allocated to them. The first, Willesden, had about 70 assigned to it to carry out shunting, empty stock, freight and suburban passenger duties. We noted a total of 40 steam on shed with the following varieties represented: 'Britannia' (1), Ivatt 2MT 2-6-0 (2), Ivatt 4MT 2-6-0 (1), '8F' (4), 'Jinty' (3), Fairburn 2-6-4T (5), Stanier 2-6-4T, (3), standard 5MT 4-6-0 (1), standard 4MT 2-6-0 (3), standard 2MT 2-6-0 (5) and 'Black 5' 4-6-0 (12). Also present was LMS Type '3' diesel No. 10001. Following a brief swansong for the depot when 'Britannia' Pacifics were serviced here while working the Great Central semi-fast expresses, the shed's steam stock would no longer be required after the electrification of the main line into Euston. The depot would close completely exactly seven months after our visit on 27th September.

After a short walk from Willesden, we were soon making note of the few steam locos on Old Oak Common. Of the 17 engines logged twelve were 0-6-0 PT's. The remainder were as follows: Churchward 2-8-0 No. 3854, 'Grange' No. 6862 Derwent Grange, 'Modified Hall' No. 6952 Kimberley Hall, 'Castle' No. 7022 Hereford Castle and 'Black 5' 4-6-0 No. 45292. The shed's demise was hard to believe; only a few years earlier our notebooks would have been full to overflowing with the numbers of 'Kings', 'Castles', and 'Halls'. I remember reading somewhere that at its peak it employed almost 2,000 people, but those days had long gone. As far as steam was concerned, it would close its doors to this form of motive power three weeks after our visit, on 21st March.

Following visits to Hither Green, Stratford, Finsbury Park and Cricklewood sheds, we found ourselves back at Paddington. An 0-6-0PT, No. 9404, on empty-stock duties, was the only steam engine to be found in the station. The chance of a steam-hauled return journey was extremely unlikely, and although a balanced working with No. 70051 would have rounded off the day brilliantly, our true expectations were confirmed when we found Brush Type '4', No. D1707, in charge of our train home.

As an aside, No. 70051 appears to have worked the last steam-hauled passenger train from New Street to Walsall via Sutton Park when, on 21st December 1964, with four corridor coaches, she substituted for a dmu on the 17.47 ex-New Street and 18.54 return. This particular route closed to such trains about a month later and became a freight only line from 18th January 1965.

Initially allocated to Polmadie (Glasgow) on entering service on 11th August 1954, 'Britannia' Pacific No. 70051 was given the name Firth of Forth the following January. Seen passing through Shap station during the winter of 1962-63, she might be just a little more presentable than she was when in charge of our train to London mentioned earlier. Author's collection.

While travelling back to Snow Hill I realised that No. 9404, one of hundreds of pannier tanks that used to be employed on the GWR, and indeed BR, would most probably be the last steam engine I would see in Paddington. Nevertheless, both of us knew how fortunate we had been at the start of our day out - being hauled fractionally over 110 miles by steam, and on a route now fully dieselised, was something very special. I couldn't have wished for a better birthday present. Altogether we had seen a total of 86 steam during the day representing 24 different classes.

As our train made its way north through the darkness, we took time to talk about visiting Scotland to see the last of the 'A4's. We were aware that the cost of such a trip would be a major problem, but as I explained to Dennis, if we joined the YHA, and camped whenever possible, we could do it reasonably cheaply... oh yes, and if we cycled there and back! Once Dennis had taken in the cycling bit, we agreed that asking our parents to allow us to travel so far from home would have been the death knell for the whole idea, so we decided on suggesting Newcastle and Carlisle as our ultimate destinations in the hope that they would be more acceptable.

March

During March I made fourteen visits to Saltley on 7th, 9th, 10th, 16th, 18th, 19th, 20th, 21st, 22nd, 24th, 25th, 27th, 28th and 29th. Totals for steam engines present and classes represented were respectively as follows: 50/15, 38/11, 34/11, 32/8, 31/10, 28/9, 33/8, 47/8, 30/8, 22/8, 21/6, 32/6, 51/8 and 31/8. Throughout the month the variety of locos found on shed broadly reflected its allocation, but there were occasional visitors that added a little extra to the shed's own familiar assortment of engines. WD's accounted for most of these, although there were one or two others worthy of note: 'K1' No. 62010, 'B1' No. 61050 (reported at the head of an iron ore train heading through Bilston Central on 4th March) and 'Grange' No. 6874 Haughton Grange on 7th; 'B1' No. 61259 on 10th; 'Britannia' No. 70004 William Shakespeare on 16th; 'Manor' No. 7811 Dunley Manor on 20th and 'B1' 61275 on 29th.

Soon to be transferred to Retford, Canklow 'B1' No. 61050 rests in the yard of Saltley MPD on Sunday 7th March 1965. After further re-allocations to Doncaster and Langwith, the 'B1' would become Service locomotive No. 30 and be based at Canklow once more.

Dieselisation of the Birmingham area continues apace and is reflected in this picture taken in Saltley MPD on 7th March 1965. No. D1724 is one of several Brush Type '4's standing in the yard of the shed.

Ivatt 2-6-0 No 43143, a Staveley (Barrow Hill) engine, rests in the yard of Saltley next to No.3 roundhouse. This engine would remain in use for a further three months before being condemned. 7th March 1965.

Saltley MPD forty-three years later on 3rd August 2008. The buildings in line with the rails are those seen to the left of the pictures of 48669 (next) and 43143 (above). The coaling stage was located to the left of the track and in line with the tall building dominating the skyline to the left of centre. Roundhouse two and three were located behind and slightly to the right of the shrubs in the right foreground.

Stanier '8F' No. 48669 stands over one of the ash pits in the yard of Saltley shed on 7th March 1965. This engine, and her feat of hauling two coal trains joined together, is mentioned in Terry Essery's book about the time he spent at the depot as a fireman in the 1950's.

I took a number of photographs on 7th March, including one of '8F' No. 48669, which featured in Terry Essery's book 'Firing Days at Saltley'. He recalls when this engine was called upon to work a special coal train one Sunday morning from Water Orton to the Corporation sidings at Washwood Heath. On arrival at Water Orton, it was discovered that the train was indeed something special - with a total of 105 wagons, it consisted not of one but two coal trains resulting in a load of approximately 1,500 tons! Nevertheless, with some careful coaxing, the engine managed admirably, and successfully delivered its very heavy and lengthy load without any problems. The wide variety of engines present on this day, with 15 different classes represented, would not be matched again before the closure of Saltley to steam two years later.

Aston and Tyseley sheds were visited on 21st March. The former had 6 varieties of steam power amongst the 14 engines on shed, while Tyseley had no fewer than 42 steam present (32 of which were ex-GWR engines) representing a total of 12 different classes.

Residing in Saltley for a couple of days, and photographed on 7th March 1965, Leicester-based '9F' No. 92109 would shortly find itself transferred to Birkenhead, where it would see out its days before withdrawal in November 1967.

Stanier 'Black 5' No. 44944 is seen standing alongside Saltley No. 3 roundhouse on 7th March 1965. At the end of September the engine would be re-allocated to Oxley, then Chester and finally Crewe South, where it would remain until withdrawal in September 1967.

On Sunday 28th March, having already mentioned to our parents the idea of Dennis and I going on a cycling and camping holiday during the summer holidays (which fortunately hadn't been dismissed out of hand), we decided to use our bikes to visit Bescot, Oxley and Bushbury MPD's. This would give us the opportunity to demonstrate that we were capable of safely cycling to other places rather than just locally and, at the same time, to start improving our fitness levels in preparation for far longer journeys than we had ever made before. How we would respond to two weeks of peddling bikes with pannier bags fully laden with clothes, camping equipment etc., remained to be seen.

Bescot, our first stop, was still a busy shed with some 60 steam amongst its allocation of motive power. Until the end of December 1964, it had employed the last ex-LNWR 0-8-0's and one, No. 48895, was still in the yard awaiting disposal. A further 49 steam were noted in addition to the 'Super D' and in all 8 different classes were represented. The depot would close precisely one year later on 28th March 1966.

About an hour or so after leaving Bescot, we were making our way up the cinder path leading to Oxley shed. Here we recorded 14 classes among the 48 steam present, including several ex-GWR varieties as follows: 'Castle' No's 7011, 7019, 7023 and 7024 (all withdrawn), 'Modified Hall' No's 6976 and 6983, 'Manor' No's 7812, 7820, 7821 and 'Grange' No's 6815, 6831, 6857, 6862, 6864 and 6870.

Bushbury, a cycle ride of only a few minutes from Oxley, had just four steam on shed: Stanier '8F' No. 48339 and 2-6-4T No. 42604, Fairburn 2-6-4T No. 42062 and 'Black 5' No. 45405. The 4-6-0 had been a Bushbury engine for at least 15 years, but would be transferred to Aston when the depot closed two weeks later. From here we started our homeward journey, with a slight detour to see what locos were in store at Wednesbury Central.

Withdrawn the previous December, ex-LNWR 'Super D' 0-8-0 No. 48895 waits in the yard of Bescot MPD to be hauled away for scrap. The diagonal line on the cabside denotes that it was banned from travelling under the electrification wires south of Crewe. 28th March 1965.

Bearing a similar yellow diagonal line as No. 48895, Fowler '4F' No. 44210 is seen resting in the yard of Bescot MPD on the same day. Previously allocated to Cricklewood, Kentish Town, Toton and Coalville, the 0-6-0 had become a 2F engine in December 1964. The loco would continue working for a further six months before being withdrawn sometime in October.

One of three 'Manors' logged on Oxley MPD on 28th March 1965 was No. 7812 Erlestoke Manor. Allocated to nine different depots since January 1948, including Bristol Bath Road, Newton Abbot, St Blazey, Oswestry and Tyseley, the 4-6-0 would end its days as a Shrewsbury engine being withdrawn from this shed later in November. Bought by the Dowty railway Preservation Society, following eight years spent in Barry scrapyard, the engine would be restored to full working order at the Severn Valley Railway. Little did I realise that forty-nine years later I would have the pleasure of driving and firing this loco on the S.V.R.

Stanier 4-6-0 No. 45405 has her thirst quenched while resting in Bushbury, her home shed, on 28th March 1965. The depot would close the following month and the 'Black 5' would face reallocation to various depots, including Aston, Nuneaton, Stoke and finally Birkenhead before being withdrawn at the end of August 1967.

On reaching Wednesbury we discovered two 'Manor' class engines, No's. 7805 Broome Manor and No. 7818 Granville Manor, standing in the old GW and LMS exchange sidings. Last allocated to Tyseley and withdrawn in December 1964 and January 1965 respectively, they would shortly be hauled to Cashmore's of Great Bridge and be broken up. Interestingly, both locos were completely intact with connecting rods still in position. As mentioned earlier, Saltley, the last shed on our schedule, had a total of 51 steam present representing 8 different varieties. By the time we reached home we had cycled about thirty-two miles and seen 22 different classes of locomotive amongst a grand total of 155 steam logged.

The end of the line: unkempt and stripped of nameplates and brass cabside numbers, but still managing to look proud, 'Manor' class No. 7818 Granville Manor stands in the sidings next to Wednesbury Central on 28th March 1965. A further journey of a mile or so to Cashmore's scrapyard at Great Bridge would be the engines last.

To prove that it wasn't always plain sailing, I was politely asked to leave Saltley shed while noting the engines sitting in the first of the three roundhouses on 30th March. At about this time, I became aware that No. 92220 Evening Star, the last steam engine to be built at Swindon, and a mere five years old, had been withdrawn and was in store in Cardiff East Dock MPD. I found it difficult to fully understand how a virtually brand new locomotive with at least a further 30 years of life ahead of it, could be taken out of service so prematurely.

There was some good news, however. Amongst the traffic reports in the May issue of Modern Railways magazine was the heartening information that two 'A4's, No's 60019 Bittern and 60034 Lord Faringdon, together with 'A2' No. 60532 Blue Peter, had been admitted to Darlington Works during April for overhaul. This was as close to confirming that the 'streaks' would still be in use during our planned visit to Scotland later in July that we could wish for. Also featured in the Train Running and Traction Performance section of the same magazine was the noteworthy performances of two of Gresley's Pacifics. The first, concerned a run from Carlisle to Edinburgh, fittingly with No. 60007 Sir Nigel Gresley, and was described as possibly one of the finest ever over the Waverley Route. The second, with sister engine No. 60034 Lord Faringdon, highlighted what these magnificent locomotives were capable of while working the three-hour expresses from Glasgow to Aberdeen. This news served to further my resolve and determination to reach Scotland, and Glasgow in particular, later in the summer.

April

As spring progressed, frequent bike rides to Saltley continued and during the first three weeks of April I visited the shed on 4th, 6th, 8th, 10th, 11th, 13th, 16th, 18th, 19th and 20th. Locomotives present for the most part reflected its allocation. Totals for steam present and number of classes represented on these days were as follows: 43/12, 23/8, 24/9, 34/10, 31/7, 29/7, 48/15, 57/11, 56/12, and 34/10 respectively. As with the previous month, there were occasions when I recorded one or two notable visitors, including 'Britannia' No. 70047 Anzac and 'Jubilee' No. 45626 Seychelles on 4th; ex-GWR 56xx 0-6-2T's No's 6692 and 6694 on 8th; 'B1' 4-6-0 No. 61306 on 10th and on 16th ex-LNER 'V2' 2-6-0 No. 60929, ex-GWR 'Modified Hall' No's 6908 Downsham Hall and 7912 Little Linford Hall, ex-GWR 'Grange' No. 6851 Hurst Grange and Leeds Holbeck 'Jubilee' No. 45608 Gibraltar.

On Tuesday 13th I spent about three hours at Bromford Bridge, and a week later on 20th, a brief period at Bordesley. I logged 11 steam workings while at the former and five steam turns while at the latter, including The Pines Express double-headed by No. 6951 Impney Hall and No. 5944 Ickenham Hall and Churchward 2-6-2T No. 4555, which I photographed (see page 120). This charming little engine had been bought for preservation, but before being despatched to the Dart Valley Railway, was being used by Tyseley MPD on various local duties, including occasionally being employed on the 5.25pm Snow Hill to Knowle and Dorridge.

Tyseley was visited only once in April, on 4th, and produced 14 varieties amongst the 36 locos recorded. Included in these was visiting 'Britannia' pacific No. 70034 Thomas Hardy, a Crewe North engine. I managed to bunk Aston twice during the month, on 18th and 20th, and recorded totals of 18/6 and 16/5 respectively for engines and classes present. Noted on both visits were Fairburn 2-6-4T's No's 42062, 42066, 42069 and 42075, while Stanier 2-6-4T No. 42604 was also on shed on 18th.

The month's trainspotting was completed with a cycle ride to Oxley, Wolverhampton, on Sunday 25th April, where I logged a total of 51 steam on shed representing 14 different classes. Looking at the distribution of the types noted, it was soon evident that the number of ex-GWR varieties had been significantly reduced with only four represented as follows: 'Hall' (5), 'Grange' (7), 41xx 2-6-2's (2) and 57xx 0-6-0PT's (9).

'Returning the empties'. Now in the hands of diesel power rather than a '9F', the Bromford Bridge to Fawley oil train, headed by Type '3's No's. D6506 and D6520, passes through Bromford station at 1.08pm on the 13th April 1965. Nowadays, the refinery delivers 80% of its output to London, Birmingham and Bristol through underground pipelines.

Adjacent to Bromford Bridge station was the Stewart and Lloyds steelworks, and on 13th April 1965 I took the opportunity to photograph the 0-4-0ST that was on duty that day. Built, I believe, by Avonside Engine Company, the saddle tank would be made redundant with the introduction of diesel locomotives in 1967.

Summer holidays were on the horizon once again. This year Dad wanted to be able to combine his passion for angling with visits to the seaside, too, so he and Mum started looking for places near to the coast that had coarse fishing rivers close by. They eventually decided on a farm in Somerset, which we had been to a few years before and was near to the rivers Axe, Brue, Yeo and Huntspill. Also nearby was Weston-super-Mare, Brean Sands and Burnham-on-Sea. My thoughts, however, turned to what the railway might have to offer and, more specifically, what stations and sheds I might be able to visit! I knew that Bristol was only about 30mins away by train from Weston, but on consulting Dad's maps to see what other railway centres were nearby, I soon realised that there was also the Somerset and Dorset railway at Highbridge, about five miles from White House Farm - our home for two weeks.

If everything went to plan with regards the Scottish adventure, the forthcoming summer was shaping up to be something really special. To say that I was preoccupied with thoughts of Scotland, and all that such an adventure would entail, would be an obvious understatement. Dennis and I would talk about the trip whenever we were together, and gradually a list was put together of what we needed to take with us and things to arrange to make sure we would be as fully prepared as possible. Often while listening to Radio Luxemburg late at night, I would lie in bed and make notes about possible routes that needed to be considered and thought through and, of course, adding items that we might require while away to what was an ever-lengthening inventory.

Adding a little variety to the regular motive power found here, Gresley 'V2' 2-6-2 No. 60929, a York engine, stands in the yard outside Saltley's No. 3 roundhouse on 16th April 1965. After arriving in Birmingham from the North Eastern Region, these engines often returned north working the 8.05am New Street to Newcastle the following day. Withdrawal for this particular 'V2' would come by the middle of July.

Brush Type '2's No's. D5806 and D5811, both based at Wath MPD, north of Rotherham, are seen standing next to Saltley's No. 3 shed on the same day, and had most probably worked a steel train into the area together earlier in the morning.

Built in June 1937, 'Black 5' No. 45369 stands in the spring sunshine in the yard of Saltley shed on 16th April 1965. Two months later she would become a Mold Junction engine, and then after this shed closed in April 1966, a final transfer to Chester would ensure a further years employment before withdrawal at the end of March 1967.

With the camera placed on the running plate of an '8F', the resulting picture shows a number of other Stanier engines resting in No. 2 roundhouse of Saltley shed sometime in April 1965.

With a bunker full of coal that would not be needed, ex-GWR 0-6-0PT No. 3770 stands in Tyseley MPD east yard on 4th April 1965. Stencilled numbers have replaced the brass cabside plate that once identified the loco. The pannier tank had recently been withdrawn and its next journey, to the scrapyard, would be its last.

Seemingly, ex-GWR 2-6-2T No 4179 did not warrant having her number neatly stencilled on to her cabside. In place of her brass number plate for her last few months in service, identification had had to suffice with just a barely legible scrawl in chalk. A Tyseley engine from April 1964, and withdrawn earlier in February, it was only a matter of time before her removal to the scrapyard would take place.

On 20th April 1965, 2-6-2T No. 4555 is seen waiting to rejoin the ex-GWR main line from Snow Hill to Paddington at Bordesley Junction. The elegant Churchward engine was no doubt heading back to Tyseley shed where she was based after being privately purchased on withdrawal the previous November. The first of the class to be fitted with outside steam pipes, she was bought by Pat Whitehouse and was once more working out of the depot she was first allocated to forty years earlier.

Railtours would become an ever-increasing feature during the final few years of BR steam. Organised by the L.C.G.B., 'Britannia' Pacific No. 70052 Firth of Tay heads away from Wellingborough with the return working of the Notts. & Lincs. Railtour on 24th April 1965. Author's collection.

May

May and June were months that I needed to give greater attention to my studies because of impending exams. I tried hard not to succumb to the ever-present desire to go trainspotting or fishing, not to mention playing football and cricket after school, but little needs to be said about how difficult it was. As far as pursuing steam was concerned, my logbook does reflect the fact that I did make an effort to curtail my enthusiasm but, as the following records show, I couldn't resist the temptation completely! Dennis and I would still manage a few visits to the local sheds and at the end of May a trip to Crewe.

Visits to Saltley in May were made on 16th and 23rd and to Tyseley on 9th and 12th. Totals for steam present and classes represented for each depot was correspondingly as follows: 50/9, 47/9, 41/14 and 28/12. Interestingly, on 9th May, Tyseley had ten ex-GWR classes out of the total of fourteen noted and was also looking after visiting ex-LNER 'A3' No. 4472 Flying Scotsman. Of the 50 steam present on Saltley on 16th twenty-six were Stanier engines (either '8F' or 'Black 5') together with a noteworthy visitor from Leeds Holbeck, 'Jubilee' No. 45626 Seychelles. A week later on 23rd, the shed was host to two guests of note - 'B1' 4-6-0 No. 61256 and ex-GWR 'Grange' 4-6-0 No. 6803 Bucklebury Grange.

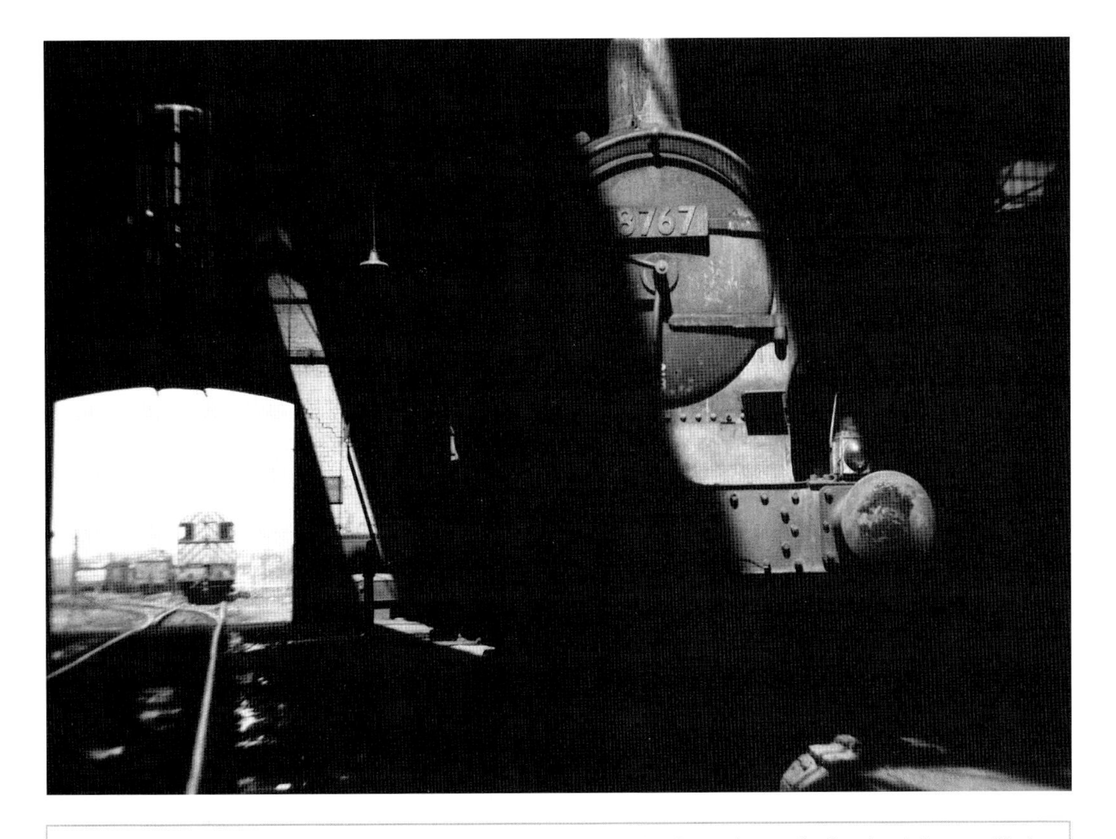

Oxley-based ex-GWR pannier tank No. 8767 is found partly bathed in sunlight inside Tyseley MPD on 9th May 1965. The loco would move to Stourbridge in twelve months time and then shortly afterwards to Croes Nwydd from where it would be withdrawn in August 1966.

On 12th May 1965, a weary and grimy looking 'Modified Hall' No. 6993 Arthog Hall takes on water in Tyseley MPD. She would shortly be transferred from Gloucester Horton Road to Oxford - her final allocation - before withdrawal at the end of the year.

A week after being photographed in Tyseley MPD No. 6993 Arthog Hall is seen next to the coaling stage of Banbury MPD. Even though the sun is doing its best to improve her appearance, the pattern of grime along her boiler hasn't changed and the 4-6-0 looks like many of her contemporaries - in need of a good wash and brush up. Author's collection.

Marginally less dirty and work-stained than her classmate (previous pictures), 'Hall' class 4-6-0 No. 5933 Kingsway Hall, allocated to Oxford MPD, is about to take up residence in Tyseley's roundhouse on 12th May 1965. Built in 1933, this particular 'maid of all work' would be withdrawn three months after this picture was taken.

Still bearing its brass cabside number plates, 5101 class 2-6-2T No. 4178, allocated to Leamington Spa, stands in the yard of Tyseley MPD on 9th May 1965. Soon to be re-allocated to Oxley (w/end. 19th June), withdrawal would come about four months later at the beginning of October.

On 16th May 1965 Saltley is home to Leeds Holbeck 'Black 5' No. 44824. Immediately behind the row of oil wagons is the chimney of the depot's sand drying oven. The Stanier 4-6-0 would continue in service for another two and a half years before withdrawal in September 1967.

Allocated to the Nottingham division, newly built BR Sulzer Type '2' No. D7544 had been in traffic just one day when photographed standing in the yard of Saltley MPD on 16th May 1965. Withdrawal would come after a little over twenty years service and, following a lengthy period of storage it would be taken to MC Metals Processing, Glasgow to be broken up.

Standard '9F's No's. 92000 and 92231 are seen standing alongside '8F' No. 48109 in the yard of Saltley shed on 16th May 1965. The former 2-10-0 had been transferred from Bristol Barrow Road to Gloucester Horton Road at the beginning of March, and within the matter of a few weeks would be removed from capital stock. The 2-8-0 would remain a Saltley engine until withdrawal in January 1966, and York-based No. 92231 would continue in revenue earning service until November 1966.

Our trip to Crewe on 30th May once more included an official tour of the Works and unofficial visits to South and North sheds. The latter, which, according to reports, had closed to steam five days earlier on 25th, had 12 such engines present - No's 44683, 44712, 45257, 45418, 48289, 48518, 48527, 48610, 70023 Venus, 70027 Rising Star, 70050, Firth of Clyde and 73096. Included in the 52 steam recorded in the Works were No. 71000 Duke of Gloucester (in store), 'Jubilees' No. 45589 Gwalior and No. 45697 Achilles and 'Britannia' Pacifics No's. 70007 Coeur de Lion, 70024 Vulcan, 70031 Byron, 70035 Rudyard Kipling, 70039 Sir Christopher Wren, and 70049 Solway Firth. 'Jubilee' No. 45589 and 'Britannia' No. 70007 (the first of the class to be made redundant) had been withdrawn and would not be receiving any sort of overhaul.

As we walked towards South MPD we could see swirls of smoke drifting high up into the sky. This was obviously an encouraging sign and suggested we could expect to see a good number of steam on shed. We weren't disappointed. Comparing my notes with those made during my previous visit in October 1964 revealed that this visit's total of 94 steam was ten more than the number recorded six months previously. Not surprisingly, the variety of motive power was slightly reduced, with 13 different classes represented - three fewer than in the previous October. By the time our train pulled in to New Street, I had logged 20 different classes of loco amongst a total of 178 steam seen during the day.

'Britannia' Pacific No. 70031 Byron, still bearing hand rails on its smoke deflectors, is seen standing in Crewe Works after overhaul. One of over fifty steam engines noted in the works during my visit on 30th May 1965, she would soon be moving north to work out of Carlisle Upperby. Withdrawal would come in November 1967.

No. 70017 Arrow, the first of eleven 'Britannia's to go into my notebook while visiting Crewe South, is seen just before leaving the depot on 30th May 1965. During the summer of the following year, the engine would be involved in a collision with a freight train while working the 11.45am Glasgow to Morecambe empty stock. Sustaining considerable damage, the Pacific would eventually be withdrawn on 1st October 1966.

Resting in Crewe south shed on 30th May 1965, and looking as though it had recently been through the Works, Fairburn 2-6-4T No. 42235 appears ready to return to Springs Branch (Wigan), its home depot. During a further two years in service the engine would initially be transferred to the NER, finally becoming a Low Moor resident in December 1966.

Caught resting between duties in Crewe south, its home shed, on 30th May 1965, Ivatt 2-6-2T No. 41212 would shortly move from 5B to Stoke. Its final transfer, in July, to Leicester Midland, would mean further employment for a total of five months before being condemned in October.

Plans for our Scottish trip were never far from our thoughts. A school notebook I was using at the time has, amongst the algebra and geometry jottings, details of our proposed route, distances between stops and projected costs of camping. YHA accommodation would provide a bit of luxury for a change and I had noted a bed for the night would cost 2/6d, a clean sheet 1/3d and, if we didn't want a cooked meal costing 3/-, we could use the kitchen to prepare our own food for 3d. It cost five shillings (25p) to join the YHA and on 1st July I received my membership card, valid until the end of the year.

June/July

June, the month synonymous with school exams, got underway, and I really tried hard to concentrate on my studies. Dennis and I were hoping to stay on and take our 'O' levels the following year, but I found it difficult to keep on task with my revision, especially with such an exciting adventure just around the corner; and as every one knows studying in the summer isn't easy so, to relieve the monotony of swotting, I occasionally got on my bike and made for Saltley and Aston sheds!

Four visits to Saltley were made before the month's end on 13th, 20th, 26th and 27th with respective totals of 54/11, 40/9, 24/7 and 31/8 for steam present and classes represented. On 13th June, it housed several visitors from the Eastern Region, including four 'WD's all allocated to Frodingham, and Thompson 'B1' No. 61013 Topi, an Ardsley engine. On 20th June Aston produced 5 different classes of engine amongst a total of 15 steam on shed. Fairburn 2-6-4T's No's 42062, 42066 and 42075 were noted as being withdrawn and awaiting removal for scrap. A trip to Tyseley on 4th July revealed no fewer than 14 varieties of motive power amongst the 48 steam recorded. Visitors included Crewe North 'Britannia' Pacific No. 70052 Firth of Tay and standard 4-6-0 No. 75006, a Stoke engine. Twenty-six of the locos present were of GWR origin.

Allocated to Saltley after being built in July 1957, '9F' No. 92139 is ready to have its tender replenished as it sits below its home shed's coaling stage on 13th June 1965. In November 1966 the loco would move to Speke Junction, and finally in August 1967 to Kingmoor, from where it would be withdrawn a month later.

While on school camp in North Wales at the end of June, I managed to visit Barmouth Junction for a few minutes and captured the picture opposite of Machynlleth-based standard 2-6-4T No. 80098, busy shunting. Previously allocated to Plaistow, Tilbury, Old Oak Common, Shrewsbury and Croes Newydd, she would be withdrawn four weeks later. Bought by Dai Woodham for scrap, the loco would be moved to Barry in January 1966. It would remain in south Wales until it was purchased for spares for sister engine No. 80080 in 1983. Fortunately, instead of being cannibalised, it would eventually be restored to full working order.

The last few days of the summer term witnessed a few alterations to our bikes with the help of our metalwork teacher, Mr Ames. Both needed to be adapted for touring purposes and be made suitable for carrying camping equipment, food, waterproofs, spare clothes, cameras, etc. Once we had arrived at a solution for the necessary framework, we set about making our designs in the school metalwork shop. Mum found some old canvas and produced the required pannier bags to fit on to the new structures and, after a few modifications, both bikes were ready at last to transport all our gear and us! On reaching home for the first time, with what was now a touring bike, I suddenly realised I had not taken into account the narrowness of the entry that ran alongside the house. Fortunately, with inches to spare, I somehow managed to squeeze it through the gate and push it into the back yard.

Our cycling exploits up until now, although frequent, had always been relatively local to where we lived, with Wolverhampton about the furthest we'd been in a day. The distances we were going to have to cover, and the variety of terrain that lay ahead would be far more demanding for us both. Our bikes, with fully laden pannier bags, would need to be handled more carefully than before - braking and steering would feel a lot different with all the extra weight being carried. How well, I wondered, would our bikes and we respond to the demands of the journey ahead?

By 9.00pm on the evening of 9th July I had finished all the packing I could do. Odd bits and pieces would go into the pannier bags in the morning, but it was time to put my bike into the shed for the night. The puncture repair kit, spanners and tools had been strategically placed at the top of one of the bags together with my waterproof top and trousers. I looked at my checklist one more time while in bed to make sure I hadn't forgotten anything and, satisfied that I couldn't think of anything else, started to listen to the radio. Unable to stop contemplating the adventure ahead and all the steam engines we were going to see, especially the A4's, I remember still being awake and fully alert in the early hours of the morning.

Left and centre left: Having travelled to the far end of Saltley MPD yard, '8F' No. 48651 moves past me towards the shed buildings. Most of the steam locos present were tucked inside the three roundhouses, but the Stanier 2-8-0 from Kirkby-in-Ashfield was on the move and, although only diesels can be seen in the background, the engine was one of twenty four steam present on 26th June 1965.

Two of the many diesels to be found in the yard of Saltley on 26th June 1965: Tinsley (Sheffield) allocated English Electric Type '3' No. D6987, which by this time had been in service about three weeks, and Brush Type '4' No. D1602.

Saturday 10th July

Having had very little sleep, I was up much earlier than I needed to be. I said my goodbyes to Dad when he left for work, and then tucked in to a full breakfast, that I'm sure was the biggest I'd ever had. As I finally cleared my plate, I wondered if I would be able to cycle anywhere after eating so much. Dennis arrived at about eight o'clock, and shortly afterwards I manoeuvred my bike down the entry and through the gate. I said farewell to Mum and continually waved goodbye as we cycled away and out of sight of the house: we were finally on our way, supposedly to Newcastle and Carlisle, but with our sights firmly fixed on Scotland.

To achieve our objective of reaching Edinburgh and Glasgow we knew it would greatly help if we could give ourselves a good start and get a reasonable distance north of Birmingham at the outset. To do so would mean taking the train for the first part of the journey; so, with our bikes safely stored in the guards van, we caught the train from New Street Station to Burton on Trent, arriving there at about 9.30am.

From the station we cycled the short distance to the shed and logged 37 steam, including Carlisle Upperby 'Britannia' Pacific No. 70022 Tornado and 'B1' No. 61313. Stanier '8F's and 'Black 5's dominated the different classes, which also included 'WD', '9F' and 'Jinty' 0-6-0T varieties.

'WD' 2-8-0's No's. 90024 and 90572 standing in the yard of Burton shed on 10th July 1965. Shedded at Frodingham and Staveley (Barrow Hill) respectively, they would escape the heavy assault on the class during the year when two hundred of their classmates would be withdrawn. Both, however, would cease working the following February.

Derby would be our next stop, so we set off for the A38, which would take us the eleven miles or so on the next leg of our journey. Its steam allocation had been steadily eroded over the last five years and had been reduced from around 110 at the beginning of 1960 to about forty at the time of our visit. The majority of its engines were now Stanier's 2-8-0's and 'Black 5's.

Thompson 'B1' No. 61313, a Langwith engine, heads a line of locos standing in the yard of Burton shed on 10th July 1965. A new diesel depot was proposed for the site but, not least because of the decline in BR's share of the town's goods traffic, the plan was abandoned and, after closure in the autumn of 1966, the shed buildings would be sold to a private company.

A view of the old Midland shed at Derby, taken from London Road Bridge on 10th July 1965. The shed was recoded 16C in September 1963, and with the advent of dieselisation its steam allocation dwindled rapidly. Closure would come in March 1967. Note the very Midland style water column in the foreground.

Once in the town centre we made our way to Midland Station and then the short distance to the bridge giving access to the shed. Getting up the steps with our bikes wasn't easy and once partly across the footbridge it was soon evident that much of the depot's motive power was being usefully employed. Indeed, we logged only 12 steam on shed representing 4 different classes of engine. Interestingly, the one 'Jubilee' present, No. 45574 India, reported as being in store at Carlisle Kingmoor at the beginning of the year, was evidently back in service and on general allocation to the North Eastern Region.

While crossing the footbridge to Derby shed, 'Black 5' No. 45267 was pictured waiting for the all clear to continue its northbound journey. Sitting with a cup of tea, and what appear to be some notes, the fireman grabs a welcome break. 10th July 1965.

This picture of an unidentified 'Black 5' travelling at speed along the Derby-Buxton line was taken rather hastily after jumping off my bike, recovering my camera from a pannier bag and quickly pointing it in the general direction of the fast approaching train. 10th July 1965.

Our next destination, Wakefield, would not be reached until the following day. However, our route along the A6 through Belper and Matlock would bring us to Rowsley and the old Midland shed that, although closed to steam by this time, had become a diesel stabling point. Our brief visit here produced four diesels - two 'Peaks' and two BR Type '2's. While on the way to Bakewell, I managed to photograph Stanier '8F' No. 48166, which had recently been allocated to Kirkby-in-Ashfield, and an unidentified 'Black 5' on the old Midland line from Derby to Buxton (see above).

After arriving in Bakewell, famous for its jam puddings topped with an egg mixture, which I can't recall us actually trying, we stopped for a rest and I wrote my first postcard to Mum and Dad. Originally we planned to use the youth hostel here, but decided instead to head for a camp site about four miles further north adjacent to the A619.

By the time we had pitched the tent and cooked our evening meal, we needed no encouragement to climb into our sleeping bags. We had cycled about forty-three miles since leaving Burton, and tomorrow faced the prospect of at least fifty miles if, after visiting Wakefield shed, we were going to get within striking distance of York. Needless to say, we slept well during our first night under canvas, and our camping fees at sixpence each were considerably less than we would have had to pay if we had stayed at the youth hostel.

Sunday 11th July

It was a warm sunny morning when we made an early start, initially for Barnsley. Here we had our first break - an early lunch on the station. The old Great Central Railway shed adjacent to the station had closed in 1960, and like Rowsley was now a diesel stabling point. Several diesels were noted during the time we were here and also 'WD' No. 90266, allocated to Staveley (Barrow Hill), with a freight train. Once rested and refreshed, we were back onto our bikes and making our way to Wakefield MPD approximately ten miles away. So far we hadn't seen a great number of engines, but we had a feeling things would change if we could manage to bunk this shed.

The depot certainly matched our expectations, even though Dennis suffered a minor hiccup while climbing over a wall to get into the shed. He snagged his trousers and left a quite a large 'L' shaped flap in the area that would normally have covered his bottom. Undaunted, he carried on until he got back to his bike and replaced them with a spare pair. Our efforts, and in the circumstances especially Dennis's, were well rewarded: a total of 69 steam locos were noted on shed, 56 of which belonged to the 'WD' class and, to just to add a little diversity to what seemed like a sea of austerities, a further 6 varieties were found amongst the remaining thirteen locos.

Neville Hill, the second of the sheds we would visit today, was reached after cycling for another hour and a half or so. It was home to ten of its own allocated engines plus visiting 'V2' from York No. 60876. A total of 5 classes of engine were represented amongst the 11 locos present. Three 'A1's were on shed - No's 60118 Archibald Sturrock, 60134 Foxhunter and 60154 Bon Accord.

On arrival at Wakefield, we found the shed shrouded in mist, and not knowing how quickly it would lift, I started taking photographs while I had the opportunity. First in the viewfinder was one of the 'Jubilees' used to cover the depot's responsibilities for excursion traffic, No. 45739 Ulster, seen here standing in the yard. 11th July 1965.

By the time this picture of 'WD's No's. 90563 (nearest the camera) and 90385 was taken, the mist had lifted and it had brightened up a little. The former engine, allocated to Aintree, would be withdrawn in September, but No. 90385, looking in much better condition, would continue in employment as a Wakefield engine until the end of March 1967.

After leaving the depot we joined the A64, which would take us further north. Having already cycled about forty-seven miles, we were determined to try and get as near to York as we could so we wouldn't have too much cycling to do the following morning. We finally succumbed to tiredness and hunger near the town of Tadcaster. After choosing a not altogether flat piece of land in the corner of a field next to the main road to pitch the tent, we quickly produced a curry for our meal courtesy of 'Vesta'. Soon afterwards, as dusk was giving way to nightfall, and despite the lumpy ground beneath our sleeping bags, we immediately fell sound asleep.

Monday 12th July

After a breakfast of cereals, tea and toast, we broke camp and set off at about 9.00am, reaching York about two hours later. We were looking forward to our time here, and because we would not be progressing any further north, we could spend virtually all the day watching the trains, visiting the shed and generally taking in the atmosphere of what was undoubtedly one of our great railway centres.

York once boasted an allocation of over one hundred and seventy steam locos in the early 1950's, and even at the end of the decade still had around one hundred and fifty. But since the start of the 60's its steam power had been much reduced and it now had somewhere close to 65 such locos to assist with its duties. Gone were the 'A2's, 'B16's and 'D49's, but we knew if we could successfully make our way round the depot we had every chance of still seeing a few 'A1's and 'V2's.

Fortunately, we did succeed, and recorded a total of 46 steam locos, including seven 'A1's and nine 'V2's. Two of the 2-6-2's worthy of a special mention were No. 60963, which would be the last to remain in service fitted with a double chimney, and No. 60847 St. Peter's School, York, A.D.627 which would be the last named member of the class to be withdrawn. Also present was 'Britannia' Pacific No. 70010 Owen Glendower. Altogether, there were 11 different classes of locomotive represented amongst the engines noted.

Once our shed bash had been completed, we cycled back to the station to have lunch. While sitting and watching the trains come and go we noted seven steam workings - all freight. Four 'Deltics' were recorded amongst the diesels, the class now fully in charge of the east coast express passenger trains that were once the responsibility of the engines we were now that little bit closer to seeing - Gresley's 'A4's.

Front ends: 'B1' No. 61276 and 'A1' Pacific No. 60121 Silurian, both York engines, are seen in the yard of their home shed on 12th July 1965. The 4-6-0 appeared to have been recently withdrawn, but the Pacific would have a little over two months of its working life to go before being condemned.

Caught resting between duties in the yard of York MPD on the same day was class 'J27' No. 65894. The 0-6-0 would remain a 50A engine until her transfer to Sunderland in September 1966. The northeast shed would continue to find employment for her for a further twelve months until her withdrawal in August 1967.

Inside the straight shed at York on 12th July 1965: with its nameplates removed, 'A1' No. 60138 Boswell stands facing 'V2' No. 60828. Both engines were nearing the end of their time and would be condemned by the end of September.

On 12th July 1965 'V2' No. 60876 moves off the turntable situated at the end of the yard in York MPD. On the evening, she would carry out an empty stock duty that remains fixed in my memory (see below). Her working life would come to an end four months after this photograph was taken.

Later in the afternoon we covered the short distance to York youth hostel, which would be our base for the night. We decided to treat ourselves and paid for a cooked evening meal, and then it was back on to our bikes to the station. After about two hours or so, we had noted mainly diesel-hauled trains with English Electric Type '4's being most evident. Four steam turns had been logged and the last of these, not long after the departure of the Tees Tyne Pullman, was undoubtedly the most spectacular and exciting.

'V2' No. 60876 had found itself with the unenviable task of removing 18 carriages of empty stock from the station. I can still see and hear her struggling to overcome inertia and move her long train from the station. Plumes of smoke and steam penetrated high into the evening sky with the engine's wheels slipping time after time as the driver tried to coax his engine to gain adhesion and start moving. Then, beginning with a gentler nudge of the regulator, the slipping was avoided and very, very slowly the heavy load began to inch forward. The exhaust reverberated around the station, its frequency gradually increasing as the engine pulled away into the fading light. Following this marvellous end to the day, we headed back to the hostel: tomorrow we would continue our journey north.

Tuesday 13th July

After breakfast we prepared ourselves for what was going to be another long day peddling our bikes, and the weather didn't look too promising. There wasn't the prospect of any shed visits until we reached Darlington, about fifty miles away. Following a brief rest at Thirsk, we had a longer break for lunch at Northallerton while relaxing on the station. Tired, but undaunted, we arrived at Darlington late in the afternoon. Once we had located the station, we followed the directions to the depot provided in our shed directory. The weather had slowly deteriorated during the day and was damp, misty and much cooler by the time we got to the shed. Nevertheless, I managed to take one or two passable photographs in the murky conditions.

Together with Buxton, this depot was the last outpost of the 'J94' 0-6-0ST's, a total of 10 of which we found on shed, although all of these had been taken out of service a few weeks prior to our visit. In addition to this variety, we logged a further 13 classes amongst the 35 steam noted. Only one other shed, which we would visit on the home leg of our journey, would match this diversity. Interestingly, and worthy of special mention, was the presence of 'A4' No. 60010 Dominion of Canada (pictured below). We didn't expect to see our first 'streak' until we reached Scotland, and although shorn of her chimney and in a somewhat ignoble state, she served as a timely and encouraging reminder of the very engines we were travelling so far to see.

Two months earlier she had been sent to Darlington Works for overhaul, but had been rejected because her boiler was in such poor condition. This, I presumed, was why the Pacific had been abandoned in the shed yard. Little did we realise that many months later, after a cosmetic overhaul in Crewe Works, she would be shipped to Canada in April 1967 and go on static display in Montreal museum. What would be an even more significant event for UK steam enthusiasts would be her return to these shores, together with sister engine No. 60008 Dwight D. Eisenhower, some forty-five years later.

Above. Seen in the yard of Darlington MPD on 13th July 1965, chimneyless 'A4' No. 60010 Dominion of Canada awaits her fate. On 5th July the loco had been earmarked and recorded in the depot's records as 'for sale to be scrapped.' Withdrawn earlier on 29th May, the 'A4' would remain at the shed for about eight months before being moved not to a scrapyard but to Crewe Works for cosmetic overhaul. BR had decided to donate the engine to the Canadian Railroad Historical Association, and from May 1966 the engine would find itself in the Canadian Railway Museum near Montreal.

To celebrate the 75th anniversary of classmate Mallard's record-breaking run, the National Railway Museum announced in 2011 that it would be reuniting both 60008 and 60010 with the four UK-based remaining 'A4's. This would be the first time that all six survivors of the class would be together since they had been preserved. After meeting up at Halifax, Nova Scotia, the engines were shipped across the Atlantic once more and arrived back in the UK at Liverpool Docks on 3rd October 2012.

No. 60008 had had a similar makeover at Doncaster Works in 1963, and had been shipped to the USA arriving in New York harbour on 11th May 1964. As far as 60010 is concerned, I've heard on good authority that Crewe's efforts regarding its repainting were at best minimal, with no real preparatory work being carried out and only a top coat being applied to most areas of the loco. This time around would be different. Once the old layers of paint had been stripped back to reveal bare metal, a far more thorough approach to the job would be made. Subsequent to the application of a primer, many further coats would follow, including several base and gloss before the lining out and numbering could be attended to. Finally, after applying several layers of varnish, Ian Matthews, having regularly worked twelve and more hours a day on the engine, must have been well satisfied with the end product (see colour section, page 43).

Signs of life: amongst the many cold and despondent looking engines, Ivatt 2-6-0 No 43102 and Kirkby-in-Ashfield '8F' No. 48272, in good external condition, rest over the ash pits in Darlington MPD on a dank and miserable 13th July 1965.

In the company of two preserved former Stockton and Darlington engines, 0-6-0 No. 25 Derwent and 0-4-0 Locomotion on static display, lunch was had on Darlington Bank Top station. In due course they would be moved from this location but, unlike the aforementioned 'A4's, they would remain much closer to where they had been built and worked. Three steam were noted before we set off for Durham, 'J94' No. 68023, 'WD' No. 90309 and 'A1' No. 60118 Archibald Sturrock, which would cease employment a few weeks later. It was nearly dark when we found somewhere to pitch the tent. We had managed a further eighteen miles or so, and were now about two miles south of Durham.

Withdrawn only a few days before I took this photograph, Stanier 2-6-4T No. 42477, minus its smokebox numberplate, still manages to appear respectable and ready to be steamed again if necessary. Indeed, records show that the tank was due to be transferred to the LMR but, at the same time, had been designated withdrawn from service. Looking every bit like an autumn day, the engine stands in the mist and gloom slowly enveloping Darlington shed on 13th July 1965.

Originally built for the Ministry of Supply and designed by Riddles, there were ten 'J94's on Darlington shed on 13th July 1965. All had been withdrawn about four weeks earlier and were awaiting removal for scrapping. Pictured is No. 68011 together with No's. 68062 (L) and 68037.

An unidentified Brush Type '4' moves quickly through Durham with an up express on 14th July 1965. A total of 512 of these engines would eventually be built at Brush's Falcon Works and Crewe between 1962 and 1968. As a testament to such a successful design, twenty-seven would still be operating on the national network, as late as autumn 2015.

Wednesday 14th July.

For the most part, today would be a cycling day. Following a brief spell of spotting on Durham station, we continued north to Newcastle and its rather grand station. Before facing the next stage of our journey, which would take us through the wilds of Northumberland and into Scotland, we spent an hour and a half or so on Central station. Our aim was to reach Hawick, about sixty miles away, before nightfall. With rest and refreshment stops, we estimated that it would take us about seven hours. Nonetheless, we were in high spirits, not least because we knew, all being well, that we would soon be leaving England and crossing over the border. Our ninety minutes on Newcastle station produced six steam turns, all freight, and hauled by 'J27's', a 'Q6' and a '9F'. Referred to earlier in the introduction, there was also a close encounter with a 'Deltic' too!

From Newcastle we headed along the A696, a quiet road that seemed to serve fewer and fewer places the further we travelled away from the city. By the time we reached Otterburn, the countryside seemed bleak and desolate with very few signs of life. We were now well and truly in the Cheviot Hills. The climb up to Carter Bar, at over 1300ft, where we would cross the border, seemed to go on forever. At this point we found the terrain really hard going and resorted to pushing our bikes for some of the way. Once over the top, though, we had the luxury of being able to put our 'feet up' and coast downhill with the need to employ our brakes much of the time so not to go too fast and part company with the road.

As the last of the evening's light was giving way to darkness, we finally reached Burnfoot camping site close to Hawick. Tired and hungry, we soon had the tent pitched and the stove set up to cook what was another late meal. Tomorrow we would visit our first Scottish shed.

Above: Built by English Electric in 1961, 'Deltic' No. D9018 Ballymoss stands next to platform 10 in Newcastle station on 14th July 1965. I was standing in the same spot as Dennis when it came to life and shook the platform and me as it started on its way again. After completing twenty years service, the engine would be withdrawn and cut up at Doncaster works in January 1982.

On the same day, following a change of crew and with the new style headboard fixed in place, there is no mistaking which famous train that 'Deltic' No. D9020 Nimbus is in charge of as it prepares to leave for Edinburgh from Newcastle's Platform 9. First used on the Flying Scotsman on 9th March 1964, the fibreglass crest depicts the thistle of Scotland in its centre, with wings spreading out from the stem similar in appearance to those on the feet of the Greek god Hermes. The idea of the crest came from the BR Board design centre.

The old and new at Newcastle: Clayton Type '1' No. D8594, a year into service, meets close to sixty years old 'J27' No. 65841 on 14th July 1965. The Clayton's were far from a successful design. By the end of 1971, all 117 members of the class would have been withdrawn.

Named after the thoroughbred racehorse, 'A3' No. 60085 Manna stands in platform 8, Newcastle Central in the summer of 1964. Transferred from Heaton to Gateshead in June 1963, no attempt had been made to furnish it with a new shedplate. Most probably not cleaned since being through Doncaster works in April 1962, the engine looks much neglected and had been withdrawn by October 1964. Many years later, in February 2015, the Pacific's nameplate would be sold for £9,500. Author's collection.

Thursday 15th July

The weather had taken a downturn by the time we awoke. The morning was misty and cool to begin with, and we took a little longer than usual to get out of our sleeping bags and have breakfast. Once we had had tea, toast and cereals it wasn't long before we were on our way to the station and shed. Hawick had never had more than about twenty-five steam engines on its books, but its allocation had now fallen to just five, all standard varieties, and we wondered whether we would find any of them at home for our visit.

Luckily, we arrived at the station in time to witness the meeting of a passenger train headed by English Electric Type '4' No. D363, and a down freight with 'V2' 2-6-0 No. 60970 in charge. After watching both trains go their respective ways, we walked the few yards to the shed and noted two standard engines - 4MT No. 76049 and 2MT No.78049 - both allocated to the depot. Six months later it would close and its handful of remaining engines would be transferred to Edinburgh St Margarets.

The next stage of our journey took us firstly to Selkirk and then to Galashiels. From here we treated ourselves to a ride on the train along the last thirty-five miles or so of the Waverley route into Edinburgh. This was a line we had heard a lot about, and that in all likelihood would become yet another casualty under the reorganisation plans. I cannot recollect what motive power we had up front, certainly not steam, but I do remember as we entered Waverley station being welcomed by 'Black '5 No. 45357 and 'B1's No. 61350 and 61244 Strang Steel.

The changing scene at Hawick: on a dull and misty 15th July 1965, Haymarket allocated English Electric Type '4' No. D363 meets 'V2' No. 60970 based at St Margarets MPD. The 2-6-0 was built at Darlington in May 1943 and was a Ferryhill engine for many years. Transferred to 64A in July 1964 this would be the engine's final home until withdrawal in February 1966.

One further 'Black Five' was noted No. 44718, a St. Rollox engine, before we set off for Edinburgh's other station, Princes Street. Formerly of the Caledonian Railway, regular passenger traffic would cease here seven weeks later, on 6th September, and the station would close. We logged only one steam engine, Stanier 4-6-0 No. 45011, allocated to Carstairs, standing at the head of a passenger train. There wasn't much activity to occupy us, so we were soon off to St Margarets MPD where we hoped we would see at close quarters one of the few 'A4's still in service. We were aware that this shed might prove very difficult to bunk. Not only would we have to pass close to the shedmaster's office, we would then have to cross the main line into Waverley to get to the main part of the depot!

Feeling distinctly uneasy and apprehensive, we walked quickly along the dim passageway, past the illuminated notice boards and once clear of the building proceeded to carefully cross the line, fortunately without being seen. Our earlier hopes were realised when, amongst the 28 steam present, we noted our first active 'A4', No. 60027 Merlin. Also present were 'A3's No's 60041 Salmon Trout and 60052 Prince Palatine, the last of its class to be overhauled at Doncaster Works and out shopped in October 1962. A further 6 different classes were represented with 'V2's (7), 'B1's (7) and standard 4MT 2-6-4T's (7) being most prolific. As soon as the last engine had been noted, we carefully retraced our steps and were soon back on our bikes and heading for Haymarket MPD, now of course home to the very diesels that had relatively recently ousted the 'A4's from their express passenger work on the East Coast Main Line.

The final shed visit of the day was the old Caledonian depot, Dalry Road, which provided the routine motive power for trains out of Princes Street station. Here, in addition to the seven members of the ill-fated Clayton Type '1' diesels present, we recorded 11 steam locos representing 3 different varieties. The day's end was drawing closer: it was time to head for Little France campsite, off the Dalkeith Road, about three miles south of the city centre, where we would stay for the next two nights.

Friday 16th July.

The weather was warm and sunny when we stirred, totally at odds with the dull and dreary day Thursday had been. This would be our first day without having to do any cycling, and we were looking forward to leaving our bikes at the campsite and travelling into the city on the bus. It would be a day of rest, a day for sitting, relaxing and watching the trains while on Waverley and Princes Street stations and, of course, a leisurely walk to St Margarets shed too.

While I sat in the bright sunshine on Waverley waiting for the next train to arrive, I wondered how Mum and Dad would respond to the postcard (depicting the Forth rail and road bridges) I had just written. If things went to plan, Dennis and I would be in Glasgow by the time they received it and ready to start heading home again. As a somewhat feeble excuse for ending up in Scotland, I explained that everything was going so well with the cycling, and because the train spotting was getting better as we ventured further north, we had decided to push on to Edinburgh; but somehow I didn't think these excuses would have much impact on the way they would react to the news. I would make sure that further cards were sent regularly in the hope that they wouldn't worry too much about how I was faring.

With Waverley 200 feet below, this picture was taken from the top of the Scott Monument as an unidentified 'Black 5' was leaving the station with what may have been an empty stock working. July 16th was turning out to be a grand day, with lots of people enjoying the good weather and sunbathing in Princes Street gardens adjacent to the station.

Haymarket-based Birmingham R.C. & W. Co. Type '2' diesel electric No. D5306, standing in Edinburgh Waverley station on 16th July 1965. Originally allocated to Hornsey when introduced in November 1958, the loco would be equipped with slow speed control apparatus in 1967 to facilitate its use on the merry-go-round coal trains serving the new Cockenzie power station situated about 8 miles east of Edinburgh.

Fitted with German style smoke deflectors, 'A3' No. 60052 Prince Palatine sits over one of the inspection pits in the yard of St Margarets shed on 16th July 1965. One of two remaining at this time, she would be the last of the class to be taken out of service in January 1966.

Waverley station, spectacularly sited right in the heart of the city, didn't produce many steam workings during the time we spent there. English Electric Type '4's and 'Peaks' were well represented, but we noted only six steam turns, the last of which I photographed from the top of the 200-foot high Scott Monument in Princes Street. Two hundred and eighty seven steps later we were back down at ground level, ready to continue on to Princes Street station. However, we decided instead to head for St Margarets to find out what motive power changes had occurred during the previous twenty-four hours.

The sun continued streaming down from a cloudless blue sky as we made the twenty-five minute walk to the depot. Once across the main line and into the yard of the shed, it was soon apparent that we had seen the majority of the engines the day before. A total of 25 steam were noted, including five new arrivals: 'B1's No's. 61029 Chamois, 61099 and 61263, 'Black 5' No. 44878 and one of the last two remaining 'Royal Scots' No. 46115 Scots Guardsman, which was destined to become the sole survivor of the class until its withdrawal at the end of the year. A further seven different varieties of locomotive were present amongst the remaining 20 engines.

Leaving St Margarets, and once again carefully crossing the main line, we walked back to Princes Street Gardens. From here we looked down on to Waverley station to see whether there were any signs of steam activity, but with only dmu's evident, we decided to get some food, head back to Little France, and have our meal at a reasonable time for a change. It was still sunny and very warm - I doubted that the weather even in the south of France would have been any better!

After we had eaten, we talked about what we would do the following day. I wanted to visit several other sheds in the area if possible, but Dennis decided to spend a further day on

Waverley and Princes Street Stations. Travelling by train would allow me to cover a reasonable area, so I thought about which depots would be worth the effort to try and bunk in the time I would have available. I eventually decided on Dunfermline, Thornton, Dundee, Perth, and Stirling and, if time permitted, one last look around St Margarets.

Saturday 17th July

Dennis and I parted company at Waverley when I set off in a dmu for Dunfermline early on the Saturday morning. The old North British Railway shed here had an allocation of about thirty engines, although on this day only 14 steam were present representing 5 different classes. There was one visiting loco, 'J37' 0-6-0 No. 64569, which was based at the shed I would be visiting next, Thornton.

Thornton was an important mining centre, and many of its shed's engines worked the local coal trains. At the start of the sixties, it still boasted an allocation of almost one hundred steam locos, but at the time of my visit this figure had been reduced to less than forty. A total of 33 steam (six of which were visitors) were recorded representing 6 different classes with 'B1's (9) and 'J38's (10) being most evident. Every steam engine I noted down was a cop.

Dundee Tay Bridge, the next depot I visited, was also well down on its allotment of steam locos compared with that of a few years earlier. Nevertheless, amongst its now small compliment, it had the last three 'A2's in service, and I was hoping to see at least one of them. As well as getting round the shed successfully, I also had the good fortune to see two of these Pacific's - No's 60528 Tudor Minstrel and 60530 Sayajirao. The latter was inside the shed, but Tudor Minstrel stood outside bathed in the warm summer sunshine and I took a couple of photographs of her. Looking quite smart, 'V2' No. 60973, also within the shed, was amongst the remaining twenty engines noted representing a total of nine different classes.

Arriving at Perth I found much to my delight another of the 'A4's I'd travelled so far to see. No. 60006 Sir Ralph Wedgwood stood at the head of the 1.30pm ex-Aberdeen to Glasgow Buchanan Street. I must have been in a dream when I took the first photograph and captured the locomotive towards the left of the picture so that carriages could be seen following the curve of the platform into the distance. I quickly realised, however, that what I thought was the rest of the train wasn't coupled to the engine! Even so, it's a picture I still enjoy looking at together with the two others I took of the 'A4' as it departed for Glasgow.

Perth station was an impressive building and equal to any other I had visited. In addition to this was the fact that steam could still be seen here in reasonable numbers, hauling not only freight and parcels trains, but also semi-fast and express passenger trains too. Conscious of the time in hand, I needed to make my way to the shed so, after noting the arrival of 'Black 5' No. 45029, a Motherwell engine, I left the station hoping that I would manage to successfully bunk the fourth shed of the day.

Fortunately my presence, if noticed, was ignored. Even so, I was conscience of the fact that I'd seen the shedmaster together with a fitter enter the depot building ahead of me, so I felt restricted in terms of photo opportunities, especially around the yard where I could easily be seen. Indeed, I only managed to take one photograph, that of St Rollox-allocated 'A4' No. 60031 Golden Plover, only realising once I'd had the film developed that she was minus her connecting rods! As soon as I had safely stored my camera in my duffel bag, I quickly made my way back to the station.

Found resting in Dunfermline MPD on 17th July 1965, 'J36' No. 65288 would soon be adopted by the local High School Railway Society. As a result, it would be cleaned and repainted and subsequently become somewhat of a celebrity, being one of two of the class built in the previous century (1897) to remain in BR service until withdrawal on 5th June 1967.

'J38' 0-6-0 No. 65915 sits in the sunshine together with a number of other engines in the yard of Thornton MPD on 17th July 1965. Transferred from St Margarets to Thornton in April, this would prove to be the locos last change of shed and she would cease working in November 1966.

With the slightest wisp of steam escaping from her safety valves, No. 65345 is a weary looking engine while resting in Thornton shed on 17th July 1965. She would be withdrawn on the same day as sister engine No. 65288 (pictured above), although rumour has it that she was used 'unofficially' after this date. Interestingly, the RCTS 1969 Locomotive Stock Book lists No. 65345 as the last representative of its type in running stock.

Named after the thoroughbred racehorse, 'A2' Peppercorn Pacific No. 60528 Tudor Minstrel bathes in the sunshine in the yard of Dundee MPD on 17th July 1965. Following her transfer to Aberdeen Ferryhill in April 1966, she would continue in service for a further few weeks before being condemned on 2nd June.

Two of the engines I found within the shed building of Dundee Tay Bridge, mentioned above, are featured here two months before my visit. 'A2' No. 60530 Sayajirao entered traffic in March 1948 and would be one of three of the class to remain in service into 1966, being withdrawn in the November. Transferred from Perth in July 1962, 'V2' No. 60973 would be the first of the final fourteen to be withdrawn (in January) during 1966. The last of her class mates, No's. 60836 and 60831, would face the final curtain in the December. G.W. Sharpe (both). Author's collection.

I had managed to record all 32 steam locos present on Perth shed, including 'A2' No. 60512 Steady Aim (withdrawn), 'Britannia' Pacifics No's 70002 Geoffrey Chaucer, 70012 John of Gaunt and 70033 Charles Dickens and 'B1' 61244 Strang Steel. Nineteen of the remaining engines were 'Black 5's', and altogether 8 different classes of locomotive had been noted. Before leaving Perth for Stirling behind standard 5MT No. 73153, a St Rollox engine, I logged three more steam locos, 'A4' No. 60019 Bittern, 'B1' No. 61262 and standard 4MT No. 76102.

Built in January 1938, 'A4' Pacific No. 60006 Sir Ralph Wedgewood, one of eleven of the class without a corridor tender, eases its way out of Perth on 17th July 1965 with a Glasgow-bound express. The two trainspotters have run from the other side of the bridge so they can watch the engine gather speed and disappear into the distance. Having passed through Doncaster works for the last time in August/ September 1961, she only had about six more weeks of employment before being withdrawn on 3rd September 1965.

Stirling's allocation had dwindled to no more than 9 Stanier 'Black 5's, yet this former Caledonian Railway depot would continue operating with a handful of steam locos until its closure almost a year later in June 1966. As I started the short walk to the shed from the station, I wasn't expecting to see more than one or two engines - I could only hope that there would be a few visitors amongst its small stud of Stanier 4-6-0's. Well, the number of steam present matched its allocation, but in addition to the expected 'Black 5's, of which there were seven, there were two guests from Carlisle Kingmoor depot in the form of 'Britannia' Pacifics No's 70008 Black Prince and 70033 Charles Dickens, seen earlier in Perth MPD.

The final leg of the day's journey, courtesy of a dmu, took me to Waverley with sufficient time to enable me to look in at St Margarets for one last time. A total of 23 steam were recorded representing 8 different classes. I didn't realise until some twenty-eight years later that, had I visited the shed earlier in the day, I would possibly have been able to take a photograph of an 'A1', 'A2', 'A3' and an 'A4' standing side by side. Steam Railway magazine of October 1993 (p32) shows a picture with No. 60121 Silurian, No. 60530 Sayajirao, No. 60052 Prince Palatine and No. 60034 Lord Faringdon in just such a pose. Mind you, this was courtesy of a very obliging shedmaster according to the details accompanying the picture.

Once back at the campsite we talked of how the day had gone and what steam we had seen etc. Dennis had remained on Waverley, which produced 13 steam workings with 'A4' N0. 60024 Kingfisher, 'A3' No. 60052 Prince Palatine and 'V2' No. 60970 all putting in appearances. We then got down to discussing the following day's journey across to Glasgow and the sheds we would visit on the way.

Sunday 18th July

We broke camp early on the Sunday morning and set off west along the A8 through Corstophine, and Broxburn to Bathgate, a distance of about twenty miles. At the shed here we would hopefully see the last named class 'J36' 0-6-0 No. 65243 Maude. The depot now had an allocation of 14 steam of 3 different types. All 14 engines were present, including Maude but, regrettably, we found her deep inside the dingy shed building, so we didn't try to photograph her. To compensate, I decided to take a picture of sister engine No. 65282 instead (see below).

Sister engine of the more well known Maude, Holmes 'J36' 0-6-0 No. 65282 is found resting in Bathgate MPD on 18th July 1965. One of four of this class allocated to the shed, she would be condemned the following January having been a 64F engine all of her BR days.

Built in 1891, Maude would become renowned in its latter years. By the time she had had a protective cab fitted in 1915, war was raging across the channel. Two years later, 25 of the class would be commandeered by the Railway Operating Division, including No. 65243, to serve in France. On their return, they were given the names of military leaders and well-known battle sites. Maude was named after Sir Frederick Stanley Maude KCB who had earned fame when commanding the allied forces in Mesopotamia (Iraq) and re-capturing Baghdad, only to die of cholera very soon afterwards. The loco would, in due course, be bought and preserved by the Scottish Railway Preservation Society.

From Bathgate we continued our journey west along the A8 through Whitburn and Newhouse, and then the A723 to Motherwell, a total of about twenty miles. The old Caledonian depot here once boasted an allocation of well over a hundred steam locos, and even at the beginning of the 1960's still had about ninety to call upon. It now had less than a quarter of this number to discharge its duties. When we started to make our way round the depot it seemed such a large place, partly I suppose because of the paucity of engines on shed. Indeed, it had a mere seventeen to service, thirteen of which were full-time residents. Nine 'Black 5's were noted together with eight standard engines representing the following types: 5MT 4-6-0 (2), 4MT 2-6-0 (3), 3MT 2-6-0 (2) and '9F' (1).

Glasgow was a further fourteen miles away, and being a Sunday we knew its sheds would be home to a generous number of engines. Consequently, we needed to get there as quickly as possible, so we decided to cover the remainder of the journey by train. This would give us sufficient time to register at the youth hostel and then visit Eastfield, Polmadie and Corkerhill MPD's before the day's end.

Having left most of our belongings at the hostel, we set off on our bikes for Eastfield. Formerly of the North British Railway, this was the second largest of the Glasgow sheds in terms of allocation of steam engines. Only five years earlier it had twenty classes of engine amongst approximately one hundred steam allotted to it. Since then its steam power had been greatly reduced and now stood at a mere six engines. Surprisingly, we recorded 28 steam present representing 10 different classes. A number of the locos were obviously in store or had been withdrawn, including Fairburn 2-6-4T's No's 42209, 42478, and 42649, 'B1' No. 61357 and standard 2-6-4T No. 80020. On a more positive note we found Stanier 'Black 5' No. 44903 to be in ex-works condition.

From Eastfield we headed for Polmadie, which like Bathgate was once part of the Caledonian Railway. In the summer of 1960 it had an allocation of approximately one hundred and sixty steam locos, including 'Jubilees', 'Royal Scots', 'Princesses', 'Coronations', 'Britannia's and 'Clans'. But its share of steam power had plummeted, too. It was now below forty, and its last express locomotives, 'A2's No's. 60522 Straight Deal and 60535 Hornet's Beauty had recently been withdrawn. Amongst the 40 Clayton Type '1' diesels present, we recorded a total of 28 steam of 7 different classes including 'Jubilee' No. 45675 Hardy and, referred to above, 'A2' Pacific No. 60535. This was a large shed covering an extensive area and had the greatest allocation of steam of all the Glasgow depots; recording any engines waiting to be turned meant one faced almost a half-mile walk from the entrance to the shed building to the turntable at the far end of the yard!

Fresh out of Cowlairs works following a non-classified overhaul, Stanier 'Black 5' No. 44903 stands in Glasgow Eastfield MPD on 18th July 1965. In the background is EE Type '1' No. D8079. The 4-6-0 would remain at its home shed, Kingmoor, until June 1966 when it would find itself re-allocated to Heaton Mersey, and from where it would be withdrawn in April 1968.

On the same day, appearing work weary, and neglected perhaps, but still looking elegant, 'A2' No. 60535 Hornet's Beauty stands in Polmadie MPD, awaiting its final fateful journey after being withdrawn on 19th June.

Corkerhill, formerly of the Glasgow and South Western Railway, was our final shed visit of the day. Like the previous sheds, it too had seen the steady erosion of its allocation and had a total of twenty-six steam by this time, about a third of its total in the summer of 1960. All of its engines, except for 'Black 5' No. 44798, were now of the standard variety, with class 5MT 4-6-0's and 4MT 2-6-4T's the most common. We noted 5 different classes of locomotive amongst the 25 steam present, including visiting Leeds Holbeck 'Jubilee' No. 45697 Achilles (see below).

We cycled back through the city to the youth hostel in Park Terrace, and after our evening meal made plans for the following day. We would leave our bikes at the hostel and walk firstly to Buchanan Street, where we hoped to see at least one 'A4' during the morning, before moving on to the city's other main stations.

Leeds Holbeck 'Jubilee' No. 45697 Achilles at rest inside Corkerhill shed on 18th July 1965. Destined to become one of a handful of this class to survive into the summer of 1967, withdrawal would come at the beginning of September after 31 years service. Following removal to J.Cashmore, Great Bridge, disposal would take place early in May 1968.

Monday 19th July

The day began bright, sunny and warm. Once showered and breakfasted, we set off to what many considered to be the least attractive of the main stations serving the city, Buchanan Street. Surrounded by tenements, warehouses, and also relatively close to a power station, didn't help its cause. Immediately after its construction, it was described as the worst of all the ugly blots on the Glasgow landscape. I don't think I found it quite that bad, and in any case it didn't really matter; I was happy to be there because it now regularly witnessed the few remaining Gresley 'A4' Pacifics, gallantly hauling some of the 3-hour expresses such as 'The Grampian' and 'The Saint Mungo' to and from Aberdeen.

We arrived there at about 9.30am and, after noting two Type '2' diesels and Brush Type '4' No. D1631 in charge of 'The Granite City', we watched the arrival (spot on time) of 'A4' No. 60019 Bittern with 'The Bon Accord'. We swiftly made our way down the platform to see the loco close up and to photograph her at the head of the train. While waiting for the empty stock to be removed we spoke to the driver and he kindly invited us up on to the footplate. He talked a little about the engines controls and what they were for until the carriages were removed from behind the engine. We thanked him for allowing us into the cab but, as we were about to climb down, he asked us if we would like to stay on the loco until we reached the other end of the platform…and didn't bother to wait for an answer!

Two 'Cheshire cats' were duly dropped off after a short but unforgettable ride. Before leaving the station, I asked the driver if he would give me a moment or two so I could take a photograph of him and Bittern, although I knew I wouldn't need a picture to remind me of what had just happened. After watching the 'A4' disappear towards St Rollox shed, two very happy trainspotters set off for St Enoch station, briefly calling in at Queen Street on the way.

The driver of 'A4' No. 60019 Bittern looks out from the cab after giving Dennis and myself a brief but unforgettable ride to the end of the platform of Buchanan Street. 19th July 1965.

St Enoch seemed to have hordes of people purposefully making their way to queue for tickets or heading quickly to the various platforms where their trains awaited departure. Lots of others, with more time available, filled the waiting and refreshment rooms or sat on the benches provided and watched the scene around them. I can't remember, and neither did I make any notes, about where the trains were heading off to, but later found out that most of them were taking holidaymakers or day trippers to the Ayrshire coast, and places like Troon, Ayr and Ardrossan from where they could catch the ferry to the Isle of Arran.

There seemed to be lots of steam activity, too, and Dennis and I were soon at the platforms' end to note down the locos heading their respective trains. We remained on the station for about four hours and logged the following engines: 'Black 5's No's. 44705, 44802, 44878, 45117, 45124 and 45480, 'Jubilee' No. 45697 Achilles and standard 5MT 4-6-0's No's 73009, 73100, 73104 and 73122, 2MT 2-6-0 No. 78026 and 4MT 2-6-4-T's No's 80004 and 80128. Corkerhill MPD supplied all of the standard locos whereas the remainder were from a mix of depots including Carlisle Kingmoor, Perth and Hurlford.

While I sat on one of the trolleys and had sandwiches and pop for lunch, I wrote another card to Mum and Dad and explained where we were and where we were staying. I also mentioned St Enoch station and what an elegant building it was. I didn't describe it in great detail, but my pictures remind me of its sharply curving tracks and marvellous glazed arch, which I discovered measured an impressive 504ft. long, 80ft. high and had a clear span of 198ft. The station would remain in use for a further eleven months, closing on 27th June 1966, when all of its traffic would be transferred to Central station, which was where we were heading to next.

An unidentified 'Black 5' heads one of a number relief trains to depart from Glasgow's imposing St Enoch station on 19th July 1965.

Left. Standard 5MT No. 73104 accelerates out of Glasgow St. Enoch with a relief passenger train, possibly bound for Ayr. Meanwhile, classmate No. 73100 has just backed on to its train and is about to be coupled up. Both locos were built at Doncaster and allocated to Corkerhill shed. The former would be withdrawn in about three months time while No. 73100 would continue to be employed until January 1967.

Above. A short while later, while EE Type '1'No. D8116 waits for its turn to depart, an unidentified standard 5MT powers its way out of St Enoch with a further relief passenger train.

A light and airy station, Central was on two levels. There were not many steam turns out of here, but a few survived to Gourock using mainly Fairburn tanks. During the time we were here we noted only two of the class, No's 42199 and 42241 with no other steam seen. After watching 'The Royal Scot' arrive with English Electric Type '4' No. D268 in charge, we made a dash for Buchanan Street station to see the arrival of 'The Grampian', which, if on time, would be in the station by 5.30pm.

The first passenger working noted was to Stirling, and according to my notes left at 5.12pm hauled by standard 5MT No. 73153. Already standing in the station, at the head of 'The St Mungo', was 'A4' No. 60019 Bittern, waiting for the signal to begin her journey to Aberdeen. Although we couldn't see him, the telltale-ringing echo from the other side of the carriages told us that the wheel-tapper was busy at work. The arrival of 'The Grampian' was imminent, so we moved to the end of the platform and waited for what we hoped would be another 'A4'. Within a couple of minutes, and right on time, No. 60024 Kingfisher eased her train into the station.

Noted while at Glasgow Central on 19th July 1965, Fairburn 2-6-4T No. 42199 is seen removing empty stock from the station. Except for a brief time allocated to Stewarts Lane in 1948, the loco would spend its whole life north of the border. The tank would continue working for a few more weeks before being withdrawn in September.

The carriage wheels having been checked, and the last of the open doors slammed shut, Bittern was ready to depart. The wheel tapper, content with what his ears had been telling him, and happy with the positive results of his work, stood at the side of the line at the end of the platform and watched the train as it accelerated briskly away from the station to begin its journey north. The ultrasonic tester, of course, would supersede the wheel-tapper; the musical ringing sound so familiar to him would no longer be used to diagnose the health of a carriage's wheels. We spent a further hour or so on the station and then caught the No.11 bus to St Rollox MPD.

Buchanan Street station, late afternoon on 19th July 1965: Gresley 'A4' No. 60019 Bittern is found once again at the head of one of the three hour expresses to Aberdeen. This working, the 'St. Mungo', departed at 5.30pm. While walking along the platform to the front of the train to take this picture, the unmistakeable sound of a wheeltapper busy at work was ringing out from the far side of the carriages.

Above. Having completed his task, the wheeltapper watches Bittern purposefully pull its load out of Buchanan Street, eager to keep to its tightly timed journey to Aberdeen. Below. As good fortune would have it, 'A4' No. 60024 Kingfisher had been left outside the shed building of St. Rollox MPD. Still carrying the single lamp, positioned to denote a light engine movement when returning to shed (after working the up 'Grampian'), the light wasn't good, but sufficient to enable me to photograph her standing in the shed yard. 19th July 1965.

Five summers earlier St Rollox still had several ex-Caledonian classes amongst its allocation of sixty-five steam engines. Only thirteen steam locos were now assigned to the depot - two 'Black 5's, ten standard 5MT's and one 'A4' No. 60031 Golden Plover. This evening's visit revealed 4 different classes represented amongst the 10 steam on shed. Included in these were two 'A4's No's 60024 Kingfisher, resting outside after working the up 'Grampian', and 60034 Lord Faringdon inside the shed building. Interestingly, the depot had been home to all four named 'Black 5's in the early 1950's.

Our time in Glasgow was fast coming to an end; tonight would be our second spent in the youth hostel and tomorrow would see us cycling south and beginning our homeward journey. We would visit one more Scottish shed before crossing back over the border, but we would delay our departure from the city and call in at Buchanan Street Station once more in the hope of catching a final glimpse of an 'A4' on express passenger duty.

Tuesday 20th July

On the morning of 20th July, we left the hostel knowing that ahead of us was a cycle ride of about sixty miles to Beattock, where we planned to stay overnight. Funds by now were very low, and we knew that it would be most unlikely that we would be able to visit all the sheds we intended to on our way home. Our itinerary would have to be reassessed once we had reached Carlisle. Interestingly, if we wanted to stay in this City's hostel now (rated as 3* by the hostel grading scheme) it would cost about £23.00 each a night. Although, it must be said that the amenities have improved somewhat over the years with private rooms, en-suite facilities, complimentary tea and coffee and a wide variety of meals on the menu!

Buchanan Street was quiet when we arrived there shortly before ten o'clock. The up 'Bon Accord' had left Aberdeen while we were still in bed. However, all being well, the train was due to arrive in a few minutes, so we walked to the end of the platform to greet what we expected to be our last 'streak' of the holiday. On time, and with No. 60019 Bittern at its head, the train eased its way into the station. After admiring the engine at close quarters, we watched her reverse out of the station and head for St Rollox and a well-earned rest. With enthusiasm in short supply, we reluctantly got on to our bikes and began the next stage of our journey to Beattock, situated at the foot of the well-known incline.

Left and next: On the morning of 20th July, 'A4' 60019 Bittern has stopped short of the buffers at Buchanan Street station with the up 'Bon Accord'. A young boy admires the engine while passengers make their way along the platform. Once the empty stock had been removed, we photographed the engine one last time while it was briefly halted before making its way to St Rollox MPD for servicing. With years of experience, and no doubt instructing his fireman to look out for the 'right away' to be given, the driver obviously feels quite relaxed and can just be seen reading the days news while standing next to the cab door.

Our route to Beattock took us through Hamilton, Lesmahagow, Abington and Elvanfoot, after which, we climbed up to and crossed over the Glasgow to Carlisle main line, to reach Beattock summit, the top of the ten-mile ascent (at an average of 1 in 77) for all north bound trains. Cycling from this point on was a lot less demanding being mostly downhill until we reached our destination.

Once at the station, we parked our bikes at the end of the down platform and walked the few yards to the shed. Beattock was primarily concerned with the provision of banking engines for the difficult and demanding climb already referred to. It was only a small two-lane shed, and rarely had more than about fifteen engines allotted to it. At the beginning of the summer, its allocation had fallen to six steam locos - three of standard design and three Fairburn 2-6-4T's. We found 8 steam on shed representing 3 different classes: Fairburn 2-6-4T No's 42125, 42129, 42169, 42274, and 42693, Stanier 'Black 5' No. 45245 and standard 4MT 2-6-4T No's 80005 and 80045.

Wednesday 21st July

The day started as the previous evening had ended, with the surrounding area echoing once again to the exhaust beats of engines battling their way up the incline on the long haul to the summit. Breakfast was very basic once again, comprising cornflakes and tea. Regrettably, we couldn't afford to eat at the truck stop across the way, and from where the smell of bacon and eggs etc. being cooked for the lorry drivers would occasionally drift by. Envious of those enjoying a full breakfast, we soon had the tent down and everything packed away. Today's journey would take us further south to Gretna and over the border into England. We would spend the night in Carlisle youth hostel, about thirty-eight miles away, but not before visiting Kingmoor MPD en-route.

Firstly, though, it was back to the bridge north of the station and a last look at one or two trains commencing their climb to slightly over one thousand feet above sea level. From this elevated position I took three or four photographs, including one of standard 4MT No. 80045 (see below) assisting English Electric Type '1' No. D8121 with a mixed freight train. On the right of the picture the line to the spa town of Moffat can clearly be seen still in situ after being closed the previous April. The branch opened in 1883 and, once connected to the main line, Moffat became a very popular and fashionable destination. The branch remained in use for 71 years, and at one time had its own train to and from Glasgow known as 'The Tinto Express'.

After noting six steam workings involving the following engines - No's 42169, 44672, 45133, 70033 Charles Dickens, 76090 and 80045 - it was time to rejoin the A74 and continue our journey south. The road passed next to the River Annan in a few places, but for the most part kept very close to the main line. Indeed, we would cross the railway on several occasions before reaching Ecclefechan, and then once more just past Kirkpatrick, after which the main line traversed the River Esk to make its way unhindered into Carlisle.

Brighton-built standard 2-6-4T No. 80045 gives a helping hand to EE Type '1' No. D8121 as it heads up the bank from Beattock. Transferred to Polmadie in November 1966, the tank would cease working in May 1967.

Once we had crossed the Waverley Route we joined the A7, the main road into the city. This in turn would take us almost, but not quite, to Kingmoor shed. Although we couldn't see it, we knew exactly where the shed was. Against a bright backdrop, an area of sky in the distance appeared grey and gloomy as a result of the smoke drifting lazily upwards from what we guessed must be a fair number of steam engines resting on shed. We were excited at the prospect of what locos we might see; after all the depot had an allocation of about 120 steam despite the massive withdrawals that had taken place over the last few years. Even back in 1950 the shed had only approximately twenty-five more steam engines in its motive power pool. Now it had the privilege to be allocated the last surviving 'Royal Scots' (4), 'Patriots' (2) and 'Clans' (5). So far, Wakefield had produced the most steam on shed and we thought if any depot would beat this figure it would be Kingmoor. Certainly we expected a good variety of steam, but would it surpass Darlington's 14 different classes?

Once in the shed I started noting the engines in the north yard. By the time I'd listed my first twenty or so, I'd already seen nine different classes of locomotive; when all 75 steam present had been logged the total number of varieties had climbed to 14. Contrary to thinking we had seen our last 'A4', we found No. 60027 Merlin together with fellow ex-LNER locos 'A3' No. 60052 Prince Palatine and 'V2' No. 60846 on shed. The other 11 classes present and number of engines of each variety was as follows: 'Black 5' (31), Stanier '8F' (3), Ivatt 4MT 2-6-0 (6), '3F' 0-6-0T ('Jinty') (3), standard 5MT (2), standard '9F' (7), 'Britannia' (9), 'Jubilee' (4), 'Royal Scot' (2), 'Patriot' (2) and 'Clan' (3).

Kingmoor had produced six more steam than Wakefield and had equalled the variety of classes we had seen on Darlington shed. Unfortunately, I had almost finished my last roll of film and couldn't afford to buy any more. Consequently, I limited myself to one or two pictures and reluctantly put my camera away so that I could finish the film the following day while visiting Upperby, Carlisle's ex-LNWR depot. With such a diverse array of engines, I still regret not being able to make the most of the photographic opportunity available to me, and often wished I had had an extra few shillings in my pocket to buy another film.

With notebooks and cameras safely stored in our pannier bags, we cycled back to the main road and to the youth hostel situated between the River Eden and the main line north of the city. This would be our last bit of luxury - we now realised that our funds were so low that we would only be able to afford to use one more official campsite on our way home. But that would be something to think about tomorrow; tonight we would relax and enjoy sleeping in comfortable beds again.

Thursday 22nd July

The morning dawned bright and sunny. If time had allowed we would no doubt have spent a few hours on Citadel station, but we needed to cycle as far as Shap, about thirty miles south, and as we also wanted to visit Upperby depot before leaving the city, we decided to head to the station so we could pick up the route to the shed as outlined in our shed directory.

Once again this depot was a prime example of how fast things were changing with regard to the allotment of steam motive power. Three and a half years earlier Upperby had had an allocation of eighty or so engines, by the end of 1963 it was down to twenty-eight, and at the time of our visit twenty-one. Its most powerful engines now were its seven 'Britannia' Pacifics, acquired between November 1964 and February 1965. Most of its duties - supplying engines for freight work - had been transferred to Kingmoor (12A), which had accelerated its decline. But the batch of 'Britannia's would continue to work from here until their transfer to 12A at the end of the following year.

As we reached the gate that would give us access to the path leading to the shed we met two lads who had already been around the depot. We asked them what Pacifics they had noted and I realised that, although based at Kingmoor, the last 'Britannia' I needed, No. 70040 Clive of India, was inside the depot. My obvious excitement at the prospect of copping my last 'Britannia' was tempered somewhat with some additional news: there were a couple of policemen in the shed, too! Dennis decided he would give the visit a miss and look after our bikes, but I couldn't resist the temptation. Anxious and apprehensive, I made my way along the cinder path towards the depot, keeping my fingers crossed that I wouldn't bump into anyone in a blue uniform.

In the excitement of finding out about the 'Britannia', I forgot to ask where it was exactly. Anyway, I started taking down the numbers of engines in the yard, and at the same time keeping a watchful eye out for any police. For some reason, I decided to take a photograph of Ivatt tank, No. 41264, from a low angle. So I squatted down, looked at the engine through the viewfinder and, at the moment I was checking the exposure, I suddenly had the feeling that I was no longer alone. I pivoted round and an Alsatian was looking straight at me - if he had put out his tongue I think he could have licked my face! Next to the dog I saw a brightly polished pair of black boots, and as I looked up at the officer they belonged to, I was asked what I thought I was up to. Well, the answer was rather obvious but, even if I hadn't been lost for words, I had no excuse for being where I was. He didn't give me time to answer anyhow and, rather forthrightly, told me to 'bugger off' and not to come back again! I think I made some sort of apology, and with *my* tail between my legs hurriedly made my way off the site, hoping that he had a firm grip of the dogs lead.

As soon as I reappeared, Dennis sensed that my mission hadn't been accomplished. I had failed to see my last 'Britannia', but at the same time was relieved that the policeman had not taken the matter any further. My notebook reminds me that I recorded 15 steam representing 8 different classes and that No. 70040 must have been in the roundhouse or a part of the yard I had not managed to cover. Having also failed to get round a shed for the first time since leaving home, we now had ahead of us a thirty-mile ride to Shap village, with some steep climbs on the way.

Several stops were made during the journey, including a break at Penrith - no incentive to call in at the station to assist us to locate the nearby shed - it had been closed for about three years. Once we had left the town, we faced the long climb up to Shap, during which we heard and caught sight of the occasional train as we stood on the peddles and did our best to keep moving. It was late afternoon by the time we reached the village, so we made straight for the campsite... only to find that it had been closed since the end of the previous summer! Fortunately, the lady who used to run the site must have sensed our disappointment and allowed us to camp in her back garden, which, although on a slope, was adjacent to the main line.

After pitching the tent and sorting out our sleeping bags and other bits and pieces, we walked along to the local shop and bought bread and milk. And because we did not have sufficient funds for some jam, I have to admit we 'borrowed' some. Back at the tent we discovered the flavour of the jam was pineapple, which neither of us liked and have never ever had since! The bread and jam would have to last us the next two days, and in that time we would need to cycle a total of one hundred and sixty five miles to reach home.

Friday 23rd July

We were up by 6.30am, and while having the last of our cornflakes for breakfast, we heard a steam engine approaching. Dennis quickly made a move to see what loco it was, and in the process slipped, knocked over the milk and his bowl of cereals and fell into a patch of nettles. Determined to get to the wall at the bottom of the garden, he ignored my laughter and just caught sight of 'Black 5' No.44767, not realising at this point in time that there would be plenty more opportunities to see this particular 'Black 5', even after steam had finished on BR!

Today we still had the incentive and motivation to make a long journey knowing that it would be punctuated by visits to at least two further sheds. But these would be the last. Tomorrow the stimulus would be somewhat different; with no money and very little food left we would have no alternative other than to get back home as quickly as possible, preferably before the end of the day.

The first leg of the day's journey took us along the A6 through Kendal and on to Carnforth, a distance of about thirty miles. Here, we had a break and, of course, visited the shed. For the previous fifteen years its allocation had remained constant with around forty steam engines assigned to it. Not knowing how things would pan out with regard to the use of steam power during the next three years or so, we were completely unaware that on a number of future visits we would record a lot more steam here than those found present today.

Reflecting its average allotment of steam power, we found exactly 40 steam on shed, including 'Britannia' Pacifics No's. 70017 Arrow, 70048 The Territorial Army 1908-1958 and 70052 Firth of Tay. 'Jinty', 'Black 5', Fairburn and Stanier 2-6-4T's, were a few of the other 10 different classes present. Carnforth shed and station seemed a hive of activity, but as much as we would have liked to have spent more time here, there was one last shed to try and get round before we continued our journey home.

No doubt someone will spot where this photograph was taken! An unidentified 'Black 5' in an unknown location heads a freight train. I cannot find any details about this picture, so whether it was taken while we were northbound or southbound I can't say. I have included it here, as I do know it was taken during our trip to Scotland in July 1965!

We made good progress over the relatively short distance to the outskirts of Lancaster, and were soon making our way round its old Midland Railway shed. Many of the depot's duties had been transferred to Carnforth, and its pool of steam locos had gradually decreased from around thirty-five in 1960 to less than twenty by the time of our visit. Indeed, we recorded a similar number on shed, the total standing at 18, amongst which were 5 different classes represented. There was nothing out of the ordinary to report; the engines present pretty much reflected its ration of steam power. However, some might say that the depot did have a significant aspect to its history - it held the record for being given the most number of different shed codes - five in all while in BR ownership.

The journey home would now begin in earnest: no further sheds would be visited, and neither would we be stopping at any stations and logging any passing trains. Our notebooks had been safely stored away and we now had to cycle for as long and as far as we could - certainly no less than fifty miles, anything more would be a bonus. So, it was back on to the A6 to head for Garstang and Preston and then, once south of the River Ribble, the A49 to Wigan and Warrington.

We passed through Warrington around 9.00pm and then, after crossing over the Manchester Ship Canal, left the A6 and joined the A50. By the time we were into open countryside again and had found a suitable field in which to camp for the night, we were pitching the tent with what little light we were getting from our torches. As soon as our sleeping bags had been laid out we were into them quickly and soon fast asleep. We had covered a little over 90 miles since leaving Shap and had exceeded the target we had set ourselves.

Saturday 24th July

We slept so well that we didn't stir until about half past eight in the morning. We reluctantly crawled out of our sleeping bags and had nothing more than tea (without milk) and bread and jam for breakfast. Once everything had been packed away, we climbed on to our bikes with little enthusiasm for the ride ahead, yet determined to reach home before nightfall.

The journey was not without incident. At one point, on the A34 between Stone and Stafford, I caught the rear wheel of Dennis' bike and careered across the road. Fortunately, nothing was overtaking us or coming in the opposite direction. I had nodded off momentarily while coasting downhill, but was fully alert in an instant when my bike lurched to one side. Luckily for my bike and me, I managed to regain control before leaving the road completely. Needless to say, we had a short rest as soon as we reached a suitable place to stop.

As we continued south, each mile seemed to take forever - even more so once we had passed through Stafford. Like a long distance runner I tried not to look too far ahead, but couldn't help doing so at times. After making our way through Walsall, leaving us with about another nine or ten miles to go, I kept willing the skyline to change. I continually scanned the horizon for the tall familiar buildings of the centre of Birmingham, which would give me a better idea of exactly where I was in relationship to home. My last postcard to Mum and Dad had been posted on 22nd July from Carlisle. At the time of writing I didn't know precisely when I would be back, and as we didn't have the luxury of a telephone, I wasn't able to let them know during the day when I was hoping to be home. I doubted they would be out, and anyway my grandma lived only two doors away, so I knew I would have somewhere to go and have someone in the family to greet me on my return.

Eventually, the familiar taller buildings I so wanted to see came into sight, and it didn't seem too long before we were skirting the city centre. We parted company when Dennis had about another mile and a half to go before reaching his house in Acocks Green, and although his route would take him past the entrance to Tyseley shed, I very much doubted he would be tempted to carry out a quick visit! I had the distinct feeling that on this occasion he would head straight home and not give the opportunity a second thought.

It was gone eight o'clock when I lifted the latch on the gate at the side of the house and pushed it open. Stretching forward from the back of the rear wheel to reach the handlebars, I pushed my bike with some difficulty up the entry and into the yard. Mum and Dad were in; tired but triumphant, I was home at last. Pleased to see me and relieved that I had got back safely both were soon listening to some of the tales of our adventure. Dad briefly mentioned about the change of plan and heading further north into Scotland, but didn't dwell on the point. Mum immediately started cooking me a meal, while listening intently to all I had to say. I was in need of more than a quick wash before eating, though, so I ran a bath and, after a quick soak, I was enjoying the first decent food I'd had in a few days.

Feeling absolutely worn out, I finished my meal, sorted out my washing and other bits and pieces and got ready for bed. Although we had used the train a few times, we had cycled a little over 600 miles, visited twenty-five steam sheds and achieved our goal of seeing the final few 'A4's still employed on express passenger duties. Later, I would discover I had seen a total of 38 varieties amongst the 714 different steam logged (see appendix 12). I fell asleep while thinking about lots of things to do with the trip, but uppermost on my mind were the films I'd taken - I really hoped that I would have a few good pictures to eventually put into my album, adding something tangible to the memories that would no doubt remain with me for years to come.

I wasn't early rising the following day. I looked down from my bedroom window and saw my bike resting against the shed wall. It was hard to believe that two weeks had passed since Dennis and I had started out on such an exciting adventure. Now it was all over, and being surrounded once again with all the familiar things associated with home, came a feeling of belonging and being safe. But, at the same time, it also brought a sense of anti-climax. Trainspotting and my enthusiasm for steam had changed as a result; it would be difficult if not impossible to get the same sense of adventure and satisfaction from the normal local locations I would soon be visiting again. There was also something else; being independent and able to make decisions without having to check with Mum and Dad, although I guess I didn't fully realise it at the time, had had a profound effect on the way I was growing up, too.

While I continued to gaze out from the window, I began to think about our forthcoming holiday in Somerset, which was only two weeks away. Fortunately, once again, and quite soon, I would be seeing steam in different surroundings - around Bristol, Weston-super-Mare and on the Highbridge branch of the former S & D Railway. I turned around and looked at the films sitting on top of my bedside table; it was time to start developing them.

Earlier in the year, I had invested in a developing tank and the necessary chemicals to enable me to produce my own negatives. What I hadn't got was a proper darkroom, or indeed any sort of space that could be adapted for the job. So, it was a question of improvising as best I could, which meant shutting my bedroom curtains, placing extra blankets on the bed and loading the tank underneath a mound of bedclothes! Sounds simple, doesn't it? Well, it was, but it all depended on how easily (once the backing paper had been removed) the film went on to the spool, which was then placed inside the tank. Once that had been achieved, and the seal and lid were safely in place, I could then come out from under the blankets, breathe a little easier and continue the process in the daylight in the kitchen.

I remember clearly the anticipation and excitement of reaching the point when it was time to open the tank, remove the first roll of film from the spool, and view the end product. As with many other films I would develop, the results were a bit of a mix bag with some pictures turning out well while others, for a variety of reasons, being rather disappointing. Sometimes the outcome was possibly linked to the developing process itself - with dilution of chemicals, or the timing and correct agitation perhaps not being carried out quite as efficiently as they should have been. All the same, I would continue to develop my own films ready for printing but, having neither the equipment or the money to complete the process, the vast majority of the negatives were popped into suitable sized envelopes and stored away in an old shoe box. It would be many years later that these, and indeed hundreds more 35mm negatives, would be retrieved and printed. Only the odd colour film taken to the chemist for processing would provide me with a positive copy and a true reflection of my efforts reasonably quickly.

By the next day I had developed all my films and, when there to listen to me, I continued to relay to Mum and Dad my exploits of the previous two weeks, being careful of course not to mention the incident while trying to bunk Upperby shed. They were both looking forward to the summer holiday, and I remember Dad servicing and cleaning the car ready for the journey south. Fishing tackle needed to be sorted out and cleaned, too, and arrangements made for Derek, my cousin, to join us for the two weeks. He also had an interest in steam, but much preferred to be on the riverbank.

August

Both Saltley and Tyseley sheds were visited on Sunday 1st August. The former depot produced 35 steam representing 8 different types, but Tyseley on this day boasted a total of 48 such locos and a much wider variety of motive power. No fewer than 14 different classes were noted with several ex-GWR designs present, including 'Hall', 'Manor', 'Grange' '5700' and '5101'. There was also a 'Britannia' Pacific in residence, No. 70052 Firth of Tay, seen previously at Carnforth on 23rd July.

On Saturday 7th August, with the boot, roof rack and every nook and cranny inside the car used to the full to store our things, we set off from Sparkbrook for Loxton, Somerset. My thoughts were firmly fixed on where I might be heading to see steam rather than where I might be going fishing. I had a good idea of where I would like to trainspot during the coming two weeks, but realised I would have to fit in with what everyone else wanted to do. I would wait for an opportune time to ask Dad to give me a lift to a station near to where we were staying or while en-route to other fishing venues so I could then journey further afield.

Having holidayed here a few years before, it didn't take us long to settle in at White House Farm and to get to know the Isgar family again. The next two days were spent fishing, but on Tuesday 10th August we went into Weston super Mare and I managed to spend a few minutes on the station. During my brief visit, I noted a diesel shunter, a 'Hymek' and a 'Warship' No. D803 Albion. I hoped I would be back the following Saturday when the station would be much busier, though I doubted I would see any steam, even though there would be numerous excursion and relief trains arriving at this popular seaside destination.

On Friday 13th August we caught up with Grandma and Granddad at the Butlins Holiday Camp in Minehead where they were staying for the week. Heading first to Bleadon to get some petrol, I persuaded Dad to take us a little further on to Bleadon and Uphill Station, which was now a museum and had ex-Cardiff Railway 0-4-0ST No. 1338 on display. This little engine, standing on its own small section of track, was designed primarily for dock shunting. Built by Kitsons, it was about sixty-seven years old and was the last standard gauge engine to be withdrawn that had been absorbed into the GWR. Bought by two enthusiasts belonging to the Weston Transport Enthusiasts Club, they had obtained permission from Robert Smallman, the Museum owner, to put it on display together with his railway relics. The museum would close at the end of 1967, and the engine would ultimately take up residency at the Didcot Railway Centre where it would be fully restored to working order.

Once I had taken a few pictures of the saddle tank, we were on our way to Minehead via Watchet and Blue Anchor Bay. After meeting up with my grandparents and spending some time swapping holiday stories with them, I wandered off with Derek to see another two preserved engines: 'Coronation' class No. (4)6229 Duchess of Hamilton and 'Terrier' 0-6-0T No. 32678. These engines were photographed, too, but not in the best of circumstances as can be seen. Both locos were enclosed by a fence and were presented like caged animals in a zoo. I remember thinking that their presence in a holiday camp was totally inappropriate and that they should have been in steam and still usefully employed. On the other hand, as a result of their purchase from BR, they would eventually be restored to working order and be seen once again hard at work on preserved railways or in the case of the 'Duchess' on the main line.

As I had wished for earlier in the week, I spent a few hours at Weston on 14th August. Being a summer Saturday I knew that it would be a lot busier than my visit earlier in the week. Not surprisingly, I hoped that at least one excursion would be steam-hauled, but disappointingly noted only diesels. I couldn't resist taking a few photographs, however, and these included shots of 'Warships' No's D841 Roebuck, D847 Strongbow, 'Western' D1010 Western Campaigner and 'Hymek's No's D7004 and D7014. Several of these pictures featured Locking Road, which acted as an overflow station when there was an influx of such trains, and as a siding in less frenetic times. It comprised four platforms and was built because of the popularity of Weston amongst the populations of Birmingham and the Midlands in general.

Preserved engines: left, ex-Cardiff railway saddle tank No. 1338 in the Bleadon and Uphill Museum and below, Coronation Pacific No. (4)6229 Duchess of Hamilton on display at Butlin's, Minehead. The Butlin's sign to the right of the loco's chimney states she had completed 1,533,846 miles before her withdrawal from BR.
Both 13th August 1965

On 14th August 1965, Crewe-built Brush Type '4' No. D1597 is ready to return to the Eastern Region of BR from Weston super Mare Locking Road. Later named Resilient, this engine would be withdrawn at the end of February 2007.

A busy but steamless summer Saturday: 'Hymek' No. D7004 and 'Western' class No. D1010 Western Campaigner are seen standing in Weston Super Mare station on 14th August 1965. The latter engine, after withdrawal in February 1977, would eventually be restored to working order and be based at the West Somerset Railway. The 'Hymek', having entered traffic in August 1961, would be withdrawn in June 1972 and would not quite reach her eleventh year in service.

In the early part of the second week of the holiday we all fished the Rivers Yeo and Axe and had reasonable catches from what I recall, but on Wednesday 18th August I arranged to go trainspotting again, this time to Bristol, and Derek decided to have a break from the fishing and come along as well.

Although a lot livelier than Weston, we failed to note a single steam engine during almost two hours on Temple Meads. Bath Road was now a diesel depot and St.Philips Marsh had closed over twelve months earlier, so if we were going to see any steam at all, it would mean a visit to Barrow Road MPD, and that's where we set off to next.

Originally belonging to the old Midland Railway, the shed had changed hands once or twice and now came under the control of the Western Region. Under its auspices came the replacement of ex-LMS locomotives by ex-GWR engines. Only a few years earlier one would have regularly seen 'Patriots' and 'Jubilees' in the depot. Reviewing its allotment of steam over the years, one locomotive from its 1950 allocation had remained attached to the shed until this summer, namely Fowler 0-6-0 No. 44269. Recently deemed surplus to requirements, she had been transferred in June to Gloucester Horton Road. The Bristol depot had about 25 active steam locos to call upon at the time of our visit.

We found a reasonable mix of motive power on shed with 7 different classes represented amongst the 20 steam locos present. Thirteen of them were ex-LMS and standard varieties and the remainder ex-GWR, including 'Hall' class engines No's. 6908 Downham Hall and 7907 Hart Hall. Interestingly, No. 44269, was also present, and had either worked into Bristol from Gloucester or her move to Horton Road MPD hadn't yet materialised. In the company of a 'Grange' and a Brush Type '4', I would photograph this engine during a visit to Horton Road next month. This would be my last visit to Barrow Road before its closure three months later on 20th November.

Leaving the depot and climbing up the steps to the road giving the depot its name, we had one final look at the locos on shed and then made our way back to Temple Meads Station. Here, during the afternoon, five steam workings were noted, including No. 6870 Bodicote Grange, which arrived at the head of a passenger train, presumably deputising for a failed diesel. Allocated to Oxley, the engine would continue in service for only a few more days before withdrawal. Amongst the many diesels recorded was Brush experimental Type '4' No. D0280 Falcon, which had been introduced in 1961.

While travelling back to Weston, I studied my jottings for the day: a meagre 24 steam had been noted, representing 10 different classes. Nineteen months had passed since my previous visit to Bristol when I had recorded over a hundred steam during time spent on Temple Meads station and visiting the city's sheds. Steams decline here was palpable and, although there were a few regular freight turns, only the odd local passenger turn remained assigned to this form of traction, with the employment of standard 3MT 2-6-2 tanks based at Barrow Road and Bath Green Park MPD's. These engines were in dreadful external condition, and although a welcome sight amongst all the diesels, they did little to offset this gloomy picture. It seemed the Western Region's plans were very much on course to eradicate steam from its territory by the end of the year.

On Wednesday, 18th August 1965, a rather scruffy and tired looking 'Grange', which in all likelihood had filled in for a failed diesel on what appears to be an ordinary passenger train, sits in Bristol Temple Meads. No. 6870 Bodicote Grange would not have to struggle on for much longer, and would face withdrawal within the matter of a few days.

We were all up early the next day, 19th August, and straight after breakfast set off to fish the milk factory stretch of the River Brue near Bason Bridge. This spot was similar to that at Lapworth - I could watch the trains and fish at the same time. Not unexpectedly, I missed a few bites during the day when my concentration was disturbed either by a passing train or while looking along the line in anticipation. My photographs here turned out poorly, so I was pleased when I added to my collection a picture taken two years earlier of Collett 0-6-0 No. 3206 passing the factory. Even more pleasing was the fact that the photograph was taken from the very spot where I fished on this day.

The milk factory added an extra dimension to the lines traffic and, following the withdrawal of passenger services, the trains it generated would keep this part of the line open until October 1972. Ignorance it is said is bliss, and at fifteen years of age I didn't fully appreciate what had really been happening with regard to the S & D. Looked at with much affection, a lot has been written about this lovely line and many pictures taken of steam trains along its scenic route. I knew that Dad and Derek were planning to fish the River Huntspill, and that I would be able to have a lift to Highbridge where the S & D line crossed the old GWR route. So, I decided to forego the opportunity to go with them on the final day of the holiday, and spend instead a few hours in the company of one or two steam engines on part of a line that was soon to be consigned to the history books.

Friday, 20th August. Dad duly dropped me off at Highbridge station, arranging to pick me up again later on the afternoon. When I looked around from the footbridge, I was amazed at the size of the station, especially the East station with five platforms serving the former S & D Railway. From here I could see the small engine shed in the distance, which I would visit later. I knew it wouldn't be the busiest of locations, but it was a lovely warm summer's day and, although diesel hauled, there would always be a few express passenger trains to see heading to or from Bristol on the ex-GWR main line.

The S & D Joint Railway in embryonic form started life on 28th August 1854 with the opening of the section between Highbridge Wharf and Glastonbury by the Somerset Central Railway, followed by the amalgamation of the SCR with the Dorset Railway on 1st September 1862. Operated by the MR and LSWR, the joint railway came into being on 1st November 1875. The wharf played a pivotal role in the development of the railway as both dairy and agricultural produce was transported from the various market towns of Dorset and Somerset to the valleys of south Wales via Highbridge. Traffic in both directions, including the coal and industrial products from the Valleys, were carried across the Channel by the S & D's own ships, but by 1933 this arrangement had come to an end. The S & D's Locomotive Works were also built at Highbridge, and between 1862 and 1930 repaired and rebuilt the lines locomotives as well as making the majority of its carriages and trucks. At its peak it employed over 300 workers. Thirty-five years after its closure, as I stood looking down what was once the main line, it was difficult to believe what a thriving and busy part of the railway Highbridge used to be. As a railway centre it had long faded and was now a quiet backwater, but at least it could still boast an engine shed, albeit a small one.

After a while, and to prove that there were occasionally signs of life, Ivatt 2-6-2T No. 41216 backed on to its train in No. 3 platform and then waited patiently for the 'right way' to start off on its journey to Templecombe. Having witnessed her departure, I switched my attention to the ex-GWR station. Here I noted in quick succession 'Warship' No. D860 Victorious and 'Western' No. D1020 Western Hero. Before walking the short distance to the shed, knowing already that there was at least one steam loco there - almost certainly another Ivatt tank - I watched the arrival of Ivatt 2-6-2T, No. 41290, with a train from Evercreech Junction.

Once a sub-shed of Templcombe and Bath Green Park, Highbridge was reported as closed in May 1959, but in fact would continue servicing steam locos right up until the line ceased operation in March 1966. By the time of my visit, it was quite clear that it had seen better days. Even so, I was fortunate to find two locos present, both Ivatt tanks as expected - No. 41206, standing in the yard and No. 41249 inside the shed building. These engines were based at Templecombe, and the latter would have the honour of hauling the last passenger train on 5th March 1966 to Templecombe and return. After taking two pictures of the former loco, I walked back to the station where I noted several diesel workings before photographing 2-6-2T No. 41290 with an afternoon train for Evercreech Junction. I didn't record the times of the steam-hauled passenger trains, so the details are incomplete, but I am sure about both the destination and origin of the workings mentioned.

The picture opposite shows where the former S & D line crosses the main line from Taunton to Bristol at Highbridge, which three months earlier had been completely re-laid and realigned during the night of 15th/16th May. Although the job was completed successfully, and only two hours behind schedule, the first working over the new crossing didn't go quite so well. The milk train from Bason Bridge was due to use the new layout at 5.00pm on the Sunday evening. Using crowbars to move the points, which then needed to be clipped, the Ivatt tank engine crossed over the main line and, after leaving its train for transfer, was given the all clear to return light to the S & D shed. However, while negotiating the new connection the engine became derailed and had to wait until about 11.00pm for a breakdown gang to lift her back on to the tracks. When I read about the incident the locomotive involved wasn't disclosed - perhaps the engine in question had been one of the tanks I'd seen during the day.

On 20th August 1965 an unidentified 'Warship' enters Highbridge with a mixed freight. These diesel hydraulics were not destined to last very long and by the end of 1972 the vast majority of them had been withdrawn. In the foreground is the former S&D line crossing over the ex-GWR main line.

Ivatt 2-6-2T No. 41216 waits for the 'right away' to start its journey from platform 3 Highbridge (East) to Templecombe on 20th August 1965. Built at Crewe in September 1948, the engine would spend a number of years working out of Rhyl MPD before heading south. Allocated to 83G, the tank would face redundancy on the closure of the SDJR next March.

Ivatt 2-6-2T No. 41206 eventually moved south to the Western Region of BR in the early 60's. By now allotted to Templecombe, the engine is seen resting in Highbridge shed on a warm and sunny 20th August 1965. These locos had taken over passenger duties from Collett's 2251 class 0-6-0 locos.

Another view of Ivatt 2-6-0T No. 41206 resting between duties on Highbridge shed. Built at Crewe in December 1946, it had been allocated to a number of depots including Hellifield, Bank Hall, Plymouth Friary and finally Templecombe from where it would be withdrawn in March 1966. To the left of the engine can be seen the hoist and skip used for coaling purposes.

Having arrived earlier during the day, Ivatt tank No. 41290 is ready to carry out its balanced working with an afternoon train to Evercreech Junction on 20th August 1965. All of the Ivatt engines seen during this day would be withdrawn the following March after the closure of the S&D line.

A reminder of the days immediately before the introduction of the Ivatt tanks. Collett 0-6-0 No. 3206 heads a train for Evercreech Junction past the Wiltshire Dairies milk factory at Bason Bridge. Withdrawn at the end of 1963, this scene most likely shows the engine carrying out its final summer's duties. G.White. Author's collection.

The time spent at Highbridge had passed all too quickly, even though I'd only recorded a total of four steam and ten diesel workings. I had visited another shed and had spent some time on a railway that all too soon would be closing. With steam virtually ousted from Bristol and surrounding district, I would not visit the area again, and the few pictures featuring Highbridge would remain the only ones taken personally of the former S & D in my collection. I often look back and think how lucky I was to see at least a small part of this once vitally important line, colloquially known as 'the slow and dirty', and to have one or two photographs to remind me of my visit.

Many years later I had the pleasure of liasing with Major Julian Peters with regards to career opportunities in the Army and to facilitate visits to the school where I was responsible for careers and work experience. He gave a number of presentations over several years before he retired and, rather than say goodbye over the telephone, he paid a personal visit to the school to say farewell. While chatting over a cup of coffee, I happened to ask him what adventures lay in store with the prospect of having a lot more free time available. One of the things he must attend to as a priority he said, was to sort out and edit a number of films and pictures that his father hadn't got round to preparing for publication. In an instant I realised he was referring to Ivo Peters one of steams great photographers and probably best known for his pictures of the S&D railway. We both agreed that if I had known this when we first met, my focus on the purpose of our working relationship would have been somewhat affected and we would probably talked more about his father's exploits than the business in hand!

Saturday 21st August dawned and it was time to say goodbye to Jack and Mona Isgar who had made us so welcome. They had been extremely hospitable and we had thoroughly enjoyed our two-week stay with them. Would we, I wondered, be back again next year? With the car packed and the four of us seated inside, they waved us off as we travelled slowly along the lane that took us over the River Axe, away from Bleadon Hill and towards the Mendip Hills. Skirting Wavering Down we joined the A38 close to Axbridge and headed north to Birmingham and its familiar industrial surroundings.

Settling in at home didn't take long, and I was soon looking forward to seeing the results of the black and white pictures I had taken. I waited until dusk, closed the curtains in my bedroom and got under the bedclothes to transfer the first of my films to the developing tank. The colour film that featured diesels and preserved steam engines at Butlins and Bleadon & Uphill would have to wait until I could afford to take it to the chemists to be developed and printed.

My film processing continued through Sunday morning until lunch was ready. Some of the negatives looked promising, but the proof would be in their printing and that, as mentioned earlier, would have to wait quite some time. After lunch, I decided to remove the pannier bags from my bike and cycle to Saltley to see what engines it had on offer.

After making my way up the ramp leading to the depot, I left my bike outside the old wood store next to No. 1 shed as I called it which, together with No.2 shed, was at the north end of the depot (plans of the depot show them numbered vice versa). Once inside this rather gloomy part of the building, I started listing the locos present. By the time I had made my way through the other two roundhouses and checked what was in the yard, a total of 35 steam had been noted representing 9 different classes. Amongst the regular parade of motive power were several visitors, including two 'Britannia' Pacifics No's 70026 Polar Star and 70047 (the only one in the class to remain unnamed), standard 5MT No. 73140 and ex-GWR 0-6-2T No. 6656.

Before the new school year got under way, I made two further visits to Saltley on the 29th and 30th August. The above-mentioned visitors noted on 22nd were still present and, in addition to these, on both days, were 'WD's No's 90190, 90315, 90456 and 90730 and ex-GWR 'Grange' No. 6871 Bourton Grange. Engine and class totals for the two visits were 35/11 and 38/11 respectively. Also on 30th I made what turned out to be my final visit to Aston. It would close a little over six weeks later on 11th October, and most of its locomotives together with its staff would be transferred to Bescot and Saltley. Steam locos present on this day were as follows: No's 42062, 42075, 44710, 44876, 45038, 45058, 46427, 46492, 48399, 48442, 48719 and 76040. I never really felt confident or comfortable visiting this shed, hence the relatively few times I recorded steam here compared with Saltley and Tyseley.

September

During September trips were made to Saltley on 12th and Tyseley on 18th. The former was home to 10 varieties of locomotive amongst the 43 steam present while Tyseley, with 31 steam on shed, had 11 different classes represented. Seven ex-GWR 'Granges' were noted, two of which, No's 6853 Morehampton Grange and 6861 Crynant Grange, were exceptionally clean. I managed to photograph these engines leaving the shed together (see colour section page 46). Also worthy of special note was the presence of ex-LNER 'K4' No. 3442 (BR No. 61994) The Great Marquess.

Above: As the sun sets, the nearby water column casts its shadow on the boiler of 'Grange' No. 6831 Bearley Grange. Also basking in the evening sunshine is Ivatt 2-6-0 No. 46457, which had become a Tyseley engine (together with classmates No's 46428, 46442 and 46470) earlier in June. This scene was photographed sometime in September or early October 1965.

On my way home from Tyseley shed on 18th September, I reached the top end of the north yard to find standard '9F' No. 92124, allocated to Warrington (Dallam), waiting for the 'right away' to continue north with a mixed freight. The driver and fireman were deep in conversation with a railwayman standing below them and either didn't see me or completely ignored my presence.

On Saturday 25th September Dennis and I travelled southwest to Worcester and Gloucester on what was to prove an extremely dull and dreary day. Twelve months earlier these sheds had had between them an allocation of over eighty steam engines, sixty-one of which were of GWR origin including, at the latter, the last of the 'Castles'. If the planned elimination of steam on the Western Region by the end of the year materialised, both depots would only continue to service such engines for another three months.

Arriving at Worcester Shrub Hill Station we found pannier tank No. 3615 resting between duties. Following a short walk to the shed, a total of 24 steam were logged representing 9 different types, including 'Hall', 'Grange' 'Black 5' and standard 5MT 4-6-0. Eleven of the steam present were ex-GWR engines. Gloucester Horton Road, now without its allocation of 'Castles' (No's 5042, 7022 and 7034 had been withdrawn in July), had a greater number of steam on shed with a total of 38. It also had a more varied assortment with no fewer than 14 classes represented, including Stanier '8F', standard '9F', standard 2MT 2-6-0, Midland '4F' 0-6-0, Ivatt 2-6-2T, and 'Manor'. By the end of the day we had seen a total of 16 varieties amongst the 63 steam locos recorded (See appendix 13). Two days later on 27th September the former Chief Mechanical Engineer of the London, Midland & Scottish Railway, Sir William A. Stanier, died aged 89.

On a very wet and miserable 25th September 1965, 0-6-0PT No. 3615 and crew are found resting in Worcester Shrub Hill station. Built in February 1939, the engine spent a number of years allocated to Stafford Road before moving to south Wales. After spells at Barry and Neath sheds, the pannier was transferred, for the final time, to Worcester earlier in January. However, its shunting and trip freight duties would soon be coming to an end, and within three weeks it would face its inevitable withdrawal.

A drab looking engine in equally drab surroundings: Collett 2-6-2T No. 6147 sits in front of standard 4MT 4-6-0 No.75000 in the yard of Worcester shed, its home depot, on 25th September 1965. Fifteen of these fine engines remained in stock at this time, and although built for work in the London suburban area, most of them by now were assigned to Oxford MPD.

The weather was not improving as this dismal September day wore on. With the rain continuing to fall, 0-6-0PT No. 3643 was photographed from inside the repair shop in Gloucester Horton Road MPD. Prepared to brave the elements, Dennis must have been keen to be included too. Transferred from Barrow Road earlier in January, the pannier tank would officially be withdrawn at the end of December.

On the same day, standing in the drizzle, a somewhat bedraggled looking line up of engines was found in the yard of Horton Road depot. At least the contrast in the front ends of these engines adds a little interest to this picture. The line-up from left to right shows '4F' 0-6-0 No. 44269 (mentioned earlier p.174), 'Grange' 4-6-0 No. 6819 Highnam Grange and Tinsley allocated Brush Type '4' No. D1785.

October

I made five visits to Saltley during October on 3rd, 10th, 17th, 25th, and 31st. Engine and class totals were correspondingly as follows: 40/6, 50/8, 45/10, 32/7 and 45/10. On 17th I noted several engines of interest. Three of them, No's 43106, 43953 (both visiting engines) and 92139 all looked in ex-works condition. Also on shed was 'K1' No. 62012, a York engine, and standard 5MT No. 73112 Morgan le Fay, last allocated to Nine Elms before withdrawal earlier in June, minus her smokebox door.

I realised straight away that ex-Midland Railway 0-6-0 No. 43953 had good reason to be in such pristine condition; the previous day she had worked an RCTS special from Nuneaton entitled Midlands Locomotive Requiem Railtour. As the name of the special implies, this particular engine, and indeed the other two survivors of her class, had not long to go before withdrawal. In fact, No. 43953 would be the last of the three to remain active. After returning to her northwest base the engine would be reported in store at Workington on 15th November, thus rendering the Midland Railway Fowler 0-6-0's extinct. About a dozen of those built for the LMS would remain in stock at the start of the New Year. However, the last two, both allocated to Crewe Works, would be withdrawn in September 1966, and would mark the end for Fowler's 0-6-0 engines. Introduced in 1911, a total of 772 were constructed and, although designed primarily for freight work, they were also expected to turn their hand to passenger duties, too.

Above and next. On 16th October 1965, Midland Railway 0-6-0 No. 43953 arrives at Mansfield Town station with the RCTS special mentioned earlier. Later in the day, the train is seen at Seymour Junction, shortly after passing through Staveley Town. Numerous lines at the heart of the Midland area would be visited, with only a small part of the journey (Seymour Junction to Glapwell Colliery sidings) in the hands of a diesel - Beyer Peacock-built No. D8613. It would later be reported that, towards the end of the day, the 0-6-0 was not in particularly good form with time being lost and speed rarely exceeding 30mph. Author's collection.

When Leamington Spa shed closed earlier in June, four of its standard 5MT's (No's 73026, 73066, 73069 and 73156) were transferred to Tyseley. One of these, seen above but unidentified, was photographed sometime in October in the north yard. By April the following year they had all moved on to Bolton MPD, except for 73069 which would go to Carnforth and would be the final member of the class to be withdrawn.

Steam locos on Tyseley MPD were only logged twice in October, on 16th and 20th. Totals for engines noted and different classes were 39/10 and 28/11 respectively. Of the 39 steam present on 16th twenty-seven were former GWR engines, ten of which were 'Granges'. Collett 0-6-2T No. 6667 was found to be in spotless condition, having been prepared for the first leg of an SLS Special, which I would photograph on a mist shrouded Snow Hill the following morning (see below). Stanier '8F' No. 48451, another exceptionally clean engine was noted on 20th.

I'm not sure whether it was through morbid fascination or simply reverting back to my earlier trainspotting days when the objective was to collect as many numbers as possible, but on Sunday 24th October Dennis and I set off for South Wales and Barry Scrapyard where we knew we would see well over a hundred withdrawn steam locomotives.

While wandering along line after line of engines, I took a number of photos, which ironically turned out quite well. Although not the sort of pictures one wants to keep looking at, they do now, of course, serve as a reminder of the scale of the projects the preservation movement took on to restore to working order the many engines that frankly looked quite beyond salvation. Indeed, this particular dumping ground for a substantial quantity of redundant steam locos would become the only source for those interested in saving such motive power. The last engine would be removed in 1990 some twenty-two years after steam had finished on BR in 1968.

Responsible for the first leg of the Stephenson Locomotive Society (Midland Area) GWR Cavalcade special, Collett 0-6-2T No. 6667 stands in Birmingham Snow Hill platform 1 on a very misty 17th October 1965. The engine would take the train via Stourbridge, Kidderminster and Droitwich Spa to Worcester Shrub Hill. The next two stages of the round trip to Bristol would involve No. 7029 Clun Castle, 0-4-2T No. 1420 and light 0-6-0 pannier tank No. 6435.

'Dethroned Kings': nearest the camera is No. 6024 King Edward 1 with No. 6023 King Edward 11 in the background. Both engines were built in June 1930, both withdrawn in June 1962 and both arrived in Barry six months later in the December. Between them they had covered over three million miles while in service. Completely at the mercy of the elements during the previous three years of storage in the open, their condition had deteriorated fairly rapidly and would continue to do so until their purchase from Dai Woodham in March 1973 and December 1984 respectively. 24th October 1965.

I last visited Barry in August the previous year and recorded 92 locos representing 19 different classes. This time the scrapyard produced totals of 127 and 26 respectively. As the elimination of steam grew ever closer, their number would continue to grow and by the end of 1968 would peak at 223. All but two, No's 4156 and 92085, which were broken up, would be bought. Having spent 28 years in the scrapyard following its arrival in March 1962, Churchward 2-6-2T No. 5553 would be the last to leave, on 31st January 1990.

After leaving the scrapyard we bunked Barry MPD, which housed 7 English Electric Type '3' diesels; Cardiff next, and Canton shed, which was all diesel; and then Ebbw Junction where we found 10 steam on shed representing 5 different classes. All ten engines had been withdrawn yet, as close to Barry as they were, not one of them would be deposited at this particular breakers yard. Housing a few diesels, Pontypool Road was our final shed visit of the day. The last shed in South Wales employing steam, Llanelly, had closed on October 3rd and, except for two pannier tanks on steam heating duties at Swansea High Street Station and the odd isolated incursion, this part of Wales was, for all intents and purposes, now bereft of live, working steam.

Withdrawn in June 1964, Hawksworth 0-6-0PT No. 9466 sits languishing in Barry on 24th October 1965. Below the BR emblem, someone has written Dusty Springfield's name in chalk (see comments below about loco No. 7325). Taken out of service twelve years after being built, the engine would be purchased in 1975 and eventually restored to mainline standard. The present owner, Dennis Howell, has looked after the engine since 1977.

Ex-Southern Railway 'U' class No. 31618 stands in Barry scrapyard on 24th October 1965. Required to haul three of its classmates (No's. 31625, 31638 and 31806) to the yard in June 1964, the weeds are almost hiding the engines motion, but it can just be seen that it is still completely intact. Sixteen months after arriving at the yard, the 2-6-0 continues to look in reasonable condition. It would be purchased by the Southern Mogul Preservation Society, and removed to New Hythe, Kent in January 1969.

Originally named Ogmore Castle, No. 5080 was renamed Defiant in January 1941 to commemorate one of many types of aircraft used during the Battle of Britain. The loco arrived at Barry scrapyard in November 1963 where it is seen above, minus its tender, on 24th October 1965. Defiant by nature, the 4-6-0 would brave the elements for eleven years before being bought by the Birmingham Railway Museum Trust in August 1974. Following lengthy restoration, it would return to the main line on 11th June 1988.

On the same day, Churchward 2-6-0 No. 7325, looking in a sorry state, stands in Dai Woodham's scrapyard, Barry. Allocated to Pontypool Road when withdrawn in April 1964, she did not arrive at Barry until later in the November. A fan of Dusty Springfield had decided to make their admiration known not only on pannier tank No. 9466, but on this engine, too. The mogul would leave the scrapyard ten years later, and after lengthy restoration work many steam enthusiasts would have the pleasure of photographing her at the Severn Valley Railway (see colour section page 48) as well as on the main line.

Throughout the journey back to Birmingham I was preoccupied with images and thoughts about Barry scrapyard: the significance of seeing so many sad looking locomotives was for me a stark reminder of the apparent eagerness to rid the railway of what was regarded an out-moded form of motive power, even if it meant its replacement in part with some diesel locomotives that proved to be of dubious quality and reliability. I decided then, that no matter how many more engines made their way there, I would not go back again. The following day I visited Saltley, most probably because I wanted to see steam alive and kicking together with its attendant smells and sounds and, most importantly, in more functional surroundings. I found the shed home to 30 steam, including Oxford-based 'Hall' No. 7927 Willington Hall. A further 5 different varieties were present with Stanier '8F's (10) and 'Black 5's (9) dominating.

November

Once autumn half term had passed, it was back to seeing steam at weekends. My logbook shows four trips to Saltley, but there is a notable absence of visits to Tyseley during November, which may be due to lost jottings or undated records. Totals for engines present and classes represented for Saltley on 7th, 14th, 21st and 28th were 32/7, 39/8, 44/9, and 35/9 respectively. Interestingly, on 14th, named 'Black 5' No. 45154 Lanarkshire Yeomanry, allocated to Speke Junction, was noted together with fellow visitor 'B1' No. 61024 Addax, a Wakefield engine. On 21st there were another three visitors worthy of mention: Stanier 'Black 5' No. 45405, assigned to Nuneaton and in ex-works condition after a light intermediate overhaul completed on 10th November, 'Jinty' No. 47250 (withdrawn the previous June and last allocated to Westhouses) and Wakefield 'B1' No. 61040 Roedeer.

The young fireman of Tyseley-based 'Black 5' No. 44777, looks out from his cab to see if the cavalcade is about to start moving again from Bordesley (Camp Hill line) towards its most likely destination, Saltley MPD. The other engines making up the group are '8F' No. 48603, '9F' No. 92194 and heading the line-up '9F' No. 92137. Determined to see them again further along the line, I jumped on to my bike and set off for Brickyard crossing - see next photograph.

Cycling as quickly as I could, I managed to reach Brickyard Crossing (serving Adderley Park Brickworks) and photograph '9F' No. 92137, the lead engine of the four locos. Just visible in the background is the bridge carrying the line from New Street to Coventry. Next year the standard 2-10-0 would move from Saltley to Croes Newydd in the August and finally to Kingmoor in the December. Withdrawal would come in September 1967. Above and previous, 14th November 1965.

One of the four named 'Black 5's, No. 45154 Lanarkshire Yeomanry, rests in the yard of Saltley shed on 14th November 1965. Nearly half of the engine's working life was spent allocated to St Rollox before moving south of the border early in 1957. Transferred from Lancaster to Speke Junction earlier in March, she would remain at this depot until ceasing work at the end of November 1966.

After updating steam allocations in my locoshed book using the Locomotive Notes in the November issue of The Railway Magazine, I turned my attention to a regular feature - Locomotive Practice and Performance by O S Nock. This months article entitled 'Caledonian: Glasgow to Aberdeen', was in essence about the likely closure of the route between Stanley and Kinnaber Junction and a look at the recent performances of the Gresley's 'A4's on the three-hour expresses between Buchanan Street and Aberdeen. Writing as a railway enthusiast, Nock had this to say about the merits of a class widely revered by many hundreds of spotters:

'If the Caledonian route from Perth to Kinnaber is dying it is certainly going down in a blaze of locomotive brilliance - and with steam locomotives too! Admittedly the engines concerned are to some extent strangers; but one cannot think of any class more fitted to "see steam out" on any fast express route, than the Gresley "A4" Pacifics.'

The Railway Magazine, November 1965, Locomotive Practice and Performance, p.636.

Memories of last summer's trip to Scotland came flooding back as I read on and looked at the Tables giving details of the logs he'd received. One that couldn't be included, quite understandably, and which overshadowed all those detailed fully in the article, had also occurred of late. The focus on this engines breathtaking performance was between Perth and Forfar.

'The load was one of 251 tons tare, and the engine an anonymous "A4". Stanley was passed in 8 min. 51sec. and, after getting into speed on the generally level stretches that follow, the pace lay entirely between 82 and 89 m.p.h. right on to Kirriemuir Junction. The time over the 22.4 miles from Stanley was 15min. 42sec., and the average speed was 85.6m.p.h. This run also was made quite recently, and resulted in what I believe to be an unprecedented time of 27 min. 28 sec. start to stop from Perth to Forfar - an average speed of 71 m.p.h.'

The Railway Magazine, November 1965 Locomotive Practice and Performance, p. 638.

Whether substantiated at a later date or not, these sorts of reports made for very welcome news considering the plight of steam at the time. These superb engines were still with us as a result of the introduction of precision optical repair methods first used at Swindon, and then adopted by Darlington and Doncaster, together with a modified centre big end. The obvious question was: how much longer would they be retained for?

December

The music scene throughout the sixties was for many teenagers as important as any other interests and hobbies they might have. Dominated by a handful of groups with one particular band from Liverpool surpassing all. I recall buying three singles for £1 (6s 8p each) at the end of each month, but I was fortunate enough to be able to occasionally buy albums as well. On the morning of Friday 3rd December, I made my way as normal to the bus stop on Stratford Road, but instead of catching the bus to school, I walked a little further on and waited for Green's Record Shop to open. All being well, as I'd already ordered it the week before, the Beatles new LP, Rubber Soul, would be ready for me to collect. Once wrapped and paid for, I headed straight back home to meet up with Chris, mentioned earlier and who lived close by, to listen to the bands latest album. We played it several times and knew the title, order of each track and most of the words before we had to head off to school to arrive just in time for a late dinner and the start of the afternoon session!

The final month of the year witnessed more visits to Saltley and Tyseley MPD's. On the first of these, Sunday 12th December, the former shed had 40 steam in residence representing 9 different classes. Notable visitors were Wakefield 'WD' 2-8-0 No. 90373, York 'B1' No. 61216, Immingham 'B1' No. 61042 and withdrawn 'Jinty' No. 47338, last allocated to Crewe South. Tyseley on the same day housed 33 steam representing 11 different varieties. There were 21 ex-GWR engines present, although only two of these were in steam, No's 6951 Impney Hall and 6952 Kimberley Hall. I discovered sometime after the event that No. 6951, sporting a special headboard for the occasion, was the last steam loco to be entrusted with the 17.35 Birmingham Snow Hill to Lapworth local passenger train on 31st December.

On 19th December 1965, '8F' No. 48254 has its tender replenished with water while on Saltley shed. Despatched to Persia (Iran) in October 1941, the 2-8-0 was purchased by British Railways from the War Department in December 1949 and allocated to Crewe South. In October 1950, the '8F' became a Northwich engine and remained at the depot until it moved to Nottingham in March 1964. After briefly working out of Kirkby in Ashfield the 2-8-0 would be reallocated to Burton, its present home shed. In June 1966, the locos final move would be to Westhouses from where it would be withdrawn in August 1966.

On the same day, '8F's No's. 48359, allocated to Derby, and Stourbridge-based 48459 await their next turn of duty while on Saltley. After its transfer to Patricroft in July 1966, the latter loco would remain in service until April 1967. The star below its cabside number denotes improved wheel balancing, enabling the engine to work higher speed freight trains.

Nothing out of the ordinary was noted amongst the 34 steam recorded on my next visit to Saltley on 19th, other than the fact that exactly half of the locos present were Stanier '8F's and 'Black 5's. In all, 8 varieties of loco were noted. Five days later, on Christmas Eve, I cycled to Bromford Bridge to spend a couple of hours there to see what steam was still out and about before the system shut down for the holiday period. Nine steam were noted, and one or two photos taken before heading home.

After opening my presents on Christmas Day morning, which included, of course, both Locospotters' and Trains annuals, I checked what time we were having lunch and asked if it would be okay to be excused for a couple of hours. We would be eating at two o'clock (as we invariably did) so that we could all sit down afterwards and listen to the Queen's speech. As soon as I had been given the all clear, I was off to Saltley to see if there would be a generous number of steam on shed. With very little traffic about, I was soon making my way up the ramp leading to the back of the first roundhouse. By the time I'd noted the compliment of steam in the last of the three roundhouses I had logged thirty-eight in all and, with a further twelve recorded in the yard, the total reached exactly 50, with 10 different classes represented. Visiting engines present were ex-GWR 0-6-2 tanks No's 6656, 6679 and 6692 (all withdrawn ex-Stourbridge locos), standard 5MT No. 73155, an Eastleigh allocated engine, and Wakefield-based 'WD' 2-8-0 No. 90357.

Collett 0-6-2T No. 6656 spent a number of years allocated to St Philips Marsh after the forming of BR. In June 1959, the engine moved to Ebbw Junction and in 1962 briefly to Barry, before moving to Radyr. In July 1963 the 0-6-0 made its final move to Stourbridge from where it had been withdrawn earlier in September. Seen above in Saltley shed on Christmas Day 1965, the small white ticket at the bottom of the cab handrail provided information about its disposal - in this case, Cohen's scrapyard of Kettering.

Stanier line up in Saltley No. 3 roundhouse on Christmas Day 1965: from left to right 'Black 5's No's 45270 (the last of its class to sustain bomb damage while in Bath on 27th April 1942) and 45391, '8F' No. 48762 and 'Black 5' No. 44840. Just into shot is standard '9F' No. 92129. Only the 2-8-0 was allocated to Saltley. No. 45391 would outlive all the others depicted here and would not be withdrawn until February 1968.

Ivatt 2-6-0 No. 43052, a Crewe South engine, sits over the Hegenscheidt wheel turning lathe in Tyseley MPD on Christmas Day 1965. This was the first of its type installed by BR in 1962. It would appear that work had been completed on the driving and leading wheels before the shed closed for the holiday period, but there wasn't sufficient time to clear away the swarf. The loco would not see another Christmas in service, being withdrawn the following November.

Left: The view from the cab of withdrawn 'Grange' 4-6-0 No. 6861 Crynant Grange standing in the yard of Tyseley shed on the same day. The loco had been transferred from Oxley to Tyseley in November 1955 where she would remain for the next ten years. Disposal of the ex-GWR engines taken out of service at this time would take place reasonably quickly, with the majority removed by the middle of February. Although the 'Granges' escaped the mass withdrawals in 1962, not one member of the class would survive into preservation.

I wasn't the only person taking photos of steam engines on Christmas Day! Standing in the south yard of Tyseley MPD from nearest the camera are 0-6-2's No's. 6625 and 5658; Oxford allocated 'Modified Hall' No. 6937 Conyngham Hall; '9F' No. 92139 and nearly into the shed building 'Black 5' No.44658. The three ex-GWR engines had been withdrawn during the previous few weeks.

Tyseley next and, hopefully, another good number of steam locos taking a well-earned rest. With eight fewer engines than Saltley, there were 42 steam present representing 12 different varieties. Visitors worthy of note were Doncaster-based 'B1' No. 61121, 'WD' No. 90471, an Immingham loco, and Ivatt 2-6-0 No. 43098 allocated to Normanton. On the wheel turning lathe inside the diesel depot was sister engine No. 43052. A full list of engines recorded on both depots is given in appendix 14. With the second of the two rolls of film removed from my camera and tucked safely into my coat pocket, I climbed on to my bike and made the short journey home. Only five steam cops in total, but there was Christmas lunch to look forward to, and a gathering of the family on the evening.

My last visit to Saltley before the year's end was made on 27th December. Eleven engines had left the depot since Christmas day, leaving 8 classes of locomotive represented amongst the 39 steam present. New Year was just around the corner, and five days later on 1st January Dennis and I would be heading south from Birmingham to see some of the last steam locos working on the Western Region.

The Southern Region was beginning to feature more and more in our thoughts at this time - steam was continuing to play an important role with regard to a variety of duties that very much included express passenger work, which definitely added to the attraction of heading south. Perhaps, I thought, we might be able to do as we had done with the Scottish trip and cycle to places such as Eastleigh, Bournemouth and Weymouth to see some of Bulleid's wonderful Pacific engines still hard at work ...and, of course, visit a few sheds, too.

1965 had been an eventful, enjoyable and at times exciting year. I had seen, as I had hoped, the last few 'A4's still entrusted with express passenger duties and, in the process, had had a great adventure achieving this goal. Dennis and I had travelled far and wide without any adult supervision or assistance, and this in turn had helped us develop a sense of independence and greater self-confidence, which I don't think we were really aware of at the time.

Once again numerous steam locos had been withdrawn; totally at odds with the modern image BR was striving as quickly as possible to achieve, their removal from the everyday workings of our railway showed no signs of abating. Some of the classes that would no longer be seen once the New Year was underway included 'Castle', 'Hall', 'Modified Hall', 'Grange', 'Manor', 'Royal Scot' and 'Patriot', plus a host of less glamorous but hard-working freight varieties. Earlier in June, 'Britannia' No.70007 Coeur-de-Lion had been the first of the class to be withdrawn and, with 1966 on the horizon, only six of Gresley's 'A4's remained in service: No's 60004 William Whitelaw, 60007 Sir Nigel Gresley, 60009 Union of South Africa, 60019 Bittern, 60024 Kingfisher and 60034 Lord Faringdon.

Next year would undoubtedly see the cull continue and, if the plans that had been in place for a while now were realised, the Western Region would not permit steam workings over its metals from the beginning of January. As for the handful of 'A4's that remained in stock, Dennis and I doubted that they would see the winter timetable out. In all 1,987 steam locos had been withdrawn during the previous twelve months, leaving under 3,000 at the end of December.

With steam's continuing decimation came the inevitable increase in shed closures too. A number, of course, would become diesel maintenance depots, but many would close for good. Aberystwyth (standard gauge), Bushbury, Watford, Crewe North, Longsight, Reading, Willesden, Rugby, Northampton, Staveley (Barrow Hill), Canklow, Gorton and one of my local depots, Aston, were just a few of the sheds that had closed to steam during the year.

Such closures didn't quite always go to plan, however, and a small number of sheds would continue to service steam, some for months after their official shutting down. For these depots infiltrations would persist on a regular basis, primarily because neighbouring areas and divisions had no other form of motive power available. This meant that steam locos involved in such workings needed somewhere to lay over until the following day or indeed over a weekend. Fortunately, for me at least, Tyseley would find itself in a similar situation once it had officially closed to steam, but not primarily because of the need to meet any basic servicing or stabling requirements that unwelcome steam locos from further afield might demand.

1966 Jan - June (Goodbye to steam on the Western Region)

January

Planned during the final few days of 1965, the day had arrived to say farewell to steam on the Western Region. It was difficult to believe that a little over four years earlier that the 'Kings' and 'Castles' were still at the forefront of the motive power for this area of the network's express passenger services. By the time we were heading south from Snow Hill on the morning of Saturday 1st January to visit Oxford, Didcot and Banbury, there were only 108 ex-GWR steam locomotives still in capital stock. Within a few days the record books would be amended to list a small number of pannier tanks continuing in service on the London Midland region.

We arrived at Oxford courtesy of Brush Type '4's No's D1685 (to Banbury) and D1691, and headed immediately for the shed a few minutes walk away. We knew the depot was pretty full, as we had caught a glimpse of the yard as our train slowly entered the station.

Many of the engines present had had their fires dropped for the last time and would only move again when making their final journey (most likely hauled by a diesel) to the scrapyard. Nonetheless, we found a few locos in steam and one of them, No. 6998 Burton Agnes Hall, had been cleaned and polished and stood proudly gleaming in the winter sunshine. Built in 1949, we would discover later the following month that she had been the last GWR designed steam engine to be used on the Poole-York service on 3rd January, which was undoubtedly the reason why she was in such a well-groomed condition. A total of 56 steam were noted on shed representing 15 different varieties, including six ex-GWR classes.

Looking almost as eye-catching as it must have done when it first came out of Swindon works in January 1949, 'Modified Hall' No. 6998 Burton Agnes Hall stands next to Oxford MPD's coaling stage on 1st January 1966. Chosen to head the Western Region's last steam-hauled passenger train (save for some S & D services), the engine had been cleaned by a few dyed-in-the-wool ex-GWR shed staff who were determined to remind people one more time of the company's former glory.

With the sun highlighting its freshly cleaned paintwork, this side view of No. 6998 Burton Agnes Hall shows clearly the brackets for holding its left-hand side nameplate, by now in the hands of a collector. However, made by the shed's boilersmith, a wooden replica set would be employed when the 4-6-0 would work the Oxford - Banbury leg of the 10.25am Poole - York train on 3rd January. Purchased from BR by the Great Western Society soon after, the engine would move initially to Totnes under its own steam later in April.

Standing in the yard of Oxford MPD on 1st January 1966, having had their fires dropped almost surely for the final time, 'Modified Halls' No's. 7922 Salford Hall nearest the camera, and 6999 Capel Dewi Hall show the slightest signs of life as they slowly cool down.

A reminder of how 'Salford Hall' once looked. Seen here after her final overhaul at Swindon where she was built in 1950, the 4-6-0 was based at a number of depots, including Chester (GWR), Tyseley, Shrewsbury, Southhall and finally Oxford. Author's collection.

Beyer Peacock 'Hymek' No. D7053 entered traffic in October 1962, and is seen standing in Didcot shed yard on 1st January 1966. Continuing to be used as a signing on point, the depot had closed on 31st March the previous year. The shed building would be taken over by The Great Western Society in 1967, and the site would eventually evolve into the Didcot Railway Centre. The 'Hymek' would be withdrawn in January 1972.

Next on our itinerary was Didcot. The shed here had closed nine months earlier, but we hoped that there might be the odd steam loco being stored or stabled here. As it turned out only three diesel hydraulics were present, but once back on the station we were fortunate enough to see 'West Country' Pacific No. 34018 Axminster at the head of 'The Pines Express', quickly followed by standard 2-6-0 No. 76063, an Eastleigh engine, travelling light towards Reading.

Seen against a darkening sky, Eastleigh-based 'West Country' Pacific No. 34018 Axminster hurries through Didcot with 'The Pines Express'. Originally allocated to Exmouth Junction when new in December 1945, the 4-6-2 was transferred to Nine Elms in April 1951 and to Eastleigh in January 1964. Its final move, once more to Nine Elms, later in June this year, would see the loco usefully employed until 9th July 1967 when steam would be eliminated from the Southern Region.

The weather, although bright and sunny to begin with, had become decidedly gloomier; by the time we were back on Oxford station, the sky had lost what little patches of blue it had been trying to hold on to and had turned a uniform grey. As the clouds grew darker the accompanying heavy rain made for a very wet and miserable end to the day. However, we were determined to drop by the depot again as we knew that 'Axminster' would be on shed with, perhaps, one or two other engines that had completed their journeys and taken up residence since our visit earlier in the day.

Just as we were about to set off, first we heard and then saw in the distance a freight train gradually making its way towards us. At its head was 'Modified Hall' No. 7924 Thornycroft Hall, seemingly making hard work of the job in hand. With my notebook held above my camera in an attempt to keep the lens free of raindrops, I managed a reasonable photograph of her as she moved slowly through the station. Unfortunately, the same result could not be said of my efforts to capture 'Axminster' on film as the last of the day's light eventually gave up trying to break through the all pervading murkiness.

Heading a mixed freight, 'Modified Hall' No. 7924 Thornycroft Hall enters Oxford station on an extremely wet and blustery 1st January 1966. From May 1964 until the depot closed on 20th November 1965, the 4-6-0 worked out of Bristol Barrow Road. Its final transfer, to Oxford, happened sometime earlier the same month. Built in September 1950 at Swindon, this particular duty was most probably the engines last.

No other new arrivals were noted on shed, and once back on the station the rain continued to tumble down as we waited for the train that would take us on the first stage of our journey back to Birmingham. Nevertheless, our spirits were more than lifted when, out of the gloom, 'West Country' No. 34098 Templecombe appeared at the head of an express from Bournemouth and which she would remain in charge of as far as Banbury, our next destination. Once there, the Pacific would hand the train over to an awaiting diesel. We immediately made for the vestibule in the first carriage behind the engine, so we could savour the sounds of what would be a short but spirited run of 22 miles or so.

Representing 9 different classes, Banbury MPD contained 29 steam locos, including by this time No. 34098. Most evident were standard designs with '9F' 2-10-0's (12) dominating. Individual engines worthy of note were 'Britannia' Pacific No. 70050 Firth of Clyde, soon to be transferred to Carlisle Kingmoor, and Eastleigh-based standard 4MT 4-6-0 No. 75077. As if a further reminder were necessary of what would soon be happening to many of the engines we had seen during the day, we witnessed the depressing sight of Collett 'Hall' No. 6916 Misterton Hall in the process of being cut up.

During the last leg of our journey home, we sadly realised that we had experienced yet another significant step by BR to eliminate steam as swiftly as possible from its metals. But it would soon become apparent that the Western Region would have to wait a while longer before this form of traction would finally be purged from its territory. Numerous reports of steam workings over its metals would filter through during the following weeks and months and, because of the postponed closure of the Somerset and Dorset, steam would also carry on being usefully employed on this route. Indeed, it would continue to be used regularly on passenger trains such as the Poole-York and The Pines Express, often with Oliver Bullied's 'West Country' and 'Merchant Navy' engines in charge as far north as Oxford and Banbury.

Originating from Waterloo and named 'The Mendip Merchantman', the LCGB ran a steam tour on this day to mark the closure of the Somerset and Dorset line (planned originally for 3rd January) and which proved to be significant in two respects. To begin with it was the first time that a 'Merchant Navy' class engine (No. 35011 General Steam Navigation) had visited the S&D, weight restrictions being overlooked it would seem, and also because of the actions of a signalman at Binegar. In a statement to the crew and passengers he apologised for delaying the train, but was doing so by way of a protest against the 'vicious attitude' of British Railways in severely curtailing the passenger service over the route. I imagine he wasn't too bothered about being reprimanded or being sacked even, as he realised the future wasn't looking too bright and that he would be soon facing redundancy anyway.

Also of some significance on this New Year's Day, we later discovered, was the news that another famous class of locomotive had become extinct. The last serving 'Royal Scot', No. 46115 Scots Guardsman, after completing its final duty, had retired to Carlisle Kingmoor shed to have its grate cleared of clinker and ash. After joining a row other condemned locos, its wheels were locked with wooden sleepers, and it found itself officially withdrawn. Fortunately, the former LMS 4-6-0 would, in time, see further employment as a member of the growing ranks of preserved engines.

The traffic reports prepared by G.M. Kichenside for the monthly edition of Modern Railways were always eagerly read in the hope that at least a slow down in the relentless withdrawal of steam locos might be becoming evident; that the more modern forms of motive power were not having it all their own way. But large numbers continued to be condemned, and only occasionally was there news of steam making a fight of it, albeit fleetingly and without any sustained impact. The most uplifting reports for me were those of steam engines coming to the rescue of failed diesel or electric locos, and then making a spirited effort to claw back some of the inevitable time lost as a result of the breakdown.

Seeing the two 'West Country' Pacifics at Oxford and Didcot proved to be the catalyst for my next adventure in search of steam. My notebook reveals that soon after returning home I had referred to Dad's maps yet again, and that I had written out a proposed route which, if followed, would take me, and Dennis if he decided to come, too, to such centres as Salisbury, Weymouth, the Isle of Wight, Bournemouth, Eastleigh, Guildford and London. It would mean cycling about two thirds of the distance we had clocked up while on our Scottish Trip the previous summer. And if we were going to see steam between Shanklin and Ventnor on the I. of W., we would have to make the trip before 18th April, the date given for the withdrawal of services on this part of the line.

Following the news that the Ryde to Cowes service had ceased from 1st February, confirmation of the replacement of the island's 'O2' class 0-4-4T's by standard class 2MT 2-6-2T's had appeared in the February edition of Modern Railways magazine, but they would never reach further south than Eastleigh:

'The Southern received 10 standard Class 2 2-6-2T's from the LMR at the end of last year for use on the Isle Of Wight as a stop-gap steam replacement until the future of the Island lines is decided. However on arrival the SR found that they were not in best of condition and returned them to the LMR, where they were promptly condemned'

Modern Railways, February 1966, Traffic Report, p.119.

It was dispiriting to hear of the wiping out of yet another class of locomotive, but at the same time it would mean that the older, and for me more charismatic 'O2's, would be soldiering on for a while yet. And, most importantly, there would still be the opportunity to photograph a few of those remaining in service.

I resumed my routine visits to the local sheds at the start of the New Year, and by the end of January five trips had been made to Saltley MPD on 2nd / 9th / 16th / 23rd and 30th. Totals for engines present and number of classes represented were 42/12, 39/8, 42/8, 31/6 and 43/7 respectively. Of note on 2nd were visiting 'B1's No's 61017 Bushbuck (Ardsley) and 61058 (Immingham) together with 'Jubilee' No. 45697 Achilles (Leeds Holbeck). Mentioned previously, the three ex-GWR 0-6-0 tanks, No's 6656, 6679 and 6692, were still in residence. Ivatt 2-6-0 No. 43052 (see picture p196) had been moved from Tyseley and was now in No. 2 roundhouse. On 16th, I noted that No.3 roundhouse appeared to have been closed and was empty of locomotives. Indeed, I didn't log any engines in this the most southerly of the roundhouses again until 20th February but, unfortunately, failed to find out why this might have been.

Tyseley was visited twice during January on 2nd and 16th with totals for steam present and classes represented being 37/11 and 34/9 respectively. Amongst the visiting locos on 2nd was unnamed Banbury-based 'Britannia' Pacific No. 70047. Eighteen ex-GWR locos were noted on this day with no fewer than eight of these belonging to the 'Grange' class. It wouldn't be long, however, before most of these engines would be removed for scrap, leaving, of GWR origin, only the odd pannier tank still working out of the depot.

February

During February Dennis and I worked on the itinerary for our next cycling expedition, trying to decide whether the centres I had initially suggested could be visited in the time we had available; we also started casually mentioning the idea to our parents, reminding them, of course, how well things had gone with our trip to Scotland last summer.

By the end of the month we had managed four more visits to Saltley on 6th, 13th, 20th and 27th , with corresponding engine and class totals being 39/8, 44/8, 46/6 and 46/7. Other than the odd 'WD', the engines recorded during February mirrored the shed's allocation. Tyseley was somewhat overlooked, and I made only one trip there on 27th noting 10 different varieties amongst the 25 steam present. Two Stoke and Cockshute 'Jinties' were located in the diesel depot - No. 47273 in the yard and No. 47649 inside the shed building on the wheel turning lathe. By this date all of the 'Granges' had been removed from the shed for cutting up, leaving ex-GWR 4-6-0's No's 6951 Impney Hall and 6952 Kimberley Hall awaiting a similar fate.

Having been given the 'right away', the driver of Oxley-based 'Black 5' No. 45040 gently opens the regulator to get his mixed freight train moving. In the background is Saltley Gas Works. Like many other such plants, it was noted for its smell which, when the wind was not blowing favourably, was truly awful. February 1966.

March

By the middle of March our plans to head south to see southern steam in its 'normal' geographic area were finalised. During the last week of the month we serviced our bikes, refitted the pannier bags, borrowed one of the 'good companion' tents from school and generally got ready for another adventure in search of steam.

Eleven visits to Saltley MPD were made during the month on 6th, 7th, 12th, 13th, 19th, 20th, 21st, 22nd, 27th, 28th, and 31st. Totals for steam present and classes represented were respectively as follows: 49/9, 38/6, 47/7, 49/8, 49/7, 53/7, 39/8, 38/7, 47/7, 38/7 and 42/7. Interestingly, 'Britannia' Pacific No. 70047, although transferred from Banbury to Carlisle Kingmoor at the end of the first week of February, seemed reluctant to head north as it was noted in residence on seven different occasions. On 6th and 20th of the month, Tyseley produced totals of 21/7 and 25/9 respectively for engine and class totals. Standard 5MT No. 73137, a Patricroft engine, was the only steam loco (on 20th) waiting for attention on the WTL.

I was in possession of my brand new 35mm camera for my visit to Saltley on 31st. If judged on looks alone it would no doubt have scored top marks. Mum had ordered it the previous week out of her Grattan home shopping catalogue, and I was over the moon when I carefully loaded it with what would turn out to be the first of many films provided by my uncle, Roy Derry. However, the Halina Paulette, manufactured by Haking in Hong Kong, was not quite all what it appeared to be, as I was to find out a few weeks later.

Shadows and Steam: inside Saltley No. 3 roundhouse on 12th March 1966. Nearest the camera is ‘9F’ No. 92247, ‘8F No. 48385 centre, and shrouded in steam in the background,‘9F’ No. 92138.

Royston-based Stanier ‘8F’ No. 48337 stands alongside Saltley number 3 roundhouse on a pleasant 20th March 1966. The ‘8F’, formerly a Saltley engine from January 1948 until its transfer to Royston in November 1949, would continue working from 55D for another seventeen months before being withdrawn in September 1967.

Allocated to Tinsley (Sheffield), brand new British railways Type '2' No. D7602 stands in Saltley MPD on 20th March 1966. In the background, '9F' No. 92136 was also new when first allotted to Saltley in July 1957. Later in the year the diesel would move north and see employment in Scotland, while the 2-10-0, after a further six months of service, would cease working in October. Its disposal would take place at T.W. Wards, Beighton, Sheffield the following February.

Two years younger than the '9F' featured top, No. 92204 with double-chimney, continues to take up residence in Saltley on 20th March 1966. According to my records, she spent about three weeks here before returning across the city to Tyseley, her home shed. She would be transferred to Speke Junction later in August, and eventually face withdrawal in December 1967.

Stanier 4-6-0 No. 45264, an Oxley engine, rests in the yard of Saltley depot on Sunday 20th March 1966. Twelve months later the engine would be transferred to Crewe South (together with ten other 'Black 5's from Shrewsbury and Oxley on their closure) and would remain working from 5B until withdrawal in September 1967.

First allocated new to Saltley on 5th November 1957, Standard '9F' No. 92155 rests in the yard of the said depot on 20th March 1966. Five months later, it would find itself working out of Speke Junction from where it would be withdrawn, many years before its time, in November 1966.

Brush Type '4' No D1863 stands next to Saltley coaling stage on 31st March 1966. Built at the Falcon works and allocated to Tinsley MPD, the engine entered service in May 1965. It would sport several liveries during its lifetime, but is seen here in its original two-tone green colours. After forty-years service, withdrawal would eventually come in May 2005.

April

Early on Saturday 2nd April our quest to see Southern steam began. It was a cold and miserable morning when we set off, with the threat of heavy rain looking likely to become a reality at any moment. Our route would take us along the A34 through Stratford-upon-Avon, Shipston-on-Stour, and Woodstock and on into the centre of Oxford. Three months had passed since we witnessed the end of steam here, and we thought it might be interesting to see if any of the locos recorded on 1st January were still to be found in store at the shed.

The depot did indeed have a number of locos in store, and the atmosphere and mood of the place reflected the fact that steam had been driven out and replaced by diesels. It was now void of all the smells, sounds and noises normally associated with a busy working steam shed. Standing triumphant, but lacking any character, the few diesel locos present only served to emphasise their achievement, and the sight was a thoroughly sad and depressing one. The remaining steam engines, their services now long dispensed with, sat huddled together awaiting their final fateful journey. Out of a total of 26 present, representing 5 different classes, 23 were ex-GWR locomotives. The other three locos were standard 4-6-0's No's 73003 and 73166 and 'WD' No. 90258, which it would seem, had got caught up in the net of mass withdrawals that occurred at the beginning of the year. Last allocated to Langwith (41J), she would never return to her Eastern Region home. Only one or two photographs were taken - the atmosphere was so disheartening it reminded me of my visit to Barry, although ironically not one of the engines present would find their way to that particular South Wales scrapyard.

Rather than continuing by bike, we decided to catch the train to Swindon via Didcot. This would enable us to spend some time on Didcot Station, visit Swindon Works and shed, and still have sufficient time to get a reasonable distance across Salisbury plain before nightfall. Steam was still penetrating the Western Region at this time, with Gloucester in particular seeing fairly frequent visits mainly by Stanier 4-6-0's and 2-8-0's. Steam passenger turns across its territory persisted on the Poole-York service, too, and we hoped that we would see this train while at Didcot. Unfortunately, another steam-hauled intruder, the 'Pines Express', had recently become a diesel turn but, interestingly, four days earlier, on 29th March, 'A4' 60024 Kingfisher had been pencilled in for the northbound run to help facilitate its eventual return to the Scottish Region after powering enthusiasts' specials the previous week-end. However, the loco developed a minor defect causing a change of plan, and it departed for home light engine.

By the time we alighted our train, the ever-present dark, intimidating clouds had given up holding their moisture and decided to release it all while we spent the next hour or so on Didcot Station. Undaunted, we made notes of the various diesel movements while waiting for the passing of the northbound Poole-York, which we expected to be steam-hauled. Sure enough, out of the gloom and persistent rain, we saw in the distance the heartening sight of 'Black 5' No. 45493 looking in really good shape after being out shopped from Crewe Works only five days earlier after a heavy casual overhaul. I reeled off three photos as she glided through the station, but none of them were any better than disappointing. It transpired that this particular loco, together with sister engine No. 44942, would dominate the rostering for this service well into May. A few minutes later we were on our way to Swindon, with No. D1025 Western Guardsman in charge of our train.

Later the same day while visiting Swindon Works, we discovered pannier tank No. 8497 looking rather inglorious as a stationary boiler. With a somewhat modified wheel arrangement and Heath-Robinson look about it, the 0-6-0, completed in November 1952, had been officially withdrawn in July 1964.

Swindon was steamless by now, except for two 0-6-0 pannier tanks No's 8466 and 8497 (both previously allocated to Radyr MPD), which had been given the demeaning duty of steam heating part of the Works. They were members of the '94xx' class designed by Hawksworth numbering 210 in all. Introduced in 1947, and not completed well into BR days in 1956, they would be the last class built to a GWR design. I suppose on a faintly positive note, one could say that these two engines were at least seeing out what remained of their very short lives helping to heat arguably the finest locomotive works in the country and, of course, the one from which they had originated. Quite what Hawksworth would have thought if he had seen them in such a state and employed in such a fashion is another matter.

As we walked back to our bikes we were brightened by the prospect of knowing that most of the steam we would see from now on would be playing a more active and purposeful role than the two pannier tanks we had left behind. So, with a sense of anticipation and expectancy, we left the outskirts of Swindon and started on the next leg of our journey towards Salisbury. All being well, tomorrow morning would see us visiting the first of a number of Southern Region sheds included in our programme. Our high spirits and optimism, however, were soon to be tempered somewhat by events about to unfold and over which we would have no control.

Just as we reached the A361 to Devizes, the weather determined it had produced enough drizzle and rain for one day, and that it was now time to send the temperature on a downward spiral. And, as if that wasn't unpleasant enough, just for good measure it decided that the wind needed to be increased in proportion with the plummeting temperature, too. By the time we had reached Devizes, it was bitterly cold and the odd snowflake had started to appear. Not surprisingly, our progress was becoming more laboured, and we were beginning to wonder how much longer we could keep going.

We were now on the A360 and, soon after leaving the small village of West Lavington, we found ourselves in a blizzard with the snow readily sticking to the tarmac. After another mile or so, we knew that we were not likely to get much further and certainly not across the plain. It was clear, too, that we would need to take shelter pretty quickly. The next village was about fifteen minutes away, so we decided to press on in the hope that it would offer shelter for the night - pitching our tent and sleeping under canvas was not going to be an option.

We found ourselves in Tilshead as darkness enveloped the small village. Ahead of us, its bright and welcoming lights penetrating the gloom and acting like spotlights on the falling snow, we saw a pub - the Black Horse. We hadn't budgeted for bed and breakfast, so what we were hoping for I can't really say. Perhaps we thought we could at least take refuge for a while to see if the weather improved and if so, try, reluctantly, to find somewhere to camp. Fortunately, the landlord was a friendly and welcoming fellow and offered us 'accommodation' in one of his outbuildings. It adjoined the pub and was divided into two areas, one for the sheep and the other for storing hay. It was in this hostelry that I had my first ever pint of beer, and its effects meant that, once into my sleeping bag under a few layers of hay, I was instantly fast asleep.

Sunday 3rd April

The temperature had climbed back above freezing during the night, and although the morning didn't dawn exactly bright and sunny, at least the snow had disappeared as quickly as it had arrived. The landlord must have taken pity on us and provided us with a breakfast of bacon, sausage and eggs, which set us up for the next stage of our journey. So, as we left Tilshead with eighteen miles to go to reach Salisbury MPD, we were in far better spirits than we had been the night before. With enthusiasm rekindled, we were once again eager to see some Southern steam.

We were not disappointed with the shed's offering of 17 locos representing 6 different classes. Unsurprisingly, nearly all ex-SR locos were either 'Battle of Britain' or 'West Country' Pacifics. However, amongst these we also found a very clean and well-polished 'Q1' 0-6-0, No. 33006. Contrary to being officially withdrawn in January, she was very much still extant and would later in the day, together with 'U' class 2-6-0 No. 31639, double-head a Locomotive Club of Great Britain steam special from Salisbury to Waterloo. After taking a few photographs, we called in briefly at the station and noted standard 4MT No. 75069 before heading off to Dorchester, about 40miles further south.

Officially listed as withdrawn in January 1966, Bullied class 'Q1' No. 33006 is clearly still very much alive and kicking. Standing in Salisbury MPD on 3rd April 1966, the 0-6-0 has been groomed ready for an LCGB rail tour later in the day.

We made good progress, and after a little over two hours, including a rest stop, we reached Blandford Forum where we decided to have a bite to eat. The weather had warmed up a little, but the sky had remained a uniform, lifeless grey. The next 16 miles were covered uneventfully in about an hour and a half, and while looking in at Dorchester Station we couldn't resist the temptation to revert to steam haulage for the last leg of our journey to Weymouth. 'West Country' Pacific No. 34024 Tamar Valley headed our train it, too, on the final part of its journey with the 1.30pm ex-Waterloo.

Even though it was only for about eight miles, it was good to be behind steam again. After passing Weymouth MPD with a number of its locos visible in the yard, we arrived at the station with the pleasant sight of two engines ready to depart with the 5.50pm to Waterloo. As soon as our train came to a halt, we retrieved our bikes from the guards van, hurried to the end of the platform so we could log the engines involved and then watch at close quarters their impending departure. With safety valves lifted on both locos, we found standard 4MT No. 76010 piloting 'Battle of Britain' No. 34071 601 Squadron. The pair were duly photographed in the dull and dreary conditions and, after noting a further three steam locos in the station, we were back on our bikes heading for the shed.

'Battle of Britain' class 4-6-2 No. 34071 601 Squadron, in filthy condition, stands in Weymouth station together with pilot engine standard 4MT 4-6-0 No. 76010 shrouded in steam. They were about to depart with a train for Waterloo on a cool, wet and miserable 3rd April 1966.

Originally belonging to the GWR, Weymouth became a Southern Region depot from February 1958. It would turn out to be the last ex-GWR shed with a steam allocation, and would also be one of the last seven active steam depots on the Southern Region. Now with an allotment of 21 steam, we weren't surprised to find only 13 present, representing a small variety of 5 different classes as follows: 'Battle of Britain' (1), 'West Country' (3), 'Merchant Navy' (5), Ivatt 2-6-2T (2) and standard 5MT 4-6-0 (2). With nameplates still intact, 'Merchant Navy' No. 35028 Clan Line, looked in ex-works condition, although it would be a further four months before she would visit Eastleigh Works for a light casual overhaul. After leaving the shed, we set off for the docks. Dennis provided the entertainment for the evening as we approached the quayside when, suddenly, he found that his front wheel, rather than turning the way he wanted it to go, followed the rail track embedded in the road, resulting in a rather spectacular parting from his bike which, as can be imagined, I was most concerned and sympathetic about!

Monday 4th April

A few weeks before our trip south, Mum had contacted her aunt who ran a boarding house in Weymouth and arranged for us to stay the night. A postcard sent home the next day describes how good both the meals and accommodation had been. Following a challenging full English breakfast, and with many a thank you before leaving, we were soon bunking the shed once more to see if any new residents had turned up overnight. We discovered three new occupants: No's 34057 Biggin Hill, 41301 and 73110 The Red Knight. Several locos had been found work, and we logged a revised total of 10 steam representing the same variety of classes as the night before. After taking a number of photographs, including several of Clan Line, we climbed back on to our bikes and set off for Wareham about twenty miles away.

Previously allocated to Bricklayer's Arms, Brighton and Guildford, Ivatt 2-6-2T No. 41301 is seen in Weymouth, its last home shed, on 4th April 1966. Five months later the tank would be removed from capital stock.

About two hours later, we crossed the old London and South Western route near Worgret Junction where the line to Corfe Castle and Swanage branches off. We didn't witness any trains when we briefly stopped here, but knew that while spending sometime on Wareham Station we would see steam both on the mainline and at least one working to or from Swanage. Indeed, as we approached the station, we could see an engine sitting in the bay platform ready to depart. Standard class 4MT 2-6-4T No. 80138 was passively waiting for the all clear to begin its eleven-mile journey along the branch line to the seaside town of Swanage.

A number of further steam turns were logged, including the arrival from Swanage of Ivatt 2-6-2T No. 41316, 'West Country' Pacific No. 34018 Axminster with a semi-fast for Waterloo, and standard 5MT No. 73088 Joyous Gard with a local for Bournemouth. Once again we couldn't resist the opportunity to be hauled by steam again - this time to Bournemouth behind 'Merchant Navy' No. 35013 Blue Funnel. During the short journey, I decided to have a quick wash and brush up. In no time at all Dennis was knocking on the toilet door to tell me we were coming into Central station. In the rush to get back to the guards van I left my watch behind, a Mu Du automatic wind, which I had been told was state-of-the-art at the time. I didn't mention it for quite a while after arriving home; it had been my Christmas present from Mum and Dad!

Built at Brighton works in June 1956 and first allocated to Neasden, standard 2-6-4T No. 80138 is ready to depart from Wareham to Swanage on 4th April 1966. After ten years service, the engine would be withdrawn in October while allocated to Bournemouth MPD.

Two 'West Country' Pacifics and an Ivatt 2-6-2T were noted in Bournemouth Station prior to making the short walk to the shed via the yard at the side of the up platform. We logged 6 different classes of loco amongst the 25 steam on shed, with standard 4MT 2-6-0's and 2-6-4 tanks being most evident. Only six ex-SR steam were noted - 'West Country' Pacific's No's. 34002 Salisbury, 34026 Yes Tor, 34037 Clovelly, 34040 Crewkerne, 34047 Callington and 'Merchant Navy' No. 35027 Port Line.

Back on the station we watched the trains come and go while we had sandwiches and pop for lunch. A further seven steam were noted: ex-SR 'West Country's' No's. 34036 Westward Ho, 34093 Saunton and 34104 Bere Alston, unrebuilt 'Battle of Britain' No. 34057 Biggin Hill, two standard class 2-6-0's No's 76016 and 76064 and standard class 4-6-0 No. 73117 Vivien. After witnessing Biggin Hill leave with her train for Waterloo, we too departed the station and started off on the next stage of our journey. The relatively short ride of eighteen miles took us through Boscombe and Christchurch and on into Lymington where we would camp overnight. Early the following morning we would call in at the station, and then head to the ferry, which would take us over to the Isle of Wight.

Front ends: 'West Country' Pacifics No's. 34026 Yes Tor and 34037 Clovelly and standard 2-6-0 No. 76033 simmer on Bournemouth shed on 4th April 1966. Withdrawn in September 1966 and July 1967 respectively, the two Bullied engines would complete over 1.7 million miles between them while in service. Built at Doncaster in December 1953, the much younger 2-6-0 would be withdrawn in February 1967.

Previously carrying Rough Tor nameplates for two weeks in April 1948, 'West Country' Pacific No. 34025 Whimple stands on the turntable of Bournemouth MPD on 4th April 1966. Withdrawal for this engine would come at the end of Southern steam, on 9th July 1967.

Above. Not appearing quite as bewitching as her name from Arthurian legend might suggest, standard 5MT No. 73117 Vivien, looking grimy and unkempt is all but ready to leave Bournemouth with a semi-fast for Waterloo on 4th April 1966. Originally allocated to Nine Elms when new, the 4-6-0 would spend time based at Reading, Eastleigh and, finally from October, Guildford, from where she would be withdrawn six months later in March 1967.

Bournemouth Central, Monday 4th April 1966. Standing in the down platform is 'West Country' No. 34036 Westward Ho and standard 4MT No. 76064. Entering the station from the shed is Ivatt 2-6-2T No. 41295 which would be withdrawn in May the following year. The other two locos would continue working until 9th July 1967.

The chain hanging alongside the tender of 'Battle of Britain' No. 34057 Biggin Hill reveals that water is being taken prior to departure from Bournemouth Central for Waterloo on 4th April 1966. Fifteen years earlier, the engine was allocated to Stratford to take the place of one of three 'Britannia's' sent to the Southern Region for evaluation. After clocking up over 939,000 miles, the unrebuilt Pacific would be withdrawn on 7th May 1967.

Tuesday 5th April

Having broken camp, we made our way to Lymington Pier station and noted newly arrived standard 2-6-4T No. 80146 allocated to Bournemouth. Once across the relatively narrow expanse of the Solent, we landed at Yarmouth harbour after a journey lasting about 50minutes. We then cycled the eighteen miles across the island via Newport to Ryde where we spotted our first working 'O2' with a train for Ventnor. With No. 24 Calbourne in charge, we caught the next available train to Ryde St John's Road. Both Ryde shed and Works were adjacent to the station, and we were looking forward to bunking both, hopefully without too much difficulty.

After briefly speaking to two friendly enginemen, we strolled round the depot while the weather continued to pick up; the day was developing into the warmest since leaving home. Eight class 'O2' 0-4-4T's were noted on shed: No's. 14 Fishbourne, 16 Ventnor, 21 Sandown, 26 Whitwell, 27 Merstone, 29 Alverstone, 33 Bembridge, and No. 35 Freshwater. The Works, also visited without any problems, had a further 5 'O2's present, No's. 17 Seaview, 18 Ningwood, 22 Brading, 28 Ashey, and being cut up No. 30 Shorwell, which had been withdrawn the previous September.

Except for the photograph of ex-London tube stock, the following eight pictures were taken on Tuesday, 5th April 1966.

Adams class '02' 0-4-4T No.20 Shanklin is seen standing in Ryde St Johns Road station.

There were fourteen 02's still in capital stock at the time of our visit to the island. Here, looking very presentable, is No. 35 Freshwater resting in the yard of Ryde MPD. All of the engines had had their nameplates removed by this time, presumably either to be sold or for safekeeping. In the background is No. 33 Bembridge.

The sun started to appear while making our way round the depot, which allowed the opportunity to take a couple of pictures inside the shed building in slightly brighter conditions. The three engines seen here are No. 14 Fishbourne, No. 22 Sandown and nearest the camera No. 27 Merstone.

Above left. Another view of No. 35 Freshwater standing in Ryde shed with its Westinghouse brake equipment clearly visible and, right, No. 27 Merstone sitting above the inspection pit inside the depot. All of the engines' names related to different places on the island.

We rounded off the day spending time on Ryde St. John's Road station taking the opportunity to photograph one or two more of the tank engines, including No. 24 Calbourne with a parcels train. The picture was repeated again by Dennis 37 years later, well at least in terms of where I had been standing all those years earlier. Somehow the 'new' motive power in his photograph, for me, doesn't seem to compliment its surroundings, even though there has been some modernisation of the station since 1966. Having said that, my old monochrome picture could possibly be dated years before it was taken - time seemed to have passed the railway by in many respects, even though as early as 1909 an engineer in his report had had the foresight to suggest the complete electrification of the islands railways!

Wednesday 6th April

After a wet and miserable night under canvas, the following morning dawned cool and overcast. Even so, we were looking forward to the day ahead, not least because we had decided to take the opportunity, while we could, to ride behind steam from Ryde Esplanade to Ventnor. We didn't know if we would visit the island again, and anyway we wanted to travel over the full length of the line before the planned closure of the route south of Shanklin became a reality.

Our train was hauled by No. 35 Freshwater, which I had photographed on shed the day before. I took one photograph of the loco en-route at Wroxall, the last station before plunging into Ventnor tunnel, and it readily shows what a miserable day it was. Once at Ventnor, we climbed up to the vantage point above the station used by many photographers over the years. From here I took a picture of 'O2' No. 31 Chale arriving with its train from Ryde, with the chalk cliff caves once used by coal merchants visible in the background.

‘O2’ No. 24 Calbourne with a parcels train, waits for the bags to be attended to so that it can get on its way from St Johns Road station. The 0-4-4T would have the dubious honour of hauling the driving trailer of unit No. 037 of London Transport stock for clearance checks later in the year on 4th September.

Thirty-seven years later and the 0-4-4 tanks have long gone, their duties now in the hands of London Underground stock as seen in the photograph above taken on 1st February 2003. Interestingly, the station still retains some of its 1960’s facets including the fixtures for the telegraph wires at the gable end of the roof above the train! D.M. Perfect.

Concluding the photographs taken on 5th April, class 'O2' No. 31 Chale is seen waiting to leave Ryde St Johns with a passenger train for Ryde Esplanade. Together with No. 24 Calbourne, this engine would be retained to work engineers' trains until March 1967.

My last photograph of steam on the island (see overleaf) was taken at the start of our journey back to Ryde Esplanade and shows No.31 Chale leaving Ventnor Station at the head of our train. The IOW once boasted six different railway companies, their route mileage adding up to a little over 55 miles, but in the matter of a few days a mere 8 1/2 miles would remain. By the end of December the 'O2's normal workings would come to an end. One or two would be kept in service for engineers' trains and, No. 24 Calbourne, would be preserved and based at Haven Street. I would visit the Island again in the summer of 1969 to see, amongst many others, Bob Dylan at the music festival. But by then steam would have been well and truly consigned to the history books. The island's remaining fragment of line from Ryde to Shanklin would have been electrified for over two years and have 'tube' trains serving the route - something I don't think anyone would have predicted at the start of the 1960's.

From Ryde Esplanade we cycled the short journey to East Cowes to catch the ferry to Southampton. We left the harbour shortly before sunset, and as we cruised up Southampton Water, the liner Queen Mary came into view resting in her berth. As soon as we were off the ferry, we headed for Eastleigh, or so was our intention. By the time we reached the outskirts of Southampton it was dark and, without realising it, we took the A33 rather than the A335; instead of reaching Eastleigh we had by-passed it, and in due course found ourselves on the fringes of Winchester! This resulted in a swiftly adopted new plan - camp close to where we were and travel the seven miles back to our intended destination by train in the morning!

On a cool and misty 6th April, class 'O2' No. 35 Freshwater has been given the 'right away' and is about to leave Wroxall with its train from Ryde Esplanade to Ventnor. Ahead, through the gloom, lies Ventnor tunnel immediately at the end of which lies the engines destination.

Our return to Ryde Esplanade was courtesy of No. 31 Chale, seen here leaving Ventnor station and preparing to head into the tunnel under St Boniface Down. 6th April 1966.

Thursday 7th April

The beginning of the day started much the same as the previous one had ended - cold and wet. After a hot mug of tea and cornflakes for breakfast, we broke camp and cycled the short distance to Winchester station. Undaunted by the progressively worsening weather, we logged seven steam before catching an emu to Eastleigh: No's 34024 Tamar Valley, 34025 Whimple, 34056 Croydon, 35028 Clan Line, 41299, 73110 The Red Knight and 76053. We were looking forward to bunking both the shed, a short cycle ride from Eastleigh station, and with luck the Works, too.

Twelve months earlier Eastleigh MPD had had an allocation of a 103 steam, but this had been virtually halved by the time of our visit. However, still with a compliment of 55, we thought that the shed would be host to the most steam of any of the depots we would visit during the trip. After successfully negotiating our way round, we had recorded 14 different classes amongst 28 steam logged. Two of the engines noted, class'M7' No. 30053 and 'Schools' class 4-4-0 No. 30926 Repton, had been preserved and were destined, initially, for The Montreal Exhibition, before transfer to the Steamtown Foundation in Vermont, Virginia. The latter would be out shopped from Eastleigh Works on 28th February 1967, and would sail to Montreal on SS Roonah Head from Gladstone Dock, Liverpool in April 1967. Twenty years later she would be repatriated, arriving at the North Yorkshire Moors Railway on 11th April 1987 to be restored to working order (see colour picture of engine on Stewarts Lane shed, page 40).

'Black 5' No. 45418, a Banbury engine, withdrawn at the end of February was noted as in store and still awaiting disposal. We also saw our first 'USA' 0-6-0T's. These engines, while new to us, had been working in the area since being purchased by the old Southern Railway in 1946. With a total of 14 in the class, all of them had originally been employed on shunting duties in Southampton Docks. Altogether close to 400 had been built mainly for the war effort in Europe.

USA 0-6-0T No. DS 233 (formerly No. 30061) rests inside Eastleigh shed on 7th April 1966. On the side of the tank at the front is written Engineers Dept. This particular departmental loco worked regularly at the Redbridge Sleeper Works.

We failed in our attempt to get round the Works and noted the only two steam visible in the yard: USA Tank No. 30064 and ex-GWR 2-8-0 No. 2818 ready to be restored for preservation. Once back on Eastleigh station we recorded three steam movements, including 'Merchant Navy' No. 35013 Blue Funnel which, with nameplates still intact, came flying through at the head of a Waterloo bound express. We didn't stay here for long - it was still a thoroughly unpleasant day - time instead to make a start for our next destination, Guildford, a cycle ride of about 42 miles.

Friday 8th April

The morning of our seventh day away began marginally better than the preceding one. Our journey to the outskirts of Guildford had not been pleasant, but we had slept well and were once again looking forward to the day ahead.

Including the last few survivors of Maunsells' 'N' and 'U' class 2-6-0's, Guildford shed had 21 steam as part of its allocation of motive power. The 20 engines noted during our visit produced no fewer than 10 different classes of steam. The varieties represented being: 'Battle of Britain', 'West Country', 'N', 'U', Ivatt 2-6-0T, standard classes 5MT 4-6-0, 4MT 2-6-0, 3MT 2-6-0, 4MT 2-6-4T, and USA 0-6-0T in the form of No. 30072, which would survive acting as shed pilot until the end of Southern steam. Leaving the depot, we set our sights on cycling along the A3 to London, calling in at Nine Elms Shed before reaching our final destination, Lower Edmonton, where Dennis had arranged for us to stay with his uncle.

Above clockwise: 'U' class 2-6-0 No. 31639, 'N' class 2-6-0 No. 31411 and USA 0-6-0T No. 30072 in Guildford MPD on Friday 8th April 1966. The two 2-6-0's would be withdrawn over the next few weeks during June and April respectively, while the tank would last until steam finished on 9th July the following year.

We reached the depot by mid-afternoon - a journey time of about four and half hours with a couple of stops along the way. As we cycled down Brooklands Road towards the shed entrance, we wondered if we would make our way into and round the depot without bumping into the foreman or indeed anyone else who might think we should be elsewhere. Well, although busy with enginemen and fitters, no one seemed to pay us much attention, and after about 30mins we had listed all the locos present.

Nine Elms was now much depleted in terms of allocated steam power. Two years earlier it had had a total of 70 such locos, including 32 Bullied Pacifics. The present figure stood at 23, with only four engines originally belonging to the Southern Railway. Our visit on this occasion produced a total of 28 steam representing 7 different classes. Standard designs made up over half of this total with the remainder surprisingly all ex-SR engines. Q1 No. 33006, noted earlier in the week at Salisbury, was found inside the shed building still looking very presentable.

Cycling along the increasingly busy streets towards the centre of London, we were relieved to reach Liverpool Street after crossing the Thames via London Bridge and approaching the station along Bishopsgate. We hadn't experienced as much traffic before, and for the first time I didn't feel quite so self-assured and confident while on such hectic roads. Nevertheless, we reached the station safely, and once on the train heading north we were both looking forward to a good meal and a bath. We would be staying in London for the next three nights, giving us time to spend one day spotting at several main stations and one visiting a few of the many sheds the city had to offer.

Saturday 9th April

Following a good night's sleep and a hearty breakfast, we set off as planned to do nothing more than relax and watch the trains at a number of termini. We visited nine mainline stations at various times during the day, with steam noted at just two, Marylebone and Waterloo. At the end of the ex-Great Central station we found Stanier 'Black 5' No. 44984 taking on water. The engine provided a good example of how the reorganisation of BR was affecting its MPD's. Her Eastern Region home shed, Colwick, had been transferred at the beginning of the year to the Nottingham Division of the LMR and had been given the shed code 16B, formerly designated to Annesley, which had closed at the same time.

Waterloo station: on 9th April 1966 two enthusiasts deep in conversation, appear to be uninterested in 'Warship' No. D829 Magpie standing behind them. By now these particular diesels were familiar sights on Waterloo to Exeter services.

Seen alongside the same platform a little later is 'Merchant Navy' No. 35030 Elder Dempster Lines in charge of a Bournemouth train. Built in 1949, she would cover some 850,000 miles before withdrawal on 9th July 1967.

Waterloo produced a total of five steam while we were there: 'Merchant Navy' class No's 35010 Blue Star, 35013 Blue Funnel and 35030 Elder Dempster Lines, and standard 3MT 2-6-2T's No's. 82019 and 82029. Western Region 'Warship' class diesels had, of course, been partly responsible for displacing Bullied's Pacifics on services to Salisbury and other destinations west of Exeter and two of the class - No's. D820 Grenville and D829 Magpie - were also noted.

Before arriving back at Dennis's uncles, we had already decided which sheds we would visit the following day. We were determined to make the most of our time in London, and Sunday was always the best day of the week to see the maximum number of locos on shed. We reckoned we could manage seven depots if all went to plan: Stratford, Finsbury Park, Hornsey, Old Oak Common, Willesden, Nine Elms and Stewarts Lane. Unfortunately, by now, only Nine Elms was still a working steam depot.

Sunday 10th April

Not thinking we would see any steam locos until we reached Nine Elms, it came as quite a surprise to find one of the many buildings comprising Stratford Works full of stored steam engines awaiting possible preservation. Although the doors were locked, we managed to climb in through a window and were rewarded with a close-up view of the following locos: No's. 1008, 120, 6000 King George V, 30245, 30587, 30777 Sir Lamiel, 30850 Lord Nelson, 30925 Cheltenham, 33001, 42500, 49395, 61194, 63460, 63601 and National Coal Board 0-6-2T No. 67 (formerly No. 28 of the Taff Vale Railway). Nine Elms, contrary to our expectations, had fewer steam on shed than it had two days earlier. We found 7 varieties represented amongst the 25 locos noted, with standard class engines accounting for almost half of those present.

We had our second surprise of the day after dinner. Whether we had displayed an apparent lack of enthusiasm for the final part of our journey back to Birmingham I'm not sure, but Dennis's Uncle said he would treat us to our tickets for the train home. We thanked him and politely said we couldn't possibly accept his generous offer, but he would have none of it and, without too much persuading from what I remember, we very gratefully accepted his proposal.

Three of the fifteen locos found in store at Stratford on Sunday 10th April 1966, from left to right: ex-LSWR class 0298 Beattie Well tank No. 30587, ex-LSWR class M7 0-4-4T No. 30245 and ex- LNWR class G2 0-8-0 No. 49395.

Transformation of two of the engines seen in Stratford works on 10th April 1966: following a very involved and costly restoration, ex-LNER 'Super D' No. 49395 is seen in the colour section (page 48) shortly after leaving Bridgnorth with a train for Kidderminster on the SVR during the Gala weekend in September 2006 and, pictured above, standing in Doncaster Works on 26th July 2003, GCR class '04' 2-8-0 No. 63601 looking just as resplendent as the 0-8-0.

Looking far from how she would have done in March 1950 when new out of Eastleigh Works, unrebuilt 'West Country' No. 34102 is seen in a filthy state in Nine Elms shed on Sunday 10th April 1966. Her mechanical condition must have been a lot better than her appearance and, following a light casual overhaul later in May/June she would continue working until 9th July 1967.

Monday 11th April

Having thanked our host profusely, we caught the train into Liverpool Street Station and cycled somewhat cautiously the short distance to Paddington. No steam to be seen here regularly anymore, only the sight and smell of fumes from a triumphant array of now well-established diesels. Our train to Birmingham, the 11.10am Cambrian Coast Express, arrived at Snow Hill on time after the two-hour journey and, rather than set off for home, we decided to take a slight detour to see what Saltley shed had to offer! Well, on this occasion just the normal assortment of engines one would expect to find on 2E, with 7 classes featured amongst the 46 steam locos present, half of which comprised Stanier's '8F's (20) and 'Black 5's (3). One visitor worthy of mention, however, was Doncaster allocated 'WD' No. 90369, simply because her trip to Birmingham could well have been her last duty as she was withdrawn a few days later.

Excluding our visit to Saltley MPD, we had logged a total of 203 steam representing 37 different designs. Ex-SR locos totalled 82, ex-GWR 28, ex-LMS 17 and ex-LNER 3 together with 73 BR standard engines. NCB 0-6-2T No. 67 was taken into GWR stock in 1922 and withdrawn about four years later, so she is included in the twenty-eight under this company's heading. Following active duty with the Longmoor Military Railway and the NCB she would be restored to working order and find employment with the Dean Forest Railway. Total steam cops for the trip, 113. See appendix 15 for steam recorded on shed/Works.

Impatience got the better of me as soon as I arrived home. I couldn't wait to see how well my new camera had performed so, not waiting till dark, I got under the bedclothes and loaded the developing tank with the first film, which had been exposed for the most part during my visit to Saltley on 31st March. Once fixed and washed, I opened the tank expecting the best results I had achieved since I had started photographing steam. As I slowly unwound the film from the spool my heart sank; it soon became apparent that a number of my pictures had either been over or under exposed. The next film, the first of those taken during the Southern trip, fared no better, and I quickly realised that the remainder would most likely follow the same pattern.

Further disappointment would come, however, after the drying stage when, under closer inspection, I could see lots of scratch marks along the whole length of the film. Unfortunately, the rest of my films displayed similar problems both in terms of inconsistent exposure and much scratching of the emulsion. Many years later I found out more about the camera: produced cheaply, its outward appearance disguised the fact that inside it was made of poorly finished and dubious quality components - hence the scratching of the films. The built in lightmeter, which I expected to help achieve acceptable exposures, had been positively reviewed. Mine, however, proved to be the exception to the rule and failed miserably to produce consistently accurate readings.

Mum and Dad sensed my frustration and how dreadfully disappointed I was with the results. So, after checking the film cassettes and then the inside of the camera to see if the problem was possibly of my own making and agreeing it wasn't, it was duly returned together with a letter of complaint to the catalogue company Mum had ordered it from. The few negatives that had turned out reasonably well would not become positives for a while, my plan remained the same as for my medium format results - to capture as many pictures as possible and leave the printing until such time I could afford it. Little did I realise that it would be some forty years later when I would carry out this final part of the process, only to be reminded once more of my displeasure and frustration with a camera I had naively expected so much from.

'9F's No's. 92135 and 92139 and '8F' No. 48375 at rest in Saltley MPD No. 3 roundhouse on 24th April 1966. The two 2-10-0's were new when they arrived at the depot in the summer of 1957, and would both be reallocated twice before being withdrawn in June and September 1967 respectively. The 2-8-0 would also experience two further transfers, to Stoke later in November and Rose Grove in August 1967. Two months after becoming a 10F engine she would be withdrawn.

On 24th April 1966, Armstrong, Whitworth-built Stanier 'Black 5' No. 45287 stands in the North yard of Tyseley, its home shed, together with Banbury allocated '9F' No. 92004. The 4-6-0 would move on to Shrewsbury, Edge Hill, Patricroft and finally Rose Grove before being withdrawn when steam finished on BR.

The remainder of April was spent visiting a variety of familiar line side locations and local sheds. I managed six visits to Saltley on 11th, 21st, 23rd, 24th, 26th, and 30th. Totals for steam locos present and classes represented on these days were 46/7, 41/6, 42/6, 39/5, 42/5 and 59/7 respectively. Two visitors of note were class 'B1' 4-6-0 No. 61224, a Wakefield engine, on 23rd and on 30th Fairburn 2-6-2T No. 42069, allocated to Trafford Park. Four trips were made to Tyseley on 15th, 24th, 25th, and 26th with corresponding totals of 18/5, 28/8, 23/9 and 21/10. Class 'B1' No. 61012 Puku, a Hull Dairycoates loco, was noted during the last three consecutive visits. The only ex-GWR engines present were the odd one or two 0-6-0PT's and 2-6-2T No. 4176, now being used as a stationary boiler.

Named after an antelope found in Zambia and the Congo, 'B1' 4-6-0 No. 61012 Puku, a Hull Dairycoates loco, has taken up residence in Tyseley MPD after working a freight into the area from the North Eastern Region a few days earlier. 26th April 1966.

On the same day, 26th April, standard 4MT No. 76040, a Saltley engine, and Tyseley '9F' No. 92087 appear to be much alive, but the source of the cloud of steam is from a '9F' standing out of shot to the left of the 2-6-0. The former engine would be transferred to Croes Newydd later in September and withdrawn in April 1967. The 2-10-0 would become a Carnforth loco in November, from where it would be withdrawn in February 1967.

May

'O' level exams were fast approaching and, as much as I would like to say they had my undivided attention, I have to confess that they didn't. Dennis's ability to concentrate and stay focussed seemed far better than mine. At the beginning of the month I was thinking more about planning further trips, especially to Crewe, and the need to decide on a dates so the necessary Works permit could be applied for, than studying and revision. News from Scotland was filtering through at this time, too, and, contrary to our expectations, it seemed distinctly possible that a handful of 'A4's' would continue to be employed on express passenger duties for a while yet. Although I realised these reports were a further distraction from my studies, I couldn't help thinking about travelling north of the border once again to see the few that remained for what would undoubtedly be the very last time.

At the beginning of May, I contacted The Railway Society of Scotland and requested a copy of its booklet Steam Locomotives in Scotland, which had been published the previous month. At the same time Dennis sent off for the Society's other publication, which listed all remaining steam passenger turns. My pamphlet revealed that, at the end of February, there were still 338 steam engines extant north of the border. They were allocated to a total of 20 depots and represented 17 different classes. Realistically, the earliest we would be able to head north would be at the beginning of July, knowing full well of course that the statistics would have changed significantly by then and certainly not for the better. In fact, by the end of the year only 150 or so steam locos were expected to remain in stock. As for passenger turns for such motive power, there were about 100 listed as at 18th April, but with well over a half of these operating between Glasgow to Gourock and return. Nevertheless, with two regular diagrams for the 'A4's' remaining, there was a faint chance that we might travel behind one of the five still in service.

In spite of the need to focus on examinations, plans for a return to Scotland gathered pace during May. However, the 'bash' this time would be less physically demanding. Travel would be exclusively by train, with a seven-day rail-rover ticket providing us with the opportunity to cover all remaining steam areas north of the border. We were saving our pocket money and, with a little extra help from our parents, would be able to purchase a Freedom of Scotland, Silver Ticket. I still have mine (No. 5969), and as it says on the front, it provided a week of 'unlimited second-class travel at a cost of £6. 10. 0. valid between all stations on BR in the Scottish Region also Berwick and Carlisle and stations Berwick to Kelso via Coldstream'.

Camping would be one way of economically securing a roof over our heads at night, so once again we arranged to borrow one of the school's 'good companion' tents. Together with the camping gaz, plates, cutlery etc. and our clothes, cameras and notebooks we would have heavy rucksacks to lug around! While we were quite happy to pitch the tent almost anywhere to get a nights sleep, we planned a few overnight train journeys so we could get forty winks in the comfort of a compartment. If we were lucky we might even have the bonus of being hauled by steam.

Visiting Saltley, it might be argued, constituted a good deal of my misspent youth, and if further evidence was needed the nine trips I made there on 1st, 8th, 9th, 14th, 15th, 20th, 28th, 30th and 31st May would go some way to proving the point. Interesting visitors on 1st and 20th were Trafford Park allocated Fairburn 2-6-4T No. 42069, present on both days, and 'WD' No. 90645, a Royston loco, noted on 20th. There was an abundance of Stanier engines on 30th numbering 32 in all, constituting well over half of the 57 steam logged. Engine and class totals for these visits were 59/7, 56/5, 41/5, 50/5, 48/5, 48/7, 54/6, 57/5 and 50/6 respectively. Two trips were made to Tyseley on 20th and 28th May with similar totals for steam noted being 23/7 and 23/6 respectively. At Bromford Bridge on 28th I recorded amongst the more familiar engines York-based 'K1' No. 62012 and, during a further visit there on 31st, witnessed a total of 28 movements, with a quarter being steam-hauled freights.

My replacement Halina Paulette arrived on Friday 27th May, and this time I looked at the camera rather differently. It certainly appeared to be the B's and E's, yet I was not confident that it would perform any better than the previous one. Nevertheless, the following day I took photographs while at Bromford Bridge and during visits to Saltley and Tyseley sheds. Once again the results left a lot to be desired. Although the film didn't appear to be scratched like the previous ones, I was still not happy about the exposure or indeed the sharpness of a number of the negatives.

After checking with Dennis that he would be interested in an official visit to Crewe Works again, I wrote a letter on 30th May requesting permission to join one of the tours scheduled for the following month. The reply (see page 241) on behalf of Mr J.J.C. Barker-Wyatt, the Works Manager, informed me that we had been granted authorisation to visit the Works on Sunday 19th June at 12.30pm. The trip would provide a welcome change from spotting locally and, more importantly, would most likely present the last opportunity for us to see steam being overhauled here.

Bromford Bridge on a sunny 28th May 1966.

With the unmistakable outline of the Fort Dunlop factory in the background, York-based 'K1' No. 62012 heads north light engine. The Peppercorn 2-6-0 would move to Sunderland in April 1967, only to be withdrawn the next month.

Stanier '8F' No. 48710 trundles through the station with a mixed freight train, probably bound for Washwood Heath or Lawley Street sidings. Allocated to Royston, the 2-8-0 would remain working out of this depot until September 1967 when it would be deemed surplus to requirements.

Named after England's highest peak, the first of the 'Peaks', No. D1 Scafell Pike is seen at the head of an empty set of coal wagons, with its driver fully determined to be included in the shot! After 17 years of service withdrawal would come on 30th October 1976.

On the closure of Bescot shed on 28th March, several of its '8F's were transferred to Saltley including No. 48556, seen above standing in the yard on 28th May 1966. The gas works can be seen in the background and to the right the shed's stores and offices. Following a year based at Saltley, the 2-8-0 would see out its days allocated to Lostock Hall and finally Rose Grove from where it would be withdrawn in August 1967.

Striped in sunlight and shadow, '9F' No. 92151, a Saltley engine from new in October 1957, stands next to the lifting gear in No. 3 shed on 28th May 1966. Keeping the 2-10-0 company is 'Black 5' No. 45392, recently transferred from Colwick to Heaton Mersey. The former engine would become a Birkenhead loco later in November and would be withdrawn the following April, while the 4-6-0 would continue working for a month longer until 4th May 1967.

The sun continued to shine after leaving Bromford Bridge as can be seen in the photos taken while visiting Saltley - previous, above and below. Its roundhouses and most of the engines inside were streaked in sunlight. The ‘8F’ (above) has a wisp of steam coming from its safety valves and its identity, No. 48646, is clearly highlighted, as is the sign ‘Beware of the Engine’ on the wall on the left of the picture. The ‘Black 5’ seen below, a Newton Heath loco, was also in steam, but its number 45411 is not quite so easily made out. The 4-6-0 would remain in service until her home shed closed on 1st July 1968. The ‘8F’ would eventually become a Lostock Hall engine and it, too, would cease work at about the same time as the ‘Black 5’.

An hour or so after recording the engines on Saltley, I was wandering around Tyseley shed and noting down its compliment of locos. The top photograph shows three engines in the north yard: 'Black 5's No's. 44663 and 45134 and, sandwiched between them, '9F' No. 92001. Somehow the sunlight was still being reflected off the dirt, grime and grease plastered all over the double chimney 2-10-0 so, despite 'Villa' and not 'Blues' being chalked on the left smoke deflector, and although externally not particularly photogenic, I thought it merited another picture as the sun started to set. Interestingly, 'Black 5' No. 44663, with its smokebox door handles missing and cab window broken, seems to suggest that it has been withdrawn but, contrary to appearances, the engine would not be condemned until May 1968.

June

We left Snow Hill for Crewe on Sunday 19th June, initially behind the powerful combination of two English Electric Type '4's, just as we had done twelve months previously when starting out on the same trip. This time, No's D373 and D229 Saxonia were in charge, and they hauled the train via Wednesbury and Bushbury as far as Stafford. Here, for the remainder of the journey, they handed over the reins to electric traction in the form of BR class AL5 No. E3072.

Following a brief visit to Crewe North diesel stabling point, we made the short walk to the Works entrance in Mill Street and joined the queue for the afternoon tour. A total of 8 different varieties amongst the 34 steam present were logged, with the following four engines having been overhauled and repainted ready for running in: Stanier 'Black 5's No's 45001 and 45466, Stanier '8F' No. 48773 and standard '9F' No. 92017. Standard '8P' No.71000 Duke of Gloucester, minus its chimney, was still in storage some three and a half years after its withdrawal, and seemingly no closer to being preserved. Also present was Midland '4F' 0-6-0 No. 44525, which had been transferred from Gorton and assigned to the Works at the end of December 1964. She would be the last of her class to be withdrawn. The number of steam engines coming into the Works for overhaul was now down to a trickle; its focus had shifted and was now firmly fixed on the building and maintenance of diesel and electric locomotives.

Built by the Vulcan Foundry, Newton-le-Willows, Warrington, 'Black 5' No. 45041 is seen undergoing an overhaul in Crewe Works during our visit on 19th June 1966. By the time the engine was back in traffic, it had barely eighteen months of its working life left before withdrawal in December 1967. The frame performance of the 'Black 5's was nothing to write home about and welding, patching and even new sections were often necessary while in works. Indeed, it was the practice at Crewe to have a reconditioned set of frames ready for an engine requiring them, so that repairs would not be impeded.

Also in Crewe Works on the same day was 'Black 5' No. 45243 allocated to Crewe South. Built by Armstrong, Whitworth, it entered traffic in September 1936, and would be made redundant exactly thirty-one years later - only fourteen months after being overhauled. By the mid to late 1950's, the 842 4-6-0's were averaging 167,000 miles between general repairs.

The finished article: on 19th June 1966, both Stanier '8F' No. 48773, following its last 'Heavy Intermediate' repair, and standard '9F' No. 92017, following its last 'Light Casual' repair, look resplendent after their journey through Crewe Works. The fate of the 2-8-0 has already been mentioned; as for the 2-10-0, she would be withdrawn on the closure of her home shed, Carlisle Kingmoor, at the end of December 1967.

British Railways Workshops

Locomotive Works
Crewe
Cheshire
Crewe 55123 Ext.2323

J.J.C.Barker-Wyatt,A.M.I.Mech.E.
Works Manager

8th June, 1966.

y/r
o/r I XXXXX C302-1-3

Dear Sir,

VISITS TO CREWE LOCOMOTIVE WORKS.

With reference to your letter of the 30th May, I have pleasure in granting you permission to visit Crewe Works on **Sunday** the **19th June, 1966.** at **12.30pm.**

(I regret that this is the only date available from those you required)

This permission is granted subject to the conditions that the British Railways Board will not be responsible for the death or injury of any person exercising this permission whilst on the Board's premises, nor for any loss or damage to the property of any such person however such as death, injury, loss or damages may be caused, and whether or not by the act neglect or default of the British Railways Board their servants or agents.

Photographs may be taken on the Works Yard only on the understanding that they are for private collections only, and may not be published without permission.

Yours faithfully,
H. E. Lewsley (mrs)
for J.J.C. Barker-Wyatt.

B.R. 9200/29

Chief Mechanical & Electrical Engineer
A. E. ROBSON, M.B.E., M.I.Mech.E.
Works Manager
E. R. BROWN, M.I.Mech.E.
Telephone
CREWE 55123
Ext. 2323.
Our Reference L/48a.
Your Reference

BRITISH TRANSPORT COMMISSION

Chief Mech. & Elec. Engineer's Dept.
Locomotive Works
Manager's Office
London Midland Region
British Railways
Crewe

Dear Sir,

Thank you for your letter, I regret it is not possible to arrange your visit to Crewe Works on the date suggested.

Please note it is NOT the practice to arrange Friday or Saturday tours.

Sunday tours are fully booked until :

In future will you kindly enclose stamped and addressed envelope for reply.

Yours faithfully,

for J. C. SPARK.

P.S.
I return your postal order herewith.

Top. Two replies concerning requests to visit Crewe works. The one on the left relates to the visit presently being reported on. Received some years earlier after forgetting to enclose an sae with my request to visit the works, the second letter is included purely to highlight the change in appearance of such correspondence. Unfortunately, it is not dated, but seems to reflect a far higher standard of care in its presentation.
Above. 'Jinty' No. 47615, previously allotted to South shed, didn't have too far to travel when re-allocated to Crewe Works in December 1963. Left amongst discarded machinery, old boilers and other odds and ends, and appearing ready to be cut up, official withdrawal would not take place until three months after this picture was taken on 19th June 1966.

From the Works we made the 25min walk to Crewe South and found 85 steam on shed with a good diversity of classes totalling 13 in all. There had not been a great deal of change compared with the number of engines noted on 30th May the previous year when 94 steam were noted, also representing a total of 13 different varieties.

Well before reaching Snow Hill, I had checked all locos seen against those marked in my Combined Volume, and found it was necessary to underline 14 steam cops. During another enjoyable day out, a total of 124 steam representing 15 different classes had been logged. My Halina Paulette had been put to good use again, and I had taken over 70 pictures, but with every click of the shutter I was wondering how good the quality of the negatives would be. Within a couple of hours of returning home I had found out: once again the results were mixed to say the least - something I would have to put up with while having to continue to use this camera.

Built at Darlington Works in November 1954, standard 2MT No. 78036 is seen in her home depot, Crewe South, on 19th June 1966. Used on one of the legs of the RCTS 'St George' Railtour on 23rd April, the engine still looks reasonably clean two months later. Transferred from its first shed, Preston (used mainly for station pilot duties and local freight turns), to Lostock Hall in September 1961, it was reallocated to Skipton before becoming a Crewe engine. Its final move, to Shrewsbury, would take place during the second week in November 1966, but its usefulness would be short-lived. It would be condemned the following month after the introduction of BR Type '2' diesels on duties such as those to Nantmawr quarries near Oswestry, which the 2-6-0 had been rostered for.

Top. Stanier 'Black 5' No 45430 is seen standing in the yard of Crewe South on 19th June 1966. The 4-6-0 was an Aston engine for several years before being transferred to Shrewsbury in October 1965. She would remain allocated to 6D until official withdrawal on 1st October 1966. Above. On the same day, sister engine No. 44761 has the driver's full attention while he sees to its lubrication. A Crewe loco for a number of years, the 4-6-0 would be transferred initially to Springs Branch in June 1967 and, for the last time, to Lostock Hall the following December. Withdrawal from service would come in April 1968.

Chester-based 'Black 5' No. 45031 and diesel shunter No. D3800 stand in the yard of Crewe South shed on 19th June 1966. The Stanier 4-6-0 would move to Speke Junction MPD in March 1967, only to be withdrawn four months later. In the background, on the main line, is an unidentified Ivatt 4MT 2-6-0.

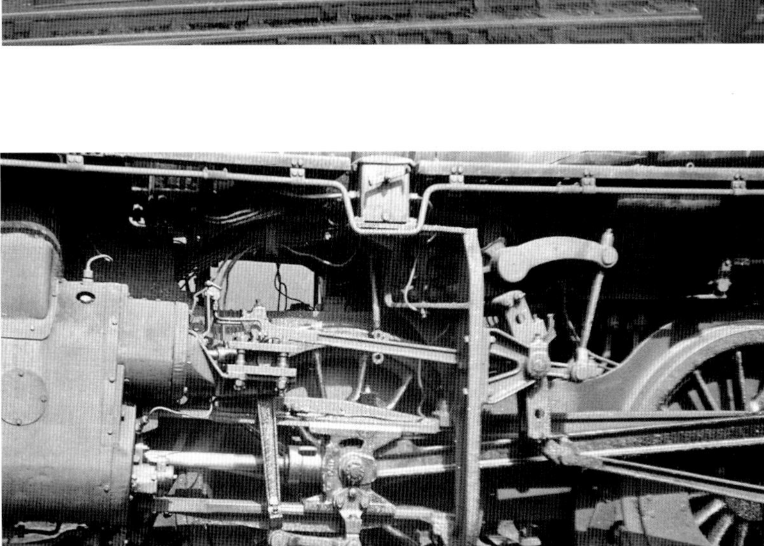

On shed the same day, with the bright sunshine highlighting its working parts, I decided to photograph the motion and valve gear of Ivatt 2-6-0 No. 43151. This engine would continue in service for a further seven months before being withdrawn in February 1967.

When new in October 1951, 'Britannia' No. 70024 Vulcan was allocated to the ex-GWR shed Laira (Plymouth). Seen here in its present home shed, Crewe South, also on 19th June, the Pacific would move eventually to Carlisle Kingmoor, from where it would be withdrawn in December 1967.

Above. While walking back to Crewe from South shed we came across Stanier '8F' No. 48646 in the sidings just south of the station. Being a Saltley engine, the loco was a familiar sight (see previous picture page 237) and would continue to be so until its transfer to Lostock Hall shed in February 1967. It would remain in capital stock until its withdrawal in July 1968.

Below. Resting between shunting duties in Crewe station on 19th June 1966 is 0-6-0T No. 47397. A Crewe South engine, its working life was fast coming to an end and it would be taken out of service about three months after this picture was taken.

Above. Another ill-fated class of diesel: known to spotters and others as 'Metrovicks' the Metropolitan-Vickers Type '2' locos had Crossley two stroke engines, which proved unreliable from the start. Rather than re-engine the whole class, BR decided they would all have to go. No. D5702, seen in Crewe North stabling point on 19th June, would be withdrawn in August 1968. By September 1969 the whole class would have suffered a similar fate.

Right. The new order of things at Crewe station: one spotter watches the departure of an electric-hauled express, while the one nearest the camera carefully underlines his latest cop. 19th June 1966.

By the end of June, I had completed my 'O' level exams and visited Saltley eight times on 4th, 7th, 12th, 14th, 16th, 22nd, 25th and 27th. Totals for steam present and classes represented were 52/6, 40/7, 34/6, 42/6, 37/7, 39/7, 42/5 and 39/5 respectively. On the afternoon of Tuesday 7th, York allocated 'B1' No. 61021 Reitbok was on shed, and a week later on 14th 'Black 5' No. 45322, allocated to Stoke & Cockshute, was receiving attention in the yard after being derailed, but with no visible damage to the engine. Two trips were made to Tyseley on 2nd and 11th with corresponding totals of 14/6 and 27/8 for engines and classes noted. During the latter visit standard 5MT No. 73131, allocated to Patricroft, was waiting outside the diesel depot ready to have its wheels reprofiled.

Top. On 22nd June 1966 'Black 5' No. 44944, allocated to Crewe South, rests in Saltley No. 3 roundhouse. Built at Horwich Works, the engine entered traffic in January 1946 and its final transfer, from Chester to 5B, had taken place earlier in April. The 4-6-0 would be withdrawn in September, three months after this picture was taken.
Above. Standing in front of the original Midland Railway office block of Saltley MPD on the same day is Ivatt 2-6-0 No. 46443. Later in October, the 2MT would be transferred from Saltley to Newton Heath. Although removal from capital stock would take place in March 1967, the engine would have the good fortune to be preserved.

In Part Two of The Final Few Years of British Steam, my recollections and records of journeys, trips and expeditions in search for steam continues and covers the last two years of the determined, unwavering effort by British Railways to rid itself as quickly as possible of the last locomotives representing this form of motive power.

Glossary of Terms /Abbreviations.

1. ATC Automatic Train Control.
2. BSA Birmingham Small Arms.
3. Bunk or Bunking. Entering a railway shed, works or such buildings without permission.
4. Cabbed. Climbing up on to the footplate of an engine.
5. Cop. Recording an engine for the first time.
6. CLC Cheshire Lines Committee.
7. CW Crewe Works.
8. dmu Diesel Multiple Unit.
9. EE English Electric.
10. ER, WR, SR and MR. Post Nationalisation abbreviations for Eastern, Western, Southern and Midland Regions.
11. emu Electric Multiple Unit.
12. GSWR Glasgow and South Western Railway.
13. GWR Great Western Railway.
14. LCGB Locomotive Club of Great Britain.
15. LMR London Midland Railway.
16. LMSR London Midland & Scottish Railway.
17. LNWR London North Western Railway.
18. LNER London North Eastern Railway.
19. LSWR London & South Western Railway.
20. L&Y Lancashire & Yorkshire Railway.
21. MR Midland Railway.
22. MPD Motive Power Depot (also referred to as a shed or depot).
23. NBL North British Locomotive Company.
24. NCB National Coal Board.
25. NRM National Railway Museum.
26. NYMR North Yorkshire Moors Railway.
27. On shed. The locos actually recorded while visiting a particular shed.
28. RCTS Railway Correspondence and Travel Society.
29. RTC Railway Touring Company.
30. SLS Stephenson Locomotive Society.
31. SRPS Scottish Railway Preservation Society.
32. SR Southern Railway.
33. S&D Somerset and Dorset or SDJR Somerset and Dorset Joint Railway.
34. WD War Department.
35. WTL Wheel Turning Lathe.

Relevant Shed Codes (as at August 1958)

1A Willesden
1B Camden
1C Watford

2B Nuneaton

5A Crewe North
5B Crewe South

6A Chester (Midland)
6C Birkenhead
6E Chester (West)

8A Edge Hill
8C Speke Junction

9A Longsight (Manchester)
9E Trafford Park
9G Gorton

12A Carlisle (Kingmoor)
12B Carlisle (Upperby)
12E Barrow

14A Cricklewood

16A Nottingham

17A Derby
17B Burton

21A Saltley
21B Bournville
21D Aston
21E Monument Lane

26A Newton Heath
26F Patricroft

30A Stratford

34B Hornsey
34G Finsbury Park

36A Doncaster

50A York

70A Nine Elms

73A Stewarts Lane

81A Old Oak Common

82A Bristol (Bath Road)
82B St. Philips Marsh
82E Bristol (Barrow Road)
82F Bath (Green Park)
Highbridge

83C Exeter *

84A Wolverhampton (Stafford Road)
84B Oxley
84E Tyseley

85B Gloucester (Horton Road)
85C Gloucester (Barnwood)
85D Bromsgrove

86A Newport (Ebbw Junction)
86B Newport (Pill)
86G Pontypool Road

87A Neath
87D Swansea East Dock

88A Cardiff (Canton)

89A Shrewsbury

* Closed by time of visit.

Relevant Shed Codes (as at October 1963)

2A Tyseley
2B Oxley
2C Stourbridge
2D Banbury
2E Saltley
2F Bescot
2H Monument Lane
2J Aston
2K Bushbury
2L Leamington Spa

5E Nuneaton

6D Shrewsbury
6E Oswestry

8B Warrington (Dallam)
8C Speke Junction
8F Springs Branch (Wigan)
8H Birkenhead

10A Carnforth
10J Lancaster
14A Cricklewood East
14B Cricklewood West

16C Derby
16E Kirkby in Ashfield
16F Burton
16J Rowsley

55A Leeds (Holbeck)
55B Stourton
55H Leeds (Neville Hill)

56A Wakefield
56C Copley Hill

62A Thornton
62B Dundee
62C Dunfermline

63A Perth

64A St Margarets(Edinburgh)
64B Haymarket
64C Dalry Road
64F Bathgate
64G Hawick

65A Eastfield (Glasgow)
65B St Rollox
65J Sterling

66A Polmadie (Glasgow)
66B Motherwell
66E Carstairs
66F Beattock

67A Corkerhill (Glasgow)

70C Guildford
70D Eastleigh
70E Salisbury
70F Bournemouth
70G Weymouth
70H Ryde

75D Stewarts Lane

81E Didcot
81F Oxford

82C Swindon

83A Newton Abbot
83D Exmouth junction

84A Laira (Plymouth)

85A Worcester

86C Hereford

88B Radyr (Cardiff)
88C Barry

Note: a number of depots have been omitted from this list, e.g. Crewe North, as their code remained unaltered.

Appendix 1

Small Heath (Golden Hillock Road Bridge) / Tyseley MPD 8th August 1959

3673 3792 3840 4111 4140 4153 4155 4172 5101 4903 4907 4912
4914 4930 4932 4942 4974 4978 4979 4983 4990 5005 5008 5012
5058 5089 5096 5308 5331 5350 5911 5926 5930 5957 5964 5988
5993 6006 6008 6009 6024 6026 6029 6129 6314 6325 6348 6375
6819 6820 6822 6834 6836 6851 6853 6904 6938 6961 6967 6968
6971 6984 7015 7031 7424 7903 7910 7912 7927 8108 8468 8700
8713 44450 45199 48415 73013 92053 92240 92244

Appendix 2

'The Button Factory' 30th August 1959

1000 3664 4104 4155 4648 4902 4946 4990 5018 5063 5070 5332
5658 5909 5977 6003 6017 6022 6311 6374 6821 6851 6971 7024
8415 8700 8713 8737 9735 9753 42267 42794 42896 42925 43122 43738
44774 44818 44845 44856 44897 44931 45013 45015 45189 45401 45325 45591
45620 45651 45674 45681 45682 45690 45704 45742 46123 46409 49126 70050
73010 73013 73022 73025 73155 75021 92152

Appendix 3

Tamworth April 1960

40108 40164 42061 42761 42799 42810 42824 42870 43043 43047 43092 43248
43482 43510 43583 43668 43680 43799 43938 43963 43991 44077 44112 44130
44296 44002 44439 44839 44841 44851 44875 44890 44920 44968 45058 45111
45124 45149 45184 45186 45189 45240 45253 45305 45351 45416 45504 45512
45519 45550 45559 45580 45626 45656 45662 45663 45668 45676 45679 45726
46106 46108 46116 46138 46146 46156 46170 46204 46221 46232 46233 46242
46244 46245 46248 46250 46258 46422 48002 48005 48053 48124 48131 48193
48287 48312 48319 48392 48398 48435 48510 48563 48601 48662 48667 70049
72002 73138 75009 90391 92014 92093 92118 92135 92151 92155 92167 92218
D6 D213 D214 D215 D217 D223 D226 D227 D228 D229 D231 D234
D255 D268 D8004 D8008

Appendix 4

Derby Works Open Day 27th August 1960

En-route to Derby from Birmingham New Street

42421 42759 42890 43012 43046 43673 43709 43762 44534 44537 44591 44810 44950
44963 45058 45059 45092 45416 45690 47643 48169 48182 48267 48272 48364 48405
48683 48706 48748 48756 61010 61248

Derby Works and Motive Power Depot

80 118 158A 1000 40003 41123 41152 41528 42054 42066 42067 42146 42161 42181 42229 42288 42316 42332 42346 42384 42390 42395 42486 42514 42541 42582 42587 43013 43174 43200 43323 43359 43360 43373 43394 43435 43459 43548 43658 43679 43778 43844 43985 44037 44049 44051 44214 44225 44235 44289 44334 44344 44456 44465 44466 44591 44597 44666 44667 44756 44806 44817 44825 44851 44854 44888 45268 45348 45416 45506 45552 45598 45610 45618 45619 45626 45627 45649 45654 45660 45685 45693 46443 46489 46497 46499 46502 47000 47006 47203 47236 47284 47331 47441 47458 47516 47533 47583 47630 47638 47660 47661 48104 48124 48152 48156 48157 48220 48225 48293 48342 48356 48381 48390 48454 48694 58144 61348 61388 70042 71000 73050 73063 73065 73066 73135 73156 73167 75055 76030 90683 92114 92139

En-route from Derby to Birmingham New Street

43122 43242 43521 43563 43668 44663 44941 44945 45625 48194 48687 90719

Appendix 5

Aston MPD 30th August 1961

42552 42945 42957 42966 42974 44110 44448 44876 45058 45237 45322 45344 45448 45647 46134 46427 48718 48719 48752 70017 70024 70027 70031 70043

Saltley MPD 30th August 1961

3821 42419 42823 42903 43012 43017 43041 43435 43599 43668 43680 44137 44179 44185 44517 44571 44659 44759 44780 44791 44810 44839 44859 44919 44944 44945 44962 44981 45268 45269 45272 45532 45569 45643 45649 46122 46132 46137 46157 48183 48220 48339 92004 92055 92131 92139 92151 92155 92165 92231 D79 D80 D90 D119 D123 12066

Appendix 6 Crewe Trip 21st April 1962 (Steam recorded)

4916 5965 6827 40165 40543 41212 41229 42079 42105 42438 42678 42776 42934 42937 42962 42964 43047 43681 43955 44110 44450 44593 44679 44681 44684 44687 44762 44834 44872 45000 45002 45035 45048 45058 45089 45110 45143 45149 45189 45231 45243 45250 45257 45276 45278 45297 45317 45325 45344 45380 45413 45421 45426 45429 45445 45446 45494 45531 45534 45560 45567 45572 45584 45587 45603 45634 45644 45643 45648 45672 45673 45689 45736 45740 45742 46127 46132 46136 46137 46165 46170 46207 46228 46231 46235 46240 46241 46250 46254 46256 47213 47384 47400 47445 47450 47469 47542 47549 47588 47590 47596 47606 48054 48205 48252 48305 48348 48365 48400 48468 48478 48505 48514 48697 48728 48735 48738 48752 49414 49452 70004 70033 70043 70047 71000 73025 73070 73073 78030 84004 90655 92096

Appendix 7 Doncaster Trip (From Manchester) 11th June 1962

32545 42088 44695 44985 45594 48136 60005 60008 60009 60012 60014 60016
60021 60024 60025 60026 60028 60031 60032 60034 60036 60042 60054 60065
60082 60083 60100 60110 60113 60114 60116 60117 60118 60119 60121 60122
60134 60139 60140 60148 60152 60156 60158 60512 60515 60528 60532 60533
60537 60800 60817 60852 60871 60880 60903 60909 60921 60936 60943 61001
61003 61004 61050 61053 61055 61057 61097 61109 61115 61118 61119 61124
61127 61137 61139 61157 61170 61193 61209 61214 61234 61247 61250 61274
61279 61365 61387 61392 61446 61942 61974 62004 62026 62034 62053 62055
62069 63593 63613 63618 63663 63698 63711 63746 63786 63848 63858 63863
68961 68971 68972 68976 68989 70002 70011 70036 70053 73016 73095 73168
76033 78022 90011 90042 90063 90144 90185 90296 90340 90425 90476 90480
90500 90501 90559 90578 90636 92173 92201

Appendix 8 Bristol Trip 17th April 1963

1661 2217 2232 2251 2277 2291 2891 3606 3623 3632 3677 3696
3702 3725 3758 3832 3844 4102 4131 4613 4619 4664 4680 4970
4991 5085 5930 5934 5975 6146 6147 6148 6312 6769 6903 6963
6965 6981 7002 7034 7338 7900 8102 8401 8402 8403 8404 8405
8409 8415 8431 8795 9404 9410 9601 9729 41207 41208 41245 41248
41249 42421 42622 43949 44102 44209 44218 44223 44264 44269 44523 44534
44569 44583 44659 44963 45006 45076 45268 45280 45561 45617 45624 45656
45675 45676 45682 45685 45690 47557 48110 48431 53807 73015 73019 73028
73031 73042 73068 73093 75001 75072 78009 82003 82007 82009 82035 82037
82038 82039 82040 90433 90506 92007 92008 92070 92077 92137 92222 92243
92248

Appendix 9 London Trip 28th September 1963

Willesden MPD

41239 42080 42222 42234 42431 42478 42562 42573 42577 42581 42606 42611
44678 44772 45000 45093 45142 45272 45410 45434 45495 45529 45620 45623
45664 45735 45736 46101 46114 46156 46222 46225 46230 46235 46239 46254
47307 47501 48018 48036 48171 48279 48416 48518 48531 48600 48624 48628
48632 48649 70001 70004 70010 70012 70018 70024 70031 70032 70034 70043
73013 73014 75014 76047 78019 78038 78039 78043 78060

Old Oak Common MPD

1010 1504 1507 2836 2879 3646 3750 4089 4098 4609 4638 4701
4703 4704 4920 5001 5041 5057 5060 5065 5070 5076 5093 5098
5919 5958 6005 6010 6124 6135 6141 6142 6930 6952 6978 6986
6998 7003 7009 7013 7014 7015 7017 7019 7020 7021 7029 7032
7035 7036 7037 7904 7921 7928 8420 8436 8756 8757 8759 8763
8768 9419 9420 9423 9455 9463 9659 9700 9704 9707 9755 9784
92241

Cricklewood West MPD

42070 42086 42092 42954 44690 44984 45197 45234 45334 45342 45346 45417
47202 47432 47434 48107 48163 48306 48332 76035 76036 76037 76039 76041
76042 76089 92127

Stewarts Lane MPD

30534 30537 30540 30928 31305 31542 31822 31893 31894 31896 32337 32340
32343 32347 34090 82023

Nine Elms MPD

120 4672 30035 30249 30320 30585 30902 31613 31617 31621 31624 31634
31796 33001 33004 33040 34001 34007 34009 34019 34028 34031 34037 34048
34056 34060 34077 34078 34082 34085 34089 34095 35012 35020 35024 35026
35030 73041 73065 73081 73082 73086 73087 73110 73119 75077 80148 82010
82014 82016 82017 82018 82022

Appendix 10

Shrewsbury MPD 8th February 1964

3709 3782 3843 4647 5932 5942 5991 6810 6819 6907 6916 6922
6931 6934 6942 6945 6987 7012 7800 9657 41202 41207 42488 44814
45143 45145 45283 45363 45422 45429 45577 46525 48269 48305 48354 48369
48404 48463 48470 48524 48730 48739 48768 73025 73034 73036 73090 73095
80069 80100

Oswestry MPD 8th February 1964

1438 1638 3208 3749 5421 6907 7033 7426 7434 7820 7822 45190
46510 46512 46513 46514 46515 46516 46518 48436 73036 80097 80104 80131
82031 84004

Appendix 11 South West Holiday August 1964

Plymouth 3rd August

1363 34023 41230 41308

Exeter St Davids station 5th August

4692 4694 31845 31859

Exeter MPD 5th August

2214 3205 31812 31854 34075

Exmouth Jnct. MPD 5th August

3746 4610 4655 31837 31849 31855 31856 31859 31875 34014 34015 34017
34033 34054 34057 34058 34059 34062 34066 34070 34076 34078 34080 34082
34083 34084 34086 41295 41317 41322 41323 73161 76008 80036 80038 80064
82030 82035 82039

Exeter Central Station 5th August

3759 4610 4692 4694 31802 34013 34030 34059 35019 35028 41206 41284
82040

Exeter St Davids station 5th August

34107

Appendix 12 Scotland Trip 10th - 23rd July 1965

Burton MPD 10th July

44688 44825 44932 44941 44989 45180 45224 45253 45464 48052 48117 48194
48266 48367 48528 48621 48651 48672 48690 47250 47313 47464 47643 61313
70022 90024 90032 90129 90220 90295 90384 90474 90572 92088 92211

Derby MPD 10th July

44839 44861 45267 48064 48141 48153 48191 48282 48317 48731 45574 90078

Wakefield MPD 11th July

42108 42150 42161 42181 42406 42650 45739 48257 48323 48363 61022 61024
61161 61309 61320 61353 61040 90047 90061 90068 90074 90076 90089 90112
90113 90116 90123 90124 90135 90155 90160 90183 90200 90210 90233 90281
90300 90321 90333 90336 90339 90341 90348 90360 90361 90370 90373 90382
90385 90396 90407 90429 90470 90415 90482 90563 90587 90610 90611 90631
90639 90651 90654 90678 90679 90684 90698 90707 90723

Neville Hill MPD 11th July

42184 42196 42689 43075 60118 60134 60154 60876 63417 63420 63426

York MPD 12th July

42204 43097 43126 44945 48381 48758 60121 60124 60138 60145 60146 60152
60155 60810 60828 60831 60847 60876 60886 60895 60929 60963 61021 61049
61055 61176 61275 61276 61299 62005 62010 62049 62065 65823 65846 65894
70010 90045 90217 90223 90280 92005 92006 92035 92231 92239

Darlington MPD 13th July

42085 42213 42477 43030 43099 43102 43128 43129 45286 48100 48272 48294
48312 48387 48430 48649 60010 60124 60806 60884 60885 61216 62003 62041
62043 62045 63368 63391 65859 68010 68011 68023 68029 68037 68043 68044
68047 68053 68055 68062 90014 90059 90412 90434 90452 90493

Hawick MPD 15th July

76049 78049

St. Margarets MPD 15th July

42128 42691 46462 60027 60041 60052 60813 60816 60824 60844 60846 60931
60970 61039 61134 61191 61324 61396 61397 61404 65234 80006 80007 80022
80026 80055 80114 80122

Dalry Road MPD 15th July

42273 44702 44878 45053 45168 45469 45477 45483 61245 61308 61347

St Margarets MPD 16th July

42128 42691 44878 46115 46462 60027 60041 60052 60813 60824 60844 60931
60970 61029 61099 61134 61263 61324 61397 61404 65234 80007 80022 80055
80114

Dunfermline MPD 17th July

61072 61101 64569 64571 64626 65903 65917 65918 65288 90039 90071 90229
90515 90547

Thornton MPD 17th July

61076 61102 61132 61133 61148 61180 61261 61343 61407 64588 64595 64606
64618 64625 64632 65327 65345 65901 65905 65907 65909 65911 65915 65916
65922 65931 65932 76110 90117 90350 90444 90596 90727

Dundee MPD 17th July

46463 46464 60528 60530 60818 60973 61147 61278 61292 61293 61340 61344
61403 64558 64576 64597 64608 64624 65319 73008 80124 90628

Perth MPD 17th July

44698 44703 44722 44792 44799 44924 44925 44931 44959 44960 44973 44979
44980 45047 45138 45213 45461 45472 45473 60031 60512 61244 70002 70012
70033 73153 73145 75032 80028 80093 80126

Stirling MPD 17th July

44727 45016 45168 45357 45359 45389 45423 70008 70033

St. Margarets MPD 17th July

42128 42691 44704 46462 60041 60824 60931 60970 61029 61099 61134 61180 61191 61345 61350 61354 61397 76050 80006 80022 80026 80055 80114

Bathgate MPD 18th July

65243 65267 65282 65297 76104 76105 76106 76107 76111 78045 78046 78050 78052 78054

Motherwell MPD 18th July

44820 44850 44880 44881 44900 44908 44991 45176 45433 73055 73059 76000 76002 76003 77005 77008 92233

Eastfield MPD 18th July

42176 42209 42478 42649 44903 45160 45202 45364 45387 45442 46460 61008 61103 61116 61140 61357 64592 65910 73078 73108 75012 80020 80024 80057 80113 80118 90168 90727

Polmadie MPD 18th July

42195 42199 44802 44965 45309 45471 45481 45675 60535 73057 73062 73063 73064 73075 73098 73099 73107 73122 76004 80058 80060 80061 80086 80109 80116 80120 80121 80130

Corkerhill MPD 18th July

44699 44705 44724 44758 44798 44977 44999 45463 45697 73009 73102 73103 73106 73120 73121 73124 76114 78026 80000 80004 80046 80047 80051 80063 80112

St. Rollox MPD 19th July

44677 44718 60024 60034 61307 73101 73147 73150 73152 73154

Beattock MPD 20th July

42125 42129 42169 42274 42693 45245 80005 80045

Carlisle Kingmoor MPD 21st July

43000 43004 43028 43045 43049 43121 44668 44672 44677 44692 44724 44790
44792 44802 44870 44873 44877 44898 44900 44901 44902 44989 45012 45028
45075 45082 45129 45135 45138 45195 45235 45259 45294 45295 45340 45490
45491 45530 45531 45573 45588 45629 45742 46128 46160 47471 47641 47667
48158 48500 48536 60027 60052 60846 70002 70003 70005 70009 70016 70029
70037 70038 70039 72006 72007 72008 73033 73101 92010 92015 92018 92114
92126 92130 92233

Carlisle Upperby MPD 22nd July (visit not completed)

41217 41264 42095 42225 43025 43953 43964 44939 46434 47285 48406 70011
70020 70029 70044

Carnforth MPD 23rd July

42118 42147 42198 42247 42322 42613 43027 43066 43103 43105 44300 44778
44816 44828 44904 44905 45014 45092 45095 45212 45230 45234 45328 45342
45372 45374 45390 47201 47531 48108 48400 48519 48707 70017 70048 70052
75015 75017 75057 92016

Lancaster MPD 23rd July

41221 43036 44667 44902 44947 45054 45193 45258 45373 46431 46433 46441
46514 48077 48148 48297 48454 48679

Steam Locomotives noted elsewhere during trip.

42128 42169 42199 42241 42277 43133 43138 44670 44672 44705 44718 44758
44772 44790 44802 44878 44947 45011 45067 45091 45117 45124 45133 45357
45402 45475 45480 45697 46115 48133 48166 48214 48247 48614 48632 48660
60007 60019 60024 60118 60532 60816 60836 60843 60876 60877 60970 61094
61101 61103 61180 61262 61303 61330 61350 61244 62028 62048 63386 65790
65841 65842 65851 65930 65934 68023 70033 73009 73057 73100 73104 73122
73145 73150 73153 76090 76094 76102 78026 80004 80045 80112 80128 90045
90229 90254 90266 90309 90441 90445 90650 92097 92206

Appendix 13 Worcester MPD 25th September 1965

3616 3682 4113 4161 4680 6147 6155 6169 6813 6848 6856 6872
6937 7909 9626 44666 44691 44945 45493 48246 75000 75008 75022 75025

Gloucester Horton Road MPD 25th September 1965

3643 3675 3759 3775 4689 4698 6113 6160 6819 6855 6931 6944
7808 7814 7816 7829 7927 8745 41291 44264 44269 44683 44710 45353
45454 48266 48370 48395 48460 48643 73013 73017 73019 78001 78004 78006
80037 92230

Appendix 14

Saltley MPD Christmas Day 1965

6656 6679 6692 44057 44840 44912 45051 45182 45267 45270 45288 45391
46443 46448 46454 46526 48016 48084 48109 48117 48133 48212 48219 48220
48351 48375 48449 48514 48554 48603 48637 48671 48725 48736 48762 48767
73155 75035 76038 76040 76043 76048 90357 92029 92125 92129 92136 92138
92151 92155 D25 D36 D88 D140 D221 D228 D267 D318 D341 D379
D384 D1588 D1589 D1593 D1653 D1813 D1908 D5183 D5197 D5202 D5223 D5226
D5233 D5234 D5245 D5246 D5266 D5292 D5695 D7508 D7518 D7519 D7570 D7572
D7592

Tyseley MPD Christmas Day 1965

3625 4176 4635 5606 5658 6625 6853 6855 6857 6858 6861 6864
6879 6937 6951 6952 6953 8767 9774 43052 43098 44658 44663 44666
44859 44937 44948 45134 45292 46428 46470 48546 48755 61121 90471 92002
92004 92073 92118 92132 92134 92139 D1065 D1604 D1914 D7587

Appendix 15 South West Trip 2nd - 11th April 1966 (Depot/Works visits only)

Oxford MPD 2nd April

3677 5971 6126 6134 6136 6849 6872 6923 6932 6937 6953 6956
6959 6967 6991 6993 6999 7904 7907 7914 7919 7922 9773 73003
73166 90258

Salisbury MPD 3rd April

33006 34006 34026 34056 34066 34089 34100 34108 73065 73169 76007 76008
76012 76018 76059 76067 80152

Weymouth MPD 2nd April

34034 34037 34044 34086 35007 35017 35022 35028 35030 41284 41298 73016
73080

Weymouth MPD 4th April

34044 34057 34086 35007 35017 35022 35028 41301 73080 73110 76011

Bournemouth MPD 4th April

34002 34026 34037 34040 34047 35027 41230 41295 41312 41320 73016 76005
76009 76010 76014 76026 76033 76057 76066 80011 80013 80019 80085 80094
80134

Ryde MPD 5th April

14 16 21 26 27 29 33 35

Ryde Works 5th April

17 18 22 28 30(Cut up)

Eastleigh MPD 7th April

30053 30069 30926 31803 31816 31873 34021 34023 34025 34041 34048 34077 34079 35022 35029 41287 41294 45418 73155 75076 76018 76019 76033 76063 76064 76069 80016 80082 80139 80142 DS233

Guildford MPD 8th April

30072 31405 31408 31411 31639 31791 34088 34097 41319 73037 73043 73065 73081 73087 73089 73093 73118 76031 77014 80154

Nine Elms MPD 8th April

33006 34002 34017 34038 34057 34066 34071 34087 34095 35011 35012 35026 73080 73085 73117 73169 73171 80015 80089 80095 80144 82006 82018 82019 82023 82024 82026 82029

Stratford MPD 10th April

120 6000 1008 30245 30587 30777 30850 30925 33001 42500 49395 61194 63460 63601 NCB67

Nine Elms MPD 10th April

33006 34002 34019 34071 34102 35011 35012 35022 35028 73085 73110 73117 80012 80015 80089 80095 80133 80143 80145 82006 82019 82024 82026 82028 82029

Note. Except for Appendices 3, 5 and 14, only steam locomotives noted are listed.

Acknowledgements (including those for Part Two)

I would like to express my sincere thanks to the following, a number of whom I have pestered on numerous occasions for help, not only with regard to Bob Cooper, but on other railway matters too: Stewart Blair (Carlisle Evening News & Star) Jimmy Boyle, John Burnett, Norman Callaghan, Alan Castle, Ronnie Clough, Noel Coates, Andrew Cooper, Therese' Cooper, Heather Crook, Brian Fare, John Fletcher, Albert Ford, Ron Gardner, Bob Gregson, Harold Griffin, Peter Groom, Dennis Halliwell, John Hill, Dave Hornby, Mick Kelly, Ian Matthews, Stuart Morley, Barry Morton, Peter Norris, Mel Parker, Richard Pearson (NRM Shildon), Chris Proctor (ASLEF), Jack Procter, Peter Richardson (Lancashire Evening Post), Herbert Ridge, Tom Rudd, Derek Sharpe, Dennis Sweeney, Mike Taylor, Richard K Taylor (RCTS), Bob Tye and Peter Whalen. Thanks, too, to Steve Waddington and David Crossland at Amadeus Press. Sadly, some of the aforementioned are no longer with us.

Last and by no means least, my thanks to my old school chum, Dennis Perfect, who has read through and made corrections to the text and also helped fill in the blanks that my memory served up on numerous occasions. Any mistakes, oversights or inaccuracies are entirely my responsibility.

Bibliography

BR Motive Power Allocations 1959 – 1968 Vol. 1, by Paul Teal (Ian Allan 1985)
British Railways Locomotives 1955 and 1962 both by Chris Banks (OPC 2001 & 2005)
British Railways Steam Locomotive Allocations, by H. Longworth (OPC 2011)
British Standard Steam Locomotives Vols. 1-5 (RCTS 1994 – 2012)
British Steam Motive Power Depots, by Paul Bolger (Ian Allan 1981 – 84)
Firing Days at Saltley Vols. 1 & 2 by Terry Essery (D Bradford Barton)
LMS Engine Sheds Vols. 1-5, by Hawkins & Reeve (Wild Swan Publications Ltd. 1981- 87)
LMS Engine Sheds Vols. 6&7, by Hawkins, Reeve and Stevenson (WSP Ltd. 1989 – 90)
Locomotive Stock Book 1960, 1963, 1966 & 1969 (RCTS)
Peto's Register of Great western Railway Locomotives. Various Volumes (Erwell Press)
Steam Locomotives of British Railways, by H C Casserley (Hamlyn 1973)
Steam The Grand Finale, by Alan Castle (Mortons Media Group Ltd. 2008)
The Book of The Royal Scots, by Richard Derry (Irwell Press 1999)
The Book of The Merchant Navy Pacifics, by Richard Derry (Irwell Press 2001)
The Book of The WC & B of B Pacifics, by Richard Derry (Irwell Press 2002)
The Stanier 4-6-0's of the LMS, Rowledge & Reed (David & Charles 1981)
The Stanier Class Five 4-6-0s, Vols. 1 & 2, by John Jennison, (RCTS 2013/2015)
The Complete BR Diesel & Electric Locomotive Directory, by Marsden (OPC 1991)

Various issues of Steam Railway, Railway Magazine, Railway World, Trains Illustrated, Modern Railways and Heritage Railways.

Footnote

The accuracy of the details concerning the disposal and scrapping of BR steam locos has long been a subject of discussion, even more so since it was discovered that deliberately false and misleading information had been accepted by many as fact. It must be born in mind, therefore, that where such particulars are included here, their reliability and accuracy cannot be guaranteed.

The Final Few Years of British Steam

An enthusiast's recollection of exploits and adventures while following the decline of steam on British Railways

Part Two

Summer 1966 – Summer 1968

Les Wheeler

Introduction to The Final Few Years of British Steam Part Two.

Records of my travels and exploits in search of steam continue from the beginning of July 1966. Throughout the previous month plans and preparations had been made for returning to Scotland, hopefully to see one or two of the handful of Gresley's 'A4's still managing to find work on express passenger duties. Steam was in its death throws north of the border and would be dispensed with by the following spring. As with many other trips throughout this sad period, it would be a question of attempting to keep one step ahead of steams Grim Reaper.

Following the fortunes of BR steam during the final two years of its employment would often mean trips and visits prompted simply by hearing or reading about imminent changes concerning this form of motive power. Forthcoming closures of steam depots, withdrawal of the final member(s) of a particular class of engine or the termination of steams regular use on certain services, would all provide the motivation to respond as best I could to record such a fast changing scene. Some forays would also be made to areas or sheds where such locomotives had relatively recently capitulated to diesel power; on reflection, these visits had most likely been made out of a feeling of disbelief and the need to see first-hand that steam had indeed been dispensed with. Of course, with any luck, there might also possibly be one final opportunity to photograph a few engines still stored on shed or in sidings while awaiting disposal.

Subsequent to what would prove to be a not entirely incident-free escapade to Scotland, other expeditions would follow to places still relatively distant from home, including the southwest and the northeast, but not for long. Steams distribution was shrinking swiftly by the month and by March 1968 it would be confined to the northwest of England. Visits to Yorkshire and Lancashire, although not a stone's throw from the West Midlands, would be made more frequently as this form of traction found itself restricted to working within the boundaries of these two counties. Once the shackles were really on, steam would only be found in Lancashire.

Steam specials would continue to attract many enthusiasts to participate in what was often a last opportunity to travel behind a certain locomotive, often the last of its class, or over a particular line that would soon be no more. From July to December 1966 a total in excess of 40 of these would take place, during 1967 the total would reach approximately 70 and during the final eight months of standard gauge steam working in 1968 there would be 33, culminating, of course, in the 'Fifteen Guinea Special' on 11th August. Engines called upon to carry out such duties were often, but not always, spruced up, and presented the many eager photographers with subjects that were far more photogenic than the vast majority of the locos remaining at the time.

However, on the subject of well-groomed locomotives, something peculiar had started to happen - for no apparent reason, there began to appear a few other clean engines, which would have no part to play in any of the planned railtours. If you found yourself in the right place at the right time (which I fortunately did once or twice) a picture of a well-presented steam loco would be an unexpected bonus, even if it had only been cleaned on one side! Why this was happening and who was responsible will become clear later.

Things would be done and dusted as far as standard gauge steam on BR was concerned by the beginning of August 1968. On Sunday 4th August the normal, everyday rostering of such motive power would come to an end, but because of my observations on this day, an extra chapter in the form of a postscript would be needed to complete to my satisfaction a true and accurate account of steams final few hours, and those of one locomotive in particular, Stanier 'Black 5' No. 45212.

A selection of photographs which will be appearing in
The Final Few Years of British Steam Part Two Summer 1966 – Summer 1968